No Names Please

SLy FOXX

Order this book online at www.trafford.com
or email orders@trafford.com

Most Trafford titles are also available at major online book retailers.

Printed in Victoria, BC, Canada.

ISBN: 978-1-4269-0754-8 (soft)
ISBN: 978-1-4269-0755-5 (hard)
ISBN: 978-1-4269-0756-2 (ebook)

*Our mission is to efficiently provide the world's finest, most comprehensive book publishing
service, enabling every author to experience success. To find out how to publish your book, your
way, and have it available worldwide, visit us online at www.trafford.com*

Trafford rev. 3/24/2010

Trafford
PUBLISHING®   www.trafford.com

North America & international
toll-free: 1 888 232 4444 (USA & Canada)
phone: 250 383 6864 ♦ fax: 812 355 4082

I dedicate this book to my grandchildren and great grandchildren. I want them, as they read the chapters of my life, and the rough roads that I have traveled, they will be cautious and appreciate any blessings they get, and not get entrapped by some of the same mistakes that I have made.

Table of Contents

Chapter 1

LIFE ON THE FARM

Being reared in the early part of the great depression, money was hard to come by and jobs were few and far between, but by living on a large farm, our family was required to purchase very little, as we were able to grow or make almost everything that we needed to survive, with the exception of salt, sugar and flour, and we could have avoided purchasing flour and sugar, if we would have been content eating cakes and pies made from corn meal and maple sugar.

We had income from the sale of calves, potatoes, maple syrup, milk and cream, and of course, timber and mine props. We were a family of seven, including my father, my mother, three older brothers and an older sister. My oldest brother was Harvey, next came Brother Everett, and then Brother Jack and of course my Sister Liz, and finally me.

My father had previously been a large road construction contractor, but after the big bust of nineteen hundred and twenty nine and as I was growing up, he had returned to make a living off of the farm.

The church that we attended, what little that we made an appearance there, was a nondenominational church, as there would not have been enough supporters of any particular group to support a church individually, in our sprawling country area. My father's family had belonged to a

Southern Baptist group and my mother's family had belonged and attended Lutheran churches.

As a young child I did not know what a Catholic was but I did know what a Jew was, as I remembered my mother reading to me about the Jews from the bible. I saw my first real live Jew when I entered high school, as there was a teacher there that taught mathematics and algebra who was Jewish.

My father always bought a new car every couple of years. He never bought one of those deluxe hand built cars but merely a small assembly line model "T" Ford.

Whenever one saw one of those large deluxe hand built cars that had a spare tire built into the running board of both sides and towards the front of the car, then you knew that it was either someone with money or someone who was important was driving it.

There was always one thing that we always had plenty of, on the farm.

Work.

If we were not milking cows or feeding the pigs, we were cutting firewood, carrying in coal, planting a garden, building haystacks or cutting hedgerows. There was always more to do than there was time to do it. I will give my parents credit though; we were never required to work on the Sabbath, with the exception of milking the cows and feeding the livestock. That was another reason that I loved going to school. At least while I was in the classroom I was not required to do work on the farm.

We had a large grove of maple trees on the farm, which we used to produce maple syrup. Early every spring, we would bore a small hole into the side of the trunk of each maple tree, and then drive into that hole a metal spout which had a hook on the bottom. We would then take a three gallon galvanized bucket, which had a small hole drilled in the side near the top, which permitted us to hang the bucket from the small metal hook that protruded from the metal spout that we had driven into the maple tree.

As the sap would rise up in the tree trunk, from the spring warm up, a small amount of that sap would drip into our buckets as sugar water. My father had built a shed in the middle of the grove of maple trees, inside of which we had built a fireplace. The fireplace was surrounded on three sides by sturdy square rocks that supported the steel rack which in turn held our maple syrup pan. The maple syrup pan was made of copper and was eight feet long, three feet wide and one foot deep.

At least twice daily we would take an empty three gallon bucket and check each tree. If the buckets were as least one third full or more, we would take it down and immediately replace it with the empty one, take the sugar water back and dump it into our maple syrup pan. This we would continue to do until we had checked every tree in the grove.

Once the pan was nearly full of sugar water, we would start a fire under the pan and keep a controlled modest fire going in the fireplace, night and day until the sugar water was reduced to maple syrup.

Maple syrup was a real treat for us kids, because my mother always made fresh pancakes from scratch every morning for breakfast for us. Hot pancakes in the morning with fresh butter made from our own cows milk and maple syrup surely was yummy. My mother would sometimes take a large copper kettle and place it on top of the kitchen stove; she then would pour a quantity of maple syrup into the copper kettle and then boil it until it was reduced to maple sugar. Maple sugar was really delicious and would keep for some time, or until it was all eaten.

Apples, cherries, blackberries, raspberries and strawberries were some of the items that we grew on the farm for our pleasure and subsistence. One time when my brother Harvey was picking cherries with my father, while my father was up on the ladder, the ladder broke and father hit the ground bending the bucket and spilling the cherries that he had already picked. Harvey said to our father, "You broke the ladder, you bent the bucket and you spilled your cherries." Our father responded with, "To hell with the ladder, to hell with the bucket and to hell with the cherries, it is your poor old Pap that is hurt."

We always kept a minimum of five milk cows on the farm to supply milk, cream, cheese and butter for our family and for sale, and any that was left over our pigs were only too happy to devour. Every morning we were awakened long before time to make the long walk to school, to enable us to have time to milk one or two of those cows before we went to school. In the evening, after school and before dark, we would have the opportunity to do it all over again.

Our family could never be gone from the farm for any period of time, as those cows had to be milked twice a day, no matter what. We also kept several bee hives full of honey bees to keep us supplied with another great source of food, honey. Honey was really a special food, as it is the only natural food known to mankind that will keep forever without any special care or refrigeration and without ever spoiling.

As a young teenager, I was able to garnish a few dollars by helping neighbors in planting their crops or by hoeing corn (that is chopping the weeds and grass out of the rows of corn with a hoe) making a whopping ten cents per hour. Looking back, I am not sure just how good a job that I was doing, because when I stopped for a lunch break, I always dug my hoe into the ground at the end of the last row that I had done, just to be sure that I did not go over the same row twice, once I returned to work from lunch.

In the fall, I could earn that same generous compensation helping my neighbors, by cutting or shucking corn, or by cutting their wheat or oats with a cradle, (but not the kind you might rock a baby in). In those days a lot of different candies could be bought for one penny, a game of pool at the local pool hall was only a nickel, tickets or a good movie like, "Gone with the Wind" or, "The Wizard of Oz" was only a quarter and of course, soft drinks were only a nickel. We thought that we were living pretty well.

In the winter time, I had steel traps and always set out a trap line, hoping that I might entrap a rabbit, an opossum, or a raccoon. Or even a skunk! Many nights I would go hunting with a buddy and a dog and try to tree these same animals. If we were successful in getting one of the animals treed, since it was winter time and there were no leaves on the trees, we could readily see the animals and shoot them with our trusty twenty two caliber rifle, and they would fall to the ground.

Any time that I was successful in capturing one of the animals, I would take it back to my home, skin the animal, stretch the hide out on a board, secure it with tacks and a few days later would take my collection into town and sell the hides to a dealer for a few much needed dollars.

We would have picnics, corn roasts, potato roasts and of course chicken roasts, all of which were much more delicious if the product were pilfered from some unsuspecting neighbor. When we had our chicken roasts we would take our corn and or potatoes and soak them in water, while at the same time we would have a roaring bonfire going in a small pit that we had dug in the ground.

In the meantime, we would take a live chicken, grab it by the head, spin the body around and then with a jerk, the body would go flying across the ground, minus a head. We would then open up the chicken and remove all of the innards from the chicken, carefully washing the chicken clean with water from a fresh spring; we would then pack the entire chicken in a mask of fresh moistened clay.

At that point we would bury our entire edible product in a bed of hot ashes, cover the ashes with hot coals and then build a roaring fire on top. We would then play games and keep the fire going hot for about two hours. When we would take the chicken out of the hot ashes, the clay would be baked hard as a rock. When we would remove the clay from the chicken, the feathers would all be stuck in the clay and the chicken would be clean as a whistle. Unless you have actually experienced this, you could never imagine the enormity of this occasion, with the moon overhead and a light breeze blowing in this outdoor setting with good teenager friends, this meal truly seemed a feast fit for the gods.

Chapter 2

SCHOOL DAYS

Growing up during the great depression, we were not blessed by having the benefit of pre-schooling or kindergarten, first grade in the elementary schools was our first opportunity for public education.

I was very fortunate that my mother was a former part time school teacher, and during the hard winter months, took the time to read books with me. By the time that I was four years old, I could easily read any of the books that any of my older siblings had brought home from the first and second grade. Reading the old McGuffy's Readers group was a piece of cake.

We also had in our home, a large library of books to choose from, and I could take any one of those books and read from them, although, I could not properly pronounce many of the words, nor understand their meaning. I remember reading "The Tin Box" by Horatio Alger, Jr. and "Glengarry School Days" by Ralph Connor and generally understood their stories.

Living out in the country, I was very fortunate that there was a one room elementary school house, called Marysville, located just one quarter of a mile from our farm house. My older sister and all three of my older brothers had been going to that school and I was very happy, because it was a distance that my little legs could easily travel.

Summer was coming to a close, but when you are at that age time seems to crawl, but finally Labor Day weekend had arrived, and I couldn't wait, as I would be going to school with the big boys on Tuesday. On Saturday afternoon I talked to my older Sister Liz, and she agreed to walk with me to the school house. When we arrived there, I just stood and stared at it. To me it looked beautiful. There was a row of windows down either side of the school building, and a bell tower above the entrance door, with a large school bell hanging in the alcove above.

My sister held me up so that I could look through the window inside and I could see rows of seats and a pot bellied stove in the middle of the room. It is hard to explain just how excited I was at that moment.

But, alas, there was a fire on Saturday night. When we went to see the Marysville School grounds on Sunday morning, all we saw left of the school house were hot coals and ashes. The only things remaining intact from the fire were the steel frames from the desks and benches and that big school bell, which was about sixteen inches in diameter.

It seems that the local county school board did not have enough money to pay the teachers to open all of the elementary schools in the county that fall, so their decision was, not to open another school, called Mountain View, which was located about three miles from our home. It was apparent that some parent or parents from the Mountain View area took it upon themselves to correct that situation and deliberately set fire to the Marysville School. Now the school board would have enough money to open the Mountain View School on Tuesday. Which they did.

Now I was relegated to walking to another one room elementary school, called Corley, which was about one and one half miles from our home. That close only, if we walked through fields and pastures, keeping a wary eye open, and out of the way of an ornery bull, or not stepping on small corn or bean plants, or walking through snow, which was up to two feet deep, depending on the time of the year.

I really enjoyed going to school, though, particularly because all eight grades were held in the one room. When the teacher wanted to conduct the class for a particular grade, he or she, would merely call those in that grade to the front of the building and they would all sit on a long wooden bench. From there, the questions and answers as well as the blackboard work were conducted.

By paying attention as to what was transpiring, I had the opportunity to glean from those classes as much information as my little brain could handle. During those first two years, my first and second grade, I missed

7

a lot of days of school. Many times the snow was deeper than my legs were long and I was just not able to walk through it. I was promoted both times though, and because of my desire to learn, I was able to keep abreast of the other students.

The third grade was a horse of a different color.

I had a young woman teacher whose name was Miss Silver, who I used to say, gave me a whipping for every day of the school week, and a couple of extra ones on Friday to keep my mind focused and in line over the weekend. She would give me a knife, have me go to the perimeter of the school yard and cut a switch, then bring it back to her and she would use it on me. I never cried though, I was too proud. I also never told my parents of the discipline that I received.

I did not realize it at the time but I was probably bored, as I was usually ahead of my class, and was probably causing distractions. At mid-term Miss Silver promoted me to fourth grade. That seemed to slow down the daily whippings.

One Saturday, as I was walking into town, a man stopped and picked me up in his car. I did not know it at the time, but found out later that he was Miss Silver's Father.

He asked me, "What school do you go to, young man?"

"Corley" I replied.

"How do you like your teacher?"

"I think that she is a good teacher, but she sure is strict."

His response was, and correctly so, "I am sure that she just wants to be sure that you have an opportunity to learn as much as possible."

In the fifth grade, I had another young woman teacher named Miss Castro, who was also a very good teacher, but I got along just fine without my daily whippings.

Internally though, I was at odds with her a lot. I would take poster board and make little signs, similar to those that you see protesters and marchers are carrying today, only smaller. I would put them on stakes and place them in the ground just outside the schoolyard fence, concerning teacher's pets, recess activities, and other items that I felt were important, so that the other students could learn about my concerns. I will give her credit though, she never retaliated. Fifty years later, I met her at a high school reunion, and she remembered me and introduced me as one of her brightest students.

I had men for teachers in the sixth and seventh grades. In those days in order to enter high school, you first had to pass an entrance exam. In the spring of your eighth grade, on a certain day, you would go to the appropriate high school as assigned to you and take your entrance exam.

While in the seventh grade, when the time came for the eighth graders in our school to take their high school entrance exams, I asked my teacher if I might be permitted to take the test also, so that in that manner I would be better prepared to know what to groom for during the next year. I must have sold him a good story as he put my name on the list that he submitted to the high school. When the results came back from the exams, my score matched the high score from the group, and I was permitted to enter high school directly from the seventh grade. The big disadvantages of that were, being so young, and with no reasonable means of transportation, I had to miss almost all of the social life that was associated with high school activities. I was able to attend almost all home games in all sports, though.

One of the highlights of the school year was the fights that always followed the basketball games when we played a certain other school in our county. The fights got so pronounced that during the final two years of my high school attendance, our principal would not schedule any team sport competition between our high school and that one other particular county high school.

I was also able to attend both the junior and senior proms. Although, with no means of transportation, I was unable to take a date to the prom, but at least I had the opportunity to dance with some of the girls while there.

Another of the highlights of our school years was twice a year, the principal would bring in a guest speaker, take the entire student body into the school auditorium and listen to the speaker. I can still recall a few of the remarks made by those speakers.

One was a statement made by one of the male speakers, which went something like this: "You may think that I do these speaking engagements for a living, but that is not the case. My father owns a large cattle ranch in Montana and is very wealthy. If I ever need any money, all I have to do is to write to my father and say, "Dear Dad, please send me five thousand dollars or even ten thousand dollars," it would not make any difference as to how much I asked for, he would not send me anything anyhow."

Another time we had a very nice looking lady who was our speaker, and she was telling us about the time that she was addressing a group of men from Alcoholics Anonymous, she said, "I was telling them about all of the bad things that alcohol was doing to their stomachs." Then she said,

"That a scuzy old drunk stood up in the rear and said 'Lady, I have been drinking all kinds of booze for over twenty seven years, and I will put my belly up against yours anytime." This brought hilarious laughter from our school group.

Another disadvantage of being the youngest student to ever graduate from that high school, was missing out on playing school sports, due to my weight and stature. When as a senior I went out for football, weighing in at 132 pounds. When I would try to tackle some of those 20 and 21 year old seniors, who weighed in at 220 to 280 pounds, they would just run over me like a freight train running over a hobo.

I never did get to play in a real football game. I did graduate though, at the age of fifteen, a time when forty percent of those starting high school in our area, failed to complete their goal.

Chapter 3

Pie Social

Living during the depression was by and large a hard life with very little pleasures to look forward to. One of those rare pleasures was called a pie social. The pie social was a fund raiser for those little one room elementary schools located out in the country. Aside from just being a fund raiser, it was also the major local social gathering for the year in our area. Mothers would bake cakes and donate them to the charity. The organizers would then display each cake, one at a time, and then would have a cake walk. In a cake walk, they put twelve chairs in a circle, with a number on each, and as each cake was displayed, they would sell twelve tickets to interested bystanders, who then would march around the chairs with music playing. When the music would stop, each participant would sit down on the chair that was currently in front of them. Which ever marcher ended up sitting on the predetermined lucky chair would win that particular cake. The lucky chair would change after each cake was won. They would then continue selling tickets and marching until all cakes were won by someone.

The high point of the social would then follow the cake walk. Thus was where young girls would bake a pie and donate it to the cause. The organizers would then display the pies, one at a time and call up the girl who had baked the pie to the front of the building. They would auction off these pies and the local young men would then bid on each pie until there was a winner. The winning bidder not only would have the privilege of sitting with the girl and sharing the pie with her, but could also walk her home after the event was over.

Earlier in the evening I had seen a cute blond girl walk in with a pie in her hand and that caught my attention. I knew that the girl's name was Donna, as I had seen her several times before and desired to talk to her, but was too shy to approach her. When Donna's pie came up for bid I immediately bid one dollar, which was about what most pies were selling for that night. Another young man apparently had his eye on this prize and bid one dollar and fifty cents. I said, "Two dollars." He bid two dollars and fifty cents. I finally bought the pie for five dollars and was happy to pay it. It had probably taken me a month or more to earn that much money, but that was what I was working for.

Donna and I sat together and shared the pie, and what we did not eat I shared with some of my less fortunate school buddies. When the festivities were over, I prepared to walk Donna home. As we were walking down the dirt road toward her home, I realized that a close neighbor of mine my the name of Bruce was also walking a girl home, whose pie that he had bought, lived in that same direction and on the same road to where Donna lived. The four of us then walked along together until we came to Donna's house. Since the girl that Bruce was with lived further down the road, I agreed that I would wait there for him until he returned, and then he and I would then walk back to our homes together. I was very willing to do this and it would give me a little more time to spend with Donna alone. We did stand and talk for a while, but when the porch light flashed on and off a couple of times, she decided she had best go into her house.

After Donna went into her house, I sat down on the road bank by her mailbox, to await the return of Bruce. It seemed that I sat there for an eternity. When Bruce finally returned I asked him, "Where in the world have you been?" He replied, "That girl lived so far back in the sticks that I had to wipe one quarter of an inch of owl shit off of the face of my wrist watch, just to see what time it was."

My arrangement with Donna did not materialize into anything, as I had no access to a car and could not afford to take her to the movies or even on a picnic, and there were no more immediate social events to attend.

Chapter 4

MISCHIEVOUS ACTIONS

Since the time and place that we lived in, we had to arrange for our own fun and recreation. My friend Walter and I had formed a bond, which we called the S T Club, which we construed to stand for the secret two clubs. We had built a small cabin in the woods, which contained a small pot bellied stove as well as a table and four chairs, for our card playing pleasures. We had a secret trap door in the floor, where we kept a thirty two caliber revolver, and any other valuables that we wanted to leave concealed in the cabin.

The door was secured by means of a two by four, which was on the inside and on a pivot and could be opened from the outside only by means of pulling a small cable, which was concealed near the roof of the cabin. We always kept a good supply of dry kindling inside the cabin and a large supply of firewood stacked outside by the side of the building. The cabin was a perfect place to meet and plan our next escapade, whether it was to be a corn roast, a bar-be-cue, a chivaree, or some mischievous Halloween tirade.

On one such Halloween outing, a group of us boys took the wheels off of a nasty neighbor's buggy and put it on top of his flat roofed shed, where we reassembled the wheels onto the buggy. We then went to the home of an older teenage girl, who we all thought that she was a snob. We had made a series of noise makers from bamboo to disturb her and attract her attention, then we intended to wave in her window the head and hide of a raccoon, which we had attached to the end of a stick.

When we arrived at her house and peeked coyly into her window to make sure that she was asleep, we were really surprised. Not only was she not asleep, but was in the midst of having sex with another local boy. We did not pull any trick or treat actions at her window bud did watch her bedroom for a while.

Then of course, we always were sure to upset two different outhouses. The second one this time was a sort of a disaster. At that point in my young life poetry was my thing, and I thought that I would grow up to be one of the world's great poets. Some of my poems I used as part of my school work and others for birthdays and holidays to amuse my buddies. The happenings on this particular Halloween night were so varied and different that I immortalized the night in a poem that I wrote. A part of which is as follows:

One boy who was wearing boots
Fell into the pit.
His boots as well as pockets
Were completely filled with s—t.

I made several copies of the poem to give to the other boys who were with me on that night, my Sister Liz, who was three years older than I, found one of the copy's and after reading it she was so amused by it that she gave the poem to one of her girl friends. That girl, after reading the poem, passed it on to another of her girl friends. That girl happened to be a young woman who was a teacher in my high school and was my Civics teacher. As a direct result of that poem, with my real name written at the bottom, I received an "F" on my next report card in Civics, the only "F" that I ever received in any of my school years.

The mother of the young girl that we spied upon that Halloween night obtained a copy of my poem and after reading it sent a scathing letter with a three cent stamp on it to my mother, about me. In those days those farm houses did not have telephones and their main way of communication was via the U S postal service. My sister happened to be the one who retrieved the mail from our mail box on the day that the letter to my mother arrived, and recognizing who the letter was from, opened and read the letter to me, but Mother never learned about it. I was so upset about all of the commotion that my poem had caused that I never again wrote a poem.

Thus a great poet was lost to the world.

On another occasion, there was a man who was always harassing us about trespassing on his property. He lived on a narrow dirt road, on which only one other family lived. He had a habit of going into town every Saturday night and returning home late, usually intoxicated. Late one Autumn Saturday night, after we were sure that all of the vehicles of the other family were safely at home, we took a shock of corn stalks and set it up right in the middle of the narrow dirt road. When he returned home late that night, we watched as he stopped his car, then threw the shock of corn to the side of the road and continued on toward his home. Continuing forward, as he rounded another bend in the road, he saw another shock of corn in the middle of the road. Again he stopped, threw the shock of corn to the side of the road and continued homeward. As he proceeded towards his home, another bend in the road and another shock of corn. This time he thought, "To hell with it" and ran right over the shock of corn.

Almost.

Right in the middle of this shock, we had placed a very large rock, which was concealed by the corn stalks. When he tried to run over it, his car became stuck on top of the rock and he was unable to move his car in any direction. It was with great joy that we watched him jack and block his car for about two hours before he was able to roll the rock from the middle of the road and continue on home. Perhaps sometimes we were not overly nice.

You have to understand that in those days we did not have television, or video games, bowling alleys or skating rinks, and the local movie theater was only open on Saturdays, matinee and night, so we had to make our own entertainment as best we could.

Christmas holidays were something that was always looked forward to by teenagers in high school. It was really one of our few free vacations. Of course we still had to milk the cows, slop the hogs and bring in the firewood, but not a lot of other work on the farm.

By this time we were old enough that we had gotten over Santa Claus and because our country was still trying to recover from a serious depression, we would not expect any extravagant gifts on Christmas morning. Our normal requests from Santa were something to wear and something to play with. We would then usually get a pair of pants with a hole in the pocket. I recall the story of the local lad who asked Santa for a pony for Christmas. When he arose on Christmas morning, he found a small pile of horse manure with his name on it under the tree. He spent the next several days looking around for his pony, as he knew that it had to be there someplace.

Wrong.

One New Year's Day, Walter and I were playing around an old coal mine, where we found an old large wash tub. Upon seeing the tub, Walter declared, "If George Washington could cross the Delaware River in a row boat, then I can cross this creek in a wash tub." With that said, I helped him carry the tub down to the edge of the creek bank. Walter then found an old pole about eight feet long. With the pole in hand, he then climbed into the wash tub and while standing up, with the pole, he pushed himself away from the creek bank. By pushing the pole against the creek bottom, he was able to propel himself out into the middle of the stream. Then the pole got stuck in the mud at the bottom, Walter lost his balance and fell into the creek, getting completely submerged. Crawling out of the creek, he was soaked from head to foot and we immediately started walking back to his house. Before we reached his home, his clothes were frozen so stiff that it was difficult for him to even walk. He had to hover over a hot Burnside stove to even be able to get undressed.

So much for trying to duplicate history.

Walter is best remembered by his world famous statement that, "I am not lazy; I was just born tired and have never had a chance to rest up." He was very ingenious though, always thinking of new ways to earn some easy money. One of his better ideas was a way to help those farmers and ranchers when they were putting up a new fence line or replacing an existing one. Since most of the property in that area was on hilly and very rocky terrain, making the digging of fence post holes very difficult. To dig a post hole there required the use of a post whole digger, a pick and a crow bar, with many of the rocks having to be removed by hand.

He came up with the idea that he and I would go to a flat meadow area of our farm, where the ground was soft and rock free. There we would dig several hundred post holes and sell them to those folks who would be building fences on that hilly, rocky terrain, so that they would not have to dig through all of those rocks. If he could only have come up with one more great idea like that, then we both could have retired as millionaires years ago.

Chapter 5

SIGNS

As we were growing up in the depression, we lived a lot by the same standards and methods that our grandparents had lived. If we had a sore, a boil or an ache, my mother would go into the field and dig up some root or other, bring it back and put it in a pot of water and let it boil for a while. She would then make a poultice of it and place it on our sore or wound. If we had a cold or sneezing attack, she would dig up an old sassafras root and make some sassafras tea for us to drink.

I felt that we were too poor to get sick, and so we just did not get sick. My first personal contact with a doctor, other than a dentist, was when I took my physical upon entering in the United States Army. My parents lived by many of the signs and omens as passed down through the generations. Farm crops were planted and harvested by the position of the moon.

My mother once told me that when her dog bayed with a certain mournful sound, that it would have a particular meaning. She said that when he made that sound and was baying towards the sky, it would mean that there was a fire nearby and that if he were baying toward the ground, which would mean that someone was dying.

I was highly skeptical at that age that a stupid dog could forewarn someone of such happenings. Little did I realize that some dogs could be used to follow a person's footprints merely by the use of his nose, even after a day or two had passed, and that dogs, by smell, would be able to detect the presence of certain drugs, the presence of explosives and even able to detect certain diseases.

I can recall one night that our dog was making that mournful sound and when my mother went to the front porch and saw her dog barking towards the ground came back into the living room and announced that someone was passing away this evening. The next morning we were to find out that the evening before that our closest neighbor, George, who lived one quarter of a mile away, had passed away. I started to believe what Mother had told me.

During the summer several months later, I was playing with two kids who lived on a farm a mile or more from our house. These two boys were about my age and lived on this farm with their mother and father, which had been owned by the boy's grandfather. Unfortunately their grandfather had died about three months before, and although their father and mother had been living on the premises for several years, there was a legal dispute over the property between his siblings, and although I did not know it at that time, there had been a court order for the family to vacate the property on that very day.

During the afternoon while I was there, their mother had done several loads of laundry and we helped to hang the clothes on an outdoor clothes line and to later fold those same items and put them in boxes. When I inquired as to why we were putting all of those clothes in boxes, their mother told me that these were all winter clothes and they were just trying to make room in the clothes closets for their summer outfits.

We spent the entire afternoon doing this type of thing, but we tried to make a sort of a game out of it. In the evening we all sat down at the dining room table for supper. After I finished eating, I thanked their mom for the meal and announced that I would have to be going home. The whole family was very insistent that I stay later in the evening, that they would have a very special surprise for me. I made myself very clear that I had to leave now, as it was imperative that I arrive home before dark and I went home.

That night Mother's old dog was back on the porch baying again, making that mournful sound, only this time he was barking toward the sky. Mother came out and watched him again for a few minutes and then went back inside the house and announced that there was a fire in the area someplace. The next day one of our neighbors stopped by our house and told us that the house, at which I had been playing the day before, had burned to the ground.

When I heard this, I asked Mother if I might be able go to look and see what remained there. With her permission, I walked back to that farm, only to find there was none of the house remaining. Only the rock chimney was still standing tall, as if it were on guard duty.

Several days later I went to visit those same boys in there new home location, and there I saw all of those same boxes that we had been packing just a few days earlier. The family had been able to save all of their personal possessions, just is if they knew that there was going to be a fire at the farm house that night. Only then did I realize that the whole family had been trying to get me involved in some manner, maybe even planning on blaming the arson on me in some way.

Chapter 6

RADIO REPAIR SHOP

Most young men from our area, upon graduating from high school or just dropping out of school, went to work in the coal mines, which were prevalent in a nearby area. I had made the determination at an early age that I was not going to go that route. At the age of ten, I was able to get my hands on some copies of electronic books. Then with the assistance of friends and neighbors, I was able to assemble a collection of non-working radios, from which I could salvage parts.

From the books, I learned how to read the color code on the resistors used in the radios at that time, as well as the value of the condensers. With this information I was able to salvage a collection of parts from some of the non-working radios, which I catalogued and kept.

On the radios that I was able to determine the problem, I would then repair them using parts from my parts salvage. I was now able to sell these working radios for from two to five dollars each. Thus, at the age of twelve I had a meager income from the electronic business. On the radios that I could not repair, I merely salvaged the parts from them.

Over the years I was able to determine the problem with almost all radios and had enough spare parts with which to repair them. By doing this for over five years, I had developed a lot of confidence in my ability.

By the time that I was fourteen years old, I was able to take a blank sheet of paper, and from memory, able to draw a complete schematic of a radio, showing sizes of the parts required and the type of vacuum tubes it would take to make the radio operate. I could then take that schematic and by using parts from my collection, I was able to assemble a radio that would work. By connecting it to an antenna that I ran from my upstairs bedroom to an adjacent tree, I was able to listen to radio stations like WLW from Cincinnati, WSN from Nashville, and WJJD from Chicago.

Having graduated from high school at the age of fifteen, I had to wait until I was sixteen to get my drivers license and social security card, then with six years of home self training, working on radios, I opened a radio repair shop in a town near my home.

Initially, I used my brother Everett's Model "A" Ford to get back and forth to work and to pick up and deliver my customer's radios and phonographs. My brother had gone to work for the Goodyear Tire and Rubber Company, a national company in Jackson, Michigan and had left his little Ford in a shed back on the farm.

I also learned to repair auto radios. In those days some of the auto manufacturers insulated the running boards on their cars and actually used the running boards as antennas for their radios.

During this time Adolph Hitler and his Nazi Army was running rampant over most of the other countries of Europe. One afternoon I had a customer from an area called Becky's Creek sitting in my shop waiting for me to complete the repairs on his radio. Another customer came in, and recognized the gentlemen waiting there. After conversing with him for a few minutes, he asked him this question, "Do you think that Hitler could take Becky's Creek?" Now Becky's Creek was well known as a source of quality moonshine and famous for the reckless use of firearms. The appearance of someone showing up at the emergency room of the local hospital by someone who either lived in or had ventured into Becky's Creek with a gunshot wound was almost a weekly occurrence and no one even bothered to make out a report on such occasions.

The man from Becky's Creek scratched his head, meditated for a few moments and then replied emphatically, "No, Hitler could never take Becky's Creek." That certainly made me feel more secure.

One evening after returning a repaired radio to an Italian family who had a cute daughter, her father asked me, "Would you care to share a glass of wine with me?" I replied, "Sure, why not, this is my last delivery and I am going straight home from here. Her father then went to a cabinet and

21

took out a bottle of vino, but her mother, who seemed to know that her daughter was sweet on me, exclaimed as she waved her arms, "No, no, not that one, get the good stuff." At that point the father went to the basement and brought up a dust covered bottle of apparently great Italian wine. At that time I did not know the difference between a good bottle of wine and a great one, but I sure could tell the difference between a good bottle of wine and a bad one!

Another time I had a customer come into my shop at a time when there were a few customers waiting. I had repaired a short wave radio for him recently and he just wanted me to know how happy that he was with the repairs. He said, "Since you have repaired my radio, I can bring in Benito Mussolini so strong that I can smell the garlic on his breath." This brought a ripple of laughter from my other customers.

Once I was repairing a car radio out of a Studebaker and the customer was sitting there waiting for me to finish the repairs. We heard a crash outside and another man came in and asked, "Does any one in here own a Studebaker car? "Yes, why do you ask?" said the Studebaker's owner. "Well, someone just backed into the side of your car, and then drove away." the man said. The customer just sat there on his chair, and I looked at him and asked, "Aren't you even going to go and look to see what damage was done?" "No, it can't be any worse than when I was driving down the highway a few weeks ago and the steering wheel came off in my hands." he said, and he never bothered to go outside and look at his vehicle.

One time a customer brought in two radios for repair. He stated to me, "If you will repair the one radio for me, I will give you the other radio as payment." One was a large RCA console radio in a beautiful wood cabinet that probably cost somewhere in the neighborhood of eighty dollars. The other was a small Emerson table radio that cost five or six dollars. Thinking that he wanted me to repair the large radio and then he would give me the small non-working radio as payment, I said, "No, I don't think so, I don't think that would be a fair proposition for me." The customer, then realizing my line of thinking replied, "I don't mean that the way you think, I mean that if you will repair the small Emerson radio for me, then I will give you the large RCA as payment for the repairs." He continued, "You see, I like to travel light, when I get ready to move on, I just want to be able to pee on the fire and call the dogs." I accepted his offer and later, after repairing the RCA, I was able to sell it for thirty five dollars, which was probably the most profitable single transaction that I had while in that repair shop location.

I almost immediately took the thirty dollars and purchased an eleven year old Chevrolet, so now I owned my own automobile. Financially, I did not do great in this business venture, but was able to buy gas for my car, pay my parts bill with a little left over to try to have a little teenager fun, but it sure beat the hell out of hoeing corn in a hot cornfield for ten cents an hour.

It also gave me great contact with people in the outside world, an opportunity that I would never have had working back on the farm. Another benefit that I received was the fact that my repair shop was not too far from the local high school, and after school started in the fall, there was a constant stream of cute little girls going by my shop, many even coming inside to talk to me, pretending to be prospective customers.

Sometimes life is just too good.

Chapter 7

Cozy Rest

It was getting late in the summer and I felt like I was sitting on top of the world. I thought that I had everything that I needed to conquer the world, and that was exactly my goal. I had a social security number, a driver's license and a high school diploma. I had opened my own radio repair shop and now had an income of cash money.

I had already earned enough money to buy a used Chevrolet four door sedan. Now that I owned my own car, I was able to have my friend Andy, who for many years had been an itinerant sign painter, to paint on both sides of the front doors of my car a picture of an antique sailing ship, and under the picture these words:

The Mayflower.

No other words or explanation was necessary, because in those days, from reading American history, whenever anyone thought of the word Mayflower, they automatically thought of the common expression, "Once you got on board the Mayflower, there was no turning back, you had to come across."

The United States was not yet involved in the Great War, and although I was only sixteen years old, I was trying to travel with the big dogs. I knew the exact latitude and longitude of every roadhouse and club in a five county area, and knew where one could purchase excellent home made Italian wine at any hour of the day or night.

You could buy gasoline for seven gallons for a dollar, so transportation was affordable. A common expression in those days was to pull up in front of the gas pump and since there was no such thing as self service, say to the attendant, "Give me fifty cents worth of regular." He would then pump your gas for you, raise your car hood and check your oil and water. He would even add air to your tires if they needed attention.

On this one particular Saturday night I would be traveling with Mike, a former classmate of mine, and Leon, a cousin of one of my neighbors who was just visiting the area. I thought that I would impress Leon a bit by going to one of the areas better clubs, an out of the county club known as the Dew Drop Inn.

As soon as we settled in there I realized that we had made a good choice. Not only was a more gentle crowd in attendance there then we would normally see in our local road houses, but there were also several unescorted girls on hand and even more unusual there was a group of three girls sitting alone. We had the bartender serve them a round of drinks, which got their attention and soon we were sitting in their booth conversing with them.

In the meantime we began to realize that we were being scrutinized by three other young men, who apparently had set a goal to try to pick up these three young ladies for themselves before we arrived. After a couple of rounds of drinks, the girls made it known that they were ready to move on to another club, called The Cozy Rest, which they said was run by a friend of theirs.

The girls had their own car and we agreed to meet them at the Cozy Rest and they then got up and went outside to their car. As we started toward the door, two of those guys stepped out and blocked our path. I did not know Leon or his background and did know just how he was going to respond to this situation. I knew how I was going to respond, and I very casually laid my right arm on the bar, nestled up to an empty long neck bottle sitting there. The two bigger fellows were the ones that were confrontational; the third one just sort of sidled away from our group. The one standing next to Leon was persistent in the fact that we were not going to get past them to go and meet with the girls. Then Leon spoke, "You know, I don't like the idea of getting embroiled in a long drawn out fight, especially just over women", he said with a slight smile on his face. Then, just as quick as a rattlesnake would strike, he came up with a right cross and smashed the man's jaw. I mean there was a loud crack, as he obviously hit the man on the lower part of his face and broke his jaw. He dropped to the floor like a ton of bricks. I was really proud of the way that Leon responded. Just as his buddy started to retaliate, I placed my fingers around the neck of that lonesome long neck bottle sitting on the bar and surgically placed it along the left side of his head just above his ear. He then joined his buddy on the floor. The third member of their group then backed away, not wanting part of us and melted into the crowd. Without any further problems, the three of us continued on out of the front door and into my car.

As we were driving away I said to Leon, "You know, that was kind of sneaky the way you handled that situation back there in the club." He replied, "I was fair about it, I told the man that I did not want to get involved in a long drawn out fight, as a fellow might get hurt in a fight like that."

I straightened out the curves a bit as I knew that we needed to make up some time in getting to the Cozy Rest. When we arrived at the Cozy Rest, the girls were settled in and had a nice large booth ready for us. We picked our conversation right where we had left off, with no mention of the confrontation that we had just encountered. We knew that this arrangement was not going to go any place because we still had their second vehicle to contend with. Mike was also well aware of this, so he went ahead and did his usual thing and got plastered. The next time the waitress came by, and after taking our order for drinks, she pointed to Mike, who was now passed out on the floor beside our booth and asked, "How about him?" I said, "Don't serve him any more drinks, he is driving."

When the bar finally closed, one of the girls said, "You may follow us over to our house, if you like." We agreed, and as they drove out of the parking lot, we were following along behind them like little puppy dogs. We did not drive too far, just to the outskirts of town. They pulled up into the drive of a large two story house, a real mansion for that part of the world, but did not get out of their car, only blowing their car horn just once.

We did not alight from our car either; we sat there and waited to see what was going to transpire. A couple of minutes passed and then we saw a man emerge from the house and walk towards our car. As he neared our car he put on his hat and then I realized that he was a state police officer. He walked up to our car and said, "What do you boys want here?" I was not going to tell him what we really wanted, but by that time Mike, who was sitting in the back seat and had sobered up a little, blurted out "Don't take any shit from him, just because he is a police officer." I thought, "Thanks a lot Mike, that is what we needed right now," but I said, "We met these young ladies at the Cozy Rest and they asked us to follow them out here, I don't know if they just wanted the security of us being behind them or what they had in mind?" He then replied "Well, they are safe at home now, and you had best be moving on." I thanked him, started my car, turned around and drove away feeling good that we did not get in more trouble after Mike's outburst. I drove my companions back to their respective homes and then went home and retired.

Forty five years later, I was back in that same general area and had the opportunity to talk to some old timers there. I had heard previously that the Cozy Rest had burned to the ground about five years after my last encounter there. I broached that subject with the old timers. They were able to confirm several things about that state police officer, now deceased.

Yes, he was the father of one of the girls.

Yes, he did, in fact, own the Cozy Rest.

Yes, he donated five hundred dollars to the local volunteer fire department, on the provision that they would not respond to any fire at the Cozy Rest in a timely manner.

Yes, the fire that burned the Cozy Rest to the ground was probably arson and was probably self inflicted.

These were interesting bits of information, but since forty five years had passed since I had last been there, I could not see any way that it was going to affect my lifestyle now.

Time to move on.

Chapter 8

BALTIMORE EMPLOYMENT

With the advent of Pearl Harbor, I closed my radio repair shop, sold my car, paid all of my bills, and with a Greyhound ticket and twenty one dollars in my pocket, I boarded a bus for the big city of Baltimore, Maryland, where I expected to get a job in some kind of factory with a defense contract.

After a full day of walking the streets of Baltimore, and riding the nickel street cars, I finally got the message that as a sixteen year old kid with no experience, I was not going to get a job of any consequence. Desperate, I accepted a job in a fast food restaurant, making a whopping forty cents per hour. They turned me on to a private home where I was able to rent a room for five dollars a week that also included board. I moved into my new quarters, which was a small bedroom, with a shared bath. I had my one suitcase, which was bulging with most of my worldly possessions, and I had a small rope tied around it to make sure that it did not pop open and lose anything.

I settled in to making nickel hamburgers, nickel coffee, and fifteen cent milk shakes. The motto of the hamburger chain was, "Buy em by the bag", which was also printed on the side of the brown paper bags, which we put the take-out hamburgers in. And they did, too. Most of the customers who came in for take-outs, would order ten or twenty hamburgers at a time. Those that ate in would usually order two or three hamburgers at a time.

I was blessed by being very good at figures, and rarely ever made a mistake with the customers money. After only three months on the job, the manager came to me and asked, "How would you like to be the night manager here?" "What are the benefits and responsibilities?" I inquired. He went on to tell me exactly what my responsibilities would be and that my salary would then be sixty cents per hour. The salary impressed me, and I never considered the fact that those shops open all night were subject to armed robbery, as they are today.

I was now making 60 cents per hour, as night manager, but, to tell you the truth, I was just a deluxe janitor. Between customers, I was required to scrub and mop the floors, clean the toilets, clean and wipe all of the stainless steel cabinets. We really only had customers during shift changes that was between 10 p.m. and midnight and from 2 o'clock until 4 o'clock in the morning, except for policemen, who would come in at all hours of the night for their free coffee.

Forty seven years later, I was back in that same area, and the same fast food chain was still operating in the same building. However when I stopped by two years after that, the hamburger restaurant was closed and an Italian take out food kitchen was operating in that building.

I lived very frugally, as I had no one close in that area to fall back on, if I had a financial or medical crisis. It did not take me too long to save one hundred dollars. That was my, "Linus Blanket," and I never, ever, let myself get below that amount on my person. I enjoyed my work at the restaurant, but felt like I was spinning my wheels, like I was going nowhere. I sent to the court house back home and got a copy of my birth certificate. With that in hand, I went to a local print shop, and had them print one just like it, only appearing to be one year older.

With my new certificate in hand, I was able to get a job as a spot welder at the Glenn Martin Company, helping build B-26 bombers. I was now making 68 cents per hour. They put me on the 11 p.m. to 7 a.m. shift. That was all right with me, as I was used to working the night shift. It was now summertime and they didn't have air conditioning in the plant. With all of the machinery running, it would get very warm in the plant. I had a partner working with me and we had an air hose that we used to blow the aluminum shreds and specks away from our work. Sometimes we would stick the air hose up our pants leg or down the neck of our shirts. One night my partner got silly and stuck the air hose in my left ear. Naturally, it ruptured my left ear drum, a fact that I had to live with for the rest of my life.

A few weeks later, Will, an old school chum from back home, contacted me to see if he might find work there. I assured him that he would have no problem finding a job. When he arrived a few weeks later, he asked if he could go to work with me to apply for a job. I assured him that he could get work there, but that he should wait until tomorrow morning and I would go with him to the shipyards, as the pay rate there would be better. The next morning we went to the shipyard and got in line for a job. After waiting in line for about half an hour, we were still at the back of the line. Out of nowhere a naval officer appeared and said, "I assume you boys are looking for work?" I replied, "My friend, Will, here is. I am currently working in Essex, at the aircraft factory." He said, "Let me take you both down to the naval storehouse, and explain what our needs are, then I will take you back to wherever you need to go." I agreed and followed him to his vehicle. He had a Chevrolet Suburban parked nearby, and we all got in and drove only a short distance to the naval storehouse, where he explained the purpose of the storehouse and what would be expected from the employees.

Will agreed to start to work immediately. The starting pay was 89 cents per hour. For me, that would be a 21 cent per hour increase. He finally convinced me to try the job for one week, to see if I would be satisfied with it. I told him that I would not be able to start until a week from Monday, as I had to give my present boss a week's notice, anyhow. He was agreeable.

That night, when I went to work, I told my boss a little fib, and said that I would have to be off work for a week or two, starting Monday, a week, as I had to go back home and resolve some personal problems. When I finally started working at the storehouse, I was surprised as to how much I liked working there. It was not the production line that I was use to, doing the same thing over and over again, for seven and one half hours a night. After only three days I called my boss at the aircraft plant and told him that I would not be returning to work and that I would stop by and pick up my last check on Friday evening.

As soon as the Navy realized that I was going to stay with them, they took me to the driver's license bureau, so I could get a chauffeur's license. With my new chauffeur's license, I was now driving that same Suburban, picking up Navy personnel, shuttling them back and forth from ships and airports, to and from hotels. I did this for over three months, and then they put me in charge of over one hundred men, who physically handled

30

the product that was stored there, and ultimately delivered it onto the merchant ships. With this, I received an increase in pay from eighty nine cents per hour, to one dollar and twenty nine cents per hour. This increase in hourly wage, plus the overtime that I would be getting, left me with a very comfortable income.

The basic work that was accomplished at this storehouse was to put enough supplies on board of American merchant ships, to last twenty eight enlisted men and one officer, for a round trip to either England or Murmansk, Russia. That consisted of life preservers, food, books, radios and record players, side arms, games and water cooled, fifty caliber machine guns. The five inch thirty eight cannons, that were mounted on the bow of the ships and the twenty and forty millimeter cannons, were all installed at another facility, that had heavy cranes, welders, etc. to handle such large equipment.

Before Pearl Harbor, the German Navy captured an American merchant ship by the name of The City of Flint that had been delivering goods to England. It was later released by the Germans, and during my tenure at Baltimore, it came into our port to get the naval armed guard installed on their ship. While at our dock, I had the opportunity to speak with some of the merchant marines who worked on the ship. They said that although they were very scared when first captured, they never had to leave the ship and were never mistreated. After leaving our facility with a full naval crew aboard, they went directly to their fuel depot, took on a full load of fuel, and headed for Murmansk, Russia.

They were destined not to complete their journey. As they went through the straights near Norway, they were located by the German Air Force and were sent to the bottom, courtesy of aerial torpedoes. I suppose the Germans felt they had let her slip through their hands once and were determined not to let that happen again. Some of the merchant marines who served on the City of Flint, came back to our dock on a different vessel, and according to them, did not lose a single merchant marine in the sinking.

One afternoon, when Will and I got back to our room, we were surprised to find two men sitting there, going through our personal items. The men produced credentials that indicated that they were from the FBI, and that our landlord had let them into our room. They seemed convincing enough, then one of them handed me a small metal box, with a telegraph key mounted on top. He asked me, "What are the limits of this transmitter?" "It is not a transmitter at all, it is only a code practice unit, that I built while learning how to use Morse code." I replied. When they left, they took with them my little code practice unit with them, they thought because I knew when various merchant ships would be leaving Baltimore harbor, I might be able to alert some foreign agents about such movements. I never saw the practice unit again.

It was soon Christmas Eve, and when Will and I got through work, we stopped at a local pub for a couple of drinks before we went home. We then decided to go visit my Sister, Liz, who was now working at Glenn Martins, helping build B-26 bombers. She had an apartment that she shared with two other girls. We caught a street car, which cost ten cents to ride, over to Liz's place. The girls were all at work, but since I had a key to their apartment, we went on inside. We looked for something to drink, but found only a bottle of rum there. We went to the end of the block, in those days, there was a pub at the end of almost every row of row houses, and bought a case of 24 bottles of beer for one dollar and ninety five cents, and took it back to Liz's apartment. We had not even finished our first beer when Liz and her girl friends came home from work, and joined right in on the beer.

Chapter 9

Army Life

I was drafted into the United States Army in 1943 and was sent to the largest infantry camp in the world, which was located at Ft. Meade, Maryland. During the first two days there I went through all of the usual procedures that all new inductees into the army go through. Standing in line waiting to take a physical examination, while watching two other soldiers carry out a third soldier, who allegedly passed out while undergoing his physical in the infirmary.

Standing in line waiting to get my new uniform issued to me.

Standing in line waiting to get my bedding issued to me.

Standing in line waiting to get most of my hair cut off, by barbers who looked and acted more like carpenters than barbers. There was an advertisement in the army newspaper, The Stars and Stripes, that stated, "Barbers, wanted, no experience necessary, bring your own tools."

Walking into the latrine (toilet to you), and stepping up to the urinal where a sign posted on the wall states, "Young bucks with short horns please stand close the next man may be barefooted."

Standing in line at the mess hall, a sign posted on the wall states, "Never in the course of history have so many waited so long for so little."

Standing in line at your first formation, and having a grumpy looking Master Sergeant who looked like he was left over from World War One, bark out at you, "Well, they REALLY did scrape the bottom of the barrel this time." And things did not get any better for me. During my second evening meal, I was sitting at the bench/table eating and not paying any attention as to who was sitting next to me, since I had only been there a couple of days I did not expect to know anyone, anyhow. Then I noticed that the soldier sitting next to me arose, picked up an aluminum pitcher from the table, walked over to the end of the chow line and from a small barrel, filled the pitcher with hot cocoa. Bringing it back to the table, he sat down and proceeded to fill his cup with cocoa and then set the pitcher down on the table on the other side of himself, away from me. At that point I turned to him and said, "Butts on the cocoa," a slang expression of those times, as per seconds on your cigarette. To which he replied, "Listen soldier, I went and got this cocoa and I am going to drink it too." I fired back at him, "You are going to shit too, if you eat regular." He then arose, took off his windbreaker and only then did I realize that he had Master Sergeant's stripes on his uniform. Upon further observance, I realized that he was MY Master Sergeant. He reached out, grabbed my dog tags and looked at my name and mumbled, "Foxx, Sly Foxx," and then spoke aloud, "Soldier, I am going to make you regret the day that you were born." The dozen or so other soldiers who were sitting close enough to hear what was going on, just looked at me and shook their heads as if they felt my pain and pitied me. During the next two days I realized that my Sergeant does not make idle threats.

It seemed that every time I turned around he was yelling at me, "Soldier, give me twenty." That meant getting down on the ground and doing twenty pushups. He did everything possible that he could to make my life miserable. I survived each day and after chow when I returned to my barracks on the second day, I was really down. Bobby, a new friend I had made said, "Let's go into town and get drunk, and then maybe things won't seem so bad." I immediately replied, "Hell, I can't get off of the base, I can't even get a pass until I finish this damn basic training, and that will be another six weeks." He then went on to tell me about the, "Hole in the wall". A place that anybody could get off of the base and back on, by just walking through a hole in the chain link fence. A place that almost everyone knew about, but apparently no one had any desire to do anything about it. I said, "Sure, why not." I figured that if we got caught we would probably get court-martialed, but that did not seem important at that moment. By the time I got out of the brig, I would probably be away from my Master Sergeant, anyhow.

I put the rest of my uniform back on and off we were, walking to an obscure section of the base, and there it was, a hole in the chain link fence big enough for even a large soldier to pass through. As soon as we stepped through the fence to the outside world, I was relieved to see a taxi there, waiting for his next fare. We climbed into the taxi and asked the driver to take us to the nearest tavern where we would find some relaxing entertainment. He was only too happy to oblige.

Once inside the tavern we settled into a booth and had a few. Probably more than we should have had, under the circumstances. When the show was over, we bought a bottle of wine to drink on our taxi ride back to the hole in the wall. Outside the tavern, we had no trouble finding a taxi whose driver knew exactly where the hole in the wall was and drove us directly to it. Once safely back inside our base, we sort of stumbled our way back to our barracks and went upstairs, as our bunks were on the second floor. By the time I reached the top of the stairs, I felt very sick and felt like everything inside of me wanted to come out. The bunks were single deckers with one soldier's head facing toward the wall and the next one facing toward the center aisle. My bunk was at the very rear of the building and as I walked about half way to it, I started to vomit. As I continued walking, some of the vomit would splash up onto ones soldiers feet and the next ones face. I did, however, make it all the way to the rear of the building and crashed onto my own bunk.

When I awoke in the morning I felt terrible. I skipped breakfast and went through the motions of making my bunk. The place smelled terrible and I really needed to get out of there. When I went down to make the early formation, I went to the Sergeant and told him that I was sick and needed to go to the infirmary. He just glowered at me and told me to fall in. I did, and as we were marching along I got sick and barfed on the back of the soldier marching in front of me. At that point my sergeant realized that indeed, I really was sick. He told me to fall out, to go to the infirmary and to then return to my barracks.

It was just my bad luck that this was the time that a base inspection was going on, and when the inspecting officers climbed the stairs of my barracks, the first question they asked was, "Soldier, what are you doing in the barracks at this hour of the day?" I explained to them that I was sick, had been to the infirmary and that my sergeant requested that I return to my barracks and rest. Their next question was, "What is that terrible odor in here?" I told them that some soldier had gotten sick here the night before but did not volunteer the information as to whom the culprit might have been.

When the rest of the troops came back around five o'clock, I was still feeling bad and did not go to the mess hall with them. When they returned from chow the sergeant ordered our group from upstairs to not only scrub our entire barracks, but also the other three barracks in our group. I was too sick to help them so I stayed in my bunk and rested. At this point I realized that not only did I have my Master Sergeant hard on my ass, but thirty nine other soldiers who were also very unhappy with me.

As usual at five o'clock the next morning a corporal came through our barracks blowing his whistle and we all knew that it was time to rise and shine. By this time I felt like I might live. After breakfast our lovely sergeant marched us down to the quartermaster's building and we were all issued full battle gear, which included a full back pack with bedding, a canteen and an old army rifle that looked like it was left over from the Spanish-American war. On this day we marched, crawled under barbed wire, and marched some more. We crawled through man made mud and marched some more. About mid morning the old sergeant yelled, "Halt, take ten men and smoke if you got em." This is the way the whole day went, but at least at the end of the day he marched us back to the quartermaster and we got rid of our excess gear.

I could see already that I was just going to love doing this for the next five weeks. We went directly to the mess hall for our evening chow, after which I drug myself back to my barracks and flopped down on my bunk. After lying there for a few, someone yelled, "Hey Foxx, you are wanted down at the orderly room." I slowly got up and walked over to the bulletin board and sure enough, there it was, a notice that said, "Sly Foxx, report to the orderly room."

Every instant of my life from the past week flashed through my mind.

"What was it?"
"What will it be this time?"
"KP duty?"
"Pulling targets on the rifle range?"
"Scrubbing barracks?"
"Court martial?"
"Firing squad?"

I mean the whole range of anything bad that could happen to me, flashed through my mind.

I broke out in a cold sweat and I was shaking, but I went back to my bunk, put on a clean uniform and walked down to the orderly room and walked up to the desk where a sergeant was sitting. He looked up at me and said, "Yes." Still shaking, I said, "My name is Foxx, Sly Foxx, there is a notice on our bulletin board for me to report to the orderly room.

He shuffled through some papers, stopped and looked at one and said, "Yes, there is a notice here that your I Q is high enough that you could qualify for Air Crew Training in the Air Corps." I was aghast! I was flabbergasted! I could not think! I said to him, "What does that mean?" He replied, "That means that you are smart enough, if you want to, you can transfer from the United States Army Infantry to the United States Air Corps." Good news like that I could never have dreamed up in a million years! I meekly asked, "When can I sign up to be transferred?" "You can sign up now and transfer to the deployment section immediately if you want to," he replied.

I thought to myself, "I have to be good to God, for only he could have gotten me out of my terrible predicament that I was in, partially, but not all, brought on by my own actions." "Give me those papers," I said, "Lets get this transfer under way!

He pushed two forms toward and said "Just sign and date these two forms here." He continued, "Turn in your bedding to the Quartermaster, put all of your personal gear into your duffel bag and report to section "O," which is the deployment section." After signing my life away, the Sergeant explained to me how to get to section "O", as this was a very large base and one could get lost very easily, particularly for someone like me who had been on the base for only a few days.

I still found it hard to believe my good fortune as I went back to my barracks, put all of my personal items in my duffel bag, rolled up my bedding and with my bedding tucked under one arm and my duffel bag over my other shoulder, held by my hand, I walked out of the building amid catcalls and, "Good riddance." I never looked back, waved or anything, I just kept walking. I turned in my bedding at our Quartermasters and walked down to the section "O" orderly room and went in with a copy of my orders in hand, got my quarter's location and then went to their Quartermaster and checked out my new bedding.

I never went back to my old barracks, even to check if I had any mail, as I was afraid that I would run into my old Sergeant who might still cause me more trouble. Two days later, I was on a train for Shepard Field, an air corps base located near Wichita Falls, Texas. The base was a sprawling place consisting of hundreds of two story barracks, built on a sand plain in North Texas.

I was assigned to barracks number three hundred and eighty eight. As a direct result of all of the exceptional activities that transpired there, the occupants became known as the commandos of three eighty eight. An example might be that if you returned from town late at night and could not locate your barracks, or you were just unable to read the numbers on the barracks, one only had to sit down on the sand and wait. Somewhere out there in a very short period of time lights would come on in some barracks and THAT would be number three eighty eight.

It seemed that long after bed check, someone in our barracks would start a conversation on a regular basis. My bunk was on the second floor, as was the room of our sergeant, which was located at the end of the building near the staircase. Soon after anyone would start a conversation, a light would come on in his room, and our sergeant would get dressed and come out of his room and yell, "All right, you sons (as he flipped on our light switch) of bitches, fall out, we are going to do some drill time and maybe that will quiet you down." We would then fall into a formation in front of the barracks and he would have us march back and forth for about an hour and then he would say "Now maybe you are tired enough to go to sleep." And he was right too, we were. After these kinds of reactions for well over a month we were all getting fed up with the Sergeant's actions so we devised a plan.

On a regular basis, our good sergeant would go into town on Saturday night and usually returned to the barracks intoxicated. On this particular Saturday night, after the Sergeant had gone into town, we went into his room, which was never locked and short sheeted his bed. Not only did we short sheet his bed, but we also sprayed the inside of his sheets with aerosol Barbasol shaving cream. We then loosened every light bulb in the second floor of our barracks and then checked to make sure that no lights came on when the light switch was turned on.

We were all in our bunks in a timely manner and then lay quietly waiting for our sergeant to return to his room. Finally, the bewitching hour came and we heard our sergeant stumbling up the stairs and into his room. We could hear one boot hit the floor and then the other one. We then saw the light coming from under his door go off, the next thing we heard emerge from the sergeants room, was an oath that only a drunken sailor could have conjured up. I mean it was difficult for our delicate ears to have to endure. We then saw the light come back showing under his door and he obviously was getting dressed. He came out of his room yelling, "All right you X#%@!(as he flipped the light switch on) but when no lights came on, all conversation stopped cold.

On Sunday morning he very politely asked us to screw all of the light bulbs back in upstairs as he knew that he had been had, and never again were we to get up in the middle of the night for drill time.

Whenever we were marching around the base, we always sang a little song to keep in step with our marching. The song went like this: Texas is a hell of a state, parley voo, Texas is a hell of a state, parley voo. Texas is a hell of a state, the ass hole of the forty eight, hinkey, dinkey, parley voo. Shepard Field is even worse, parley voo, Shepard Field is even worse, parley voo. Shepard field is even worse, the ass hole of the universe, hinkey, dinkey parley voo.

We always had formations and marching displays every Saturday and the formations would last up to two hours. It really was hot there on the desert sand and the officers in charge would keep a line of ambulances lined up near the formations. We may have been standing at attention or even at parade rest when we would hear a slight thump or a little confusion. That would mean that another soldier had passed out from heat exhaustion or dehydration. An ambulance would then pull up, stop and pick him up and deliver him to the infirmary.

A little later in the year we had a little extra excitement one day when they took us out a little deeper into the desert, gave us a little folding shovel and told us to dig a foxhole big enough for us to lie down in. The sand was frozen pretty hard at the surface and after about fifteen minutes most of us had just barely scratched the surface. About that time a sergeant came by and told us that in another fifteen minutes live ammo would be flying right where we were standing, one foot above the sand. If one were standing near us there, one would have thought that a giant sand storm had struck. I mean sand was flying in every which direction. When I finally got the hole dug deep enough to feel comfortable with, I crawled down into it and almost immediately I heard the bullets zinging by, and could also see them, as about every fifth bullet was a tracer.

Everything seemed to settle down into a pretty mundane program after that and we were all getting a little restless because the air corps had not told us whether we were to be trained as aircraft mechanics, gunners, radio operators, or flight crew engineers. One evening when I returned to the barracks from our daily routine training program, I once again found my name on the bulletin board with a notice to report to the orderly room. This time I did not go to the orderly room with a troubled mind, as I had not been getting into any problem situations. When I arrived there I was given the bad news that my father had passed away and I had been given an emergency furlough to go home. I contacted my superior officer to find out if I might be able to catch a plane ride to some airport closer to home. But no such luck, I was destined to spend the next day and a half on a train ride home.

The train ride was not bad and the time flew by. The first time that I went to the rest room I passed two older men who were playing cards. I stopped a minute or two to watch them play and then continued on. On my way back to my seat I stopped again and watched them again and when they were shuffling the cards the next time I inquired, "What is the name of the card game that you are playing?" One of the men replied, "Pinochle." I lied and said, "I have never heard of that game, I have played various types of rummy, set back, high, low, jack and game but never heard of pinochle." As a child back on the farm, I really had not heard of the game but, while working for the navy as a civilian, I had a young man working under me who was really a walking computer and when it came to remembering cards, Pinochle was his favorite card game. He taught me the secrets of winning at the game and how to count cards and keep track of every card that had been shown or played.

One of them said, "If you have played any type of card games you can easily learn this game, come on and sit with us. Three players in the game is a much better game then just playing with two people and a dummy." I came back with, "Well, if you have me in the game you will still be playing with two people and a dummy." I sat in with them and we played a few hands just to get me oriented with the game and then one of them said, "Now we will play for a nickel a hand just to make it interesting." "That will be fine with me" I said, "I let them win most of the hands until we got the stakes up to a quarter a hand, with double on spades and pay double if you went set." From then on it was every man for himself and I was able to win over eighty dollars before I detrained.

When we quit the game one of them told me, "You just had beginners luck." I replied, "I have always said that I would rather be lucky than good anytime." They seemed convinced and both offered their condolences as I left the train.

After I alighted from the train at my home town I still had to wait some time for a bus to take me to the church where my Father's funeral was being held. From the bus I went directly to the church, where the services had already started before I arrived.

My Mother was particularly glad to see me, as my Brothers were also in the service and stationed overseas. I spent the remaining few days I had on my furlough trying to console and comfort my mother but I was able to offer little consolation as she was now stuck alone on a large farm with animals to feed and look after, with a long bleak winter in front of her.

Then it was back to basic training for me at Shepard Field, Texas.

We were always able to get a class "A" pass on weekends which meant that we could come and go as we pleased just so long as we were back at our station come Monday morning. Sometimes we would cross over the state line into Oklahoma where they had real bars and served real beer and whiskey, but usually we went into Wichita Falls and drank 3.2 beer. It seemed that a small group of us always ended up at the same bar once we got off of the bus in town. I guess that I was starting to get restless and feeling mischievous again. On this one Saturday night I managed to slip away unnoticed from the other men and took a taxi back to the base. I had the driver wait, as I was only going to be there for a few minutes. I went into our barracks and short sheeted several bunks, including faking short sheeting my own bunk and then back to the bar and slipped right back into the group.

A few days later, there it was again, that notice on the bulletin board, "Sly Foxx report to the orderly room." This time I had mixed emotions about the reason, but I figured that it probably was not to transfer back to the infantry. When I went into the orderly room this time, I was really surprised when the Sergeant there said to me, "Foxx, your I Q is so high that you qualify for officer training in the air corps, if you choose. Of course, I chose and said, "What, when and where do I sign?" He gave me some papers and I immediately signed them all and the next morning I turned in my bedding and moved to the deployment section, where I was to wait for the paperwork to clear for the seven of us who would be going off to college together.

While waiting to ship out, each evening I would return to barracks three eighty eight in time for mail call to see if I had any mail from home or from other buddies in the service elsewhere. On the third evening as I walked into the barracks several of my old friends grabbed me and stripped all of the clothes off of me. They then took bottles of liquid dye-n-shine shoe polish and painted every part of my body from the neck down. They did not paint my hands and arms but did paint everything else, and I mean everything. That done, I put my clothes back on and we were friends again. It seems that one of the other men took a taxi once and it turned out to be the same taxi driver that I had taken and he was telling the driver about the short sheeting incident and between the two of them they figured out that I was the culprit. The only thing that I can say was that it looked like I had a deep suntan in the middle of the winter.

A few days later I was on a train bound for Utah State College located in Logan, Utah. Undergoing officer training was not easy, as I found out what strict regulations were all about, and making a gentleman out of a plowboy was not an easy task. I had heard about white glove inspections but this was the first time that I was to experience them. If we left a shirt hanging in the clothes closet with one button unbuttoned we would get a demerit. If they rubbed those white gloves on anything in my area, and they picked up any dust, we got a demerit. If a pair of trousers were hung with one leg slightly lower than the other one we would get a demerit. If we made up our bunk with the blanket so loose that when you dropped a quarter on it and it did not bounce back up so you could catch it we would get a demerit.

In the mess hall we always had to sit with both feet flat on the floor, with one arm under the table and had to hold our silverware in a particular way. We were taught aeronautical science, calculus, grammar and even music appreciation. We spent a lot of time studying clouds and cloud formations, studying the various factions indicating wind speed and direction, by looking at tree limbs and leaves and looking at the size and direction of waves on the water. We spent quite a bit of time on aircraft identification also.

While in an English class there I had a professor who required us to write a thesis on the theory of relativity. My theory, and that of Albert Einstein's theory, was not exactly the same but I wrote my thesis as I saw it. It started out with, "The heat of the meat plus the mass of the ass, times the angle of the dangle equals the torque of the pork." Well, you get the idea as to how the thesis went.

The professor liked my thesis so well that I received a solid "A" on it. That was Utah, nineteen hundred and forty four. Time marches on. The time is now nineteen hundred and sixty eight. The place is Ft. Lauderdale, Florida. Now, being a national distributor for Motorola products, I am having a regional sales meeting for all of my dealers. As I was talking to one of my dealers from Fort Myers, Florida, I found that we had a lot in common and during our conversation he took some papers from his briefcase and said, "Here is something that you may find interesting to read." With that he handed me an exact copy of my thesis which I had written twenty four years earlier. From whom he obtained that, I will never know. He had never been to Utah.

Small world.

While at Logan I met a lot of Mormon girls, most were very pretty and all had rosy cheeks, a healthy glow on their faces and always a broad smile. I went to parties and dances with them and even attended Mormon Church services with them on a regular basis. All in all, my training program there was a wonderful experience, but it ended all too soon. I don't know why, but I felt uneasy and had a bad premonition as I fell in for our usual formation on Saturday, April first. After our normal Saturday formalities, the officer in charge announced that the officer training program at Utah State College was being disbanded. He announced that the higher command had decided that by the time we had completed our training here, plus our pilot training to follow, would be so time consuming that our services would probably not be required in this war.

We were then offered three options. One: We could transfer back to our original command, which in my case would have been the United States Army Infantry. Two: We could transfer to Ft. Benning, Georgia to continue our officer training program but we would graduate as a Second Lieutenant in the United States Infantry. We could stay in the air corps and train to be flight crew members. I went along with option number three as I did not want to have any further connection with the infantry. After all, I still had bad memories of my old Master Sergeant and feared that I might run into him somewhere.

Since I had previous experience in the field of radio and knew the Morse code, I was able to get into the training program to become a radio operator as a flight crew member. One week later I was out of Logan, Utah and on a train to a radio operator's school located near Sioux Fall, South Dakota. There are two things that I will always remember about South Dakota. First, it snowed there on the second day of June and second, that I had to be in bed for a bed check at nine o'clock PM, and the sun was still shining in my face.

Life at the radio operator's school seemed pretty laid back, particularly just after coming out of the strict officer training program. They taught us all about the various pieces of radio equipment as used by the air corps and how to use them but nothing about how to repair them. They taught us how to send and receive Morse code but mainly we just copied code. When we copied code we would write the letters in groups of five characters and then when the message was complete we would separate the groups of letters into words.

Early in the morning of June sixth as we were copying code, the messages seemed longer than our normal practice messages. When I finally got a break and a chance to read what I had copied, I was amazed at what I was reading. I was copying the actual events of the invasion of Normandy beach as it was happening! I found it hard to believe that I was writing on paper, history as it was unfolding! Fortunately, I was correct enough in my copying of the Morse code, that what I had written actually made sense.

Outside of our school work there always seemed to be a lot of formations for which we had to line up. Sometimes it was for retreat and sometimes it was just for marching around the base. I think that they were just trying to remind us that we were still in the army and not in some private school. After I had been there for a while I had made a lot of friends with whom I would end up playing cards, shooting pool or just sitting around telling about our wild tales of life before we entered the army.

Sometimes we just did not feel like making some of the formations and would stay back in our barracks or the recreation room. When the Sergeant would call our name in the roll call, someone else who knew you and knew that you were absent would answer here or yo. The Sergeant soon got wise to that and thereafter when your name was called in the roll call you had to answer with the last four numbers of your serial number.

We countered that by having every member of our group memorize the last four numbers of the serial number of two or three other members, which worked really well for quite a while. Then one evening when it was time for us to fall out for retreat only about one fourth of our men fell out. When the Sergeant called the roll, almost everyone answered present. The Sergeant, realizing that something was seriously wrong, called the roll again, only this time he had the men fall out of the first formation and into a second one, as their name was called.

When the retreat formation was over one of my friends ran to my barracks and told me I was in a heap of trouble. He then went on to tell me just what the Sergeant had done. But again I was lucky, as this was the day that the Inspecting General was on the base and I still had fifteen minutes to get to base headquarters and file a written complaint. As long as I filed a written complaint about something that I did not like about the base operations I would be cleared for missing my formation. Done, and I never had any repercussions. I still say, "I would rather be lucky than good any time." Needless to say I did not miss any more of the required formations while still on the base at Sioux Falls.

We all had class "A" passes, which meant that we could come and go from the base as much as we wanted just so long as we did not miss any of our required classes or formations. I heard some of the fellows who had been on the base longer than I, talking about a summer resort in Iowa called Lake Okabougi. They said that the prices of things there were very reasonable and the young girls were plentiful. That sounded like a winner to me.

I talked with my best buddy about this and he agreed that we would try to go there on the next weekend. Hitchhiking was a wonderful way for soldiers to travel then, even though there were not a lot of cars on the road, when one did come by, they had a lot of respect for soldier boys and if they had any room in their vehicle for you the would always stop and pick you up and in many cases invite you into their home for lunch or dinner.

Saturday morning found me and my buddy, standing by the side of the road waiting for a ride. The very first car that came by stopped and picked us up and took us all of the way to Iowa but not as far as Lake Okabougi, only as far as Rock Rapids. In Rock Rapids we stopped at a small café to grab a bite to eat and while there we met and conversed with a couple of cute girls. After spending the afternoon with them we felt that there was no immediate need to travel any further. Life was so wonderful there, that we spent that weekend there, and also all available weekends that summer in Rock Rapids. To this day I still wonder what a weekend would have been like at Lake Okabougi, as we never got that far because life was far too good in Rock Rapids.

As fall and winter came on we started traveling to other scenic spots including Mount Rushmore National Memorial and to see the Corn Palace in Mitchell, South Dakota. The Corn Palace was a large concert hall that was beautifully decorated inside and out with corn. Corn stalks, corn leaves, ears of corn and kernels of corn. You only had to view it to appreciate its beauty.

After graduation from radio school we sewed on our corporal stripes and were on a train bound for gunnery school near

Yuma, Arizona. Our base near Yuma was really something, located well out into the desert sand with no barracks to sleep in, only tents, with temperatures exceeding one hundred degrees and of course, no air conditioning. Only the mess hall had any sort of cooling system. In one end of the building was installed a large fan that blew directly into the building over a large burlap bag filled with small wood chips that had water dripping on them constantly. As the fan blew the air over the wet wood chips, with the low humidity there, it would cause the water to evaporate and cool the inside of the building somewhat.

Another downside of living in the desert, was the ever presence of rattlesnakes, black widow spiders, and scorpions. At night it was not unusual to check under our pillows or blankets and find a black widow spider lurking there and in the morning we always had to shake our shoes to make sure that there were no scorpions resting inside. Sometimes we would go on night marches because it was cooler then, and we would always march down a paved road. It was the fall of the year and the sand would cool down fast but the paved road would stay warm and the rattlesnakes would congregate on the warm paved road. As we were marching along we could hear those rattlesnakes slithering off of the road in front of us as we marched along.

Sometimes in the evening after our normal day of training the officers would take us in trucks over into the California desert where we would dig up date palms and take them back and plant them on our base to beautify it. When we did that, we were always rewarded with two bottles of warm beer but we soon learned that we could cool the beer somewhat by dripping aviation fuel over the bottles.

During our training there we learned how to disassemble and reassemble our fifty caliber machine guns, blindfolded. We learned how to hit clay pigeons from the back of a moving pickup truck. We intensely studied aircraft identification. An art that we were so proficient in that we could identify with just a quick flash on the projection screen as to whether the plane was American, English, German or Japanese. They certainly did not want us to try to shoot down any friendly planes.

The one plus that we did have there, was the fact that there was a large swimming pool that was available only for the use of enlisted men. However, with six squadrons training there at one time, we had to divide up the time that each squadron could have use of the pool. We were required to wear a helmet liner at all times, to help protest us from the sun and also for identification as to what training squadron we belonged to. On the front of each helmet was painted a bunny rabbit, and the helmet of each squadron was painted a different color. The staff then would post a schedule as to what times each squadron could have exclusive use of the pool.

Many times when we were off duty we would put on our bathing suits and wander over to the pool and even if our squadron were not scheduled we would take off our helmet liner and jump into the pool if it was not crowded. One day, myself and other members of our squad were in the pool at a time that we were not scheduled. When a staff member came by to check the pool, he realized that some of the helmets belonged to soldiers who were not scheduled to be there at that time. He merely picked up the helmet liners of those without authorization and took them back to the quartermaster.

He knew that when we fell out tomorrow morning without our helmet liners, they would know who to discipline. Sensing that we may have a little problem we devised a risky little plan, in which one of our skinny little guys would crawl through a small window in the quartermasters that was always open and pass out enough of our colored helmet liners to accommodate all that needed them. We decided that we would go as a group because we felt that if we were caught, they might be more lenient to a large group then they might be to just two or three men. As soon as it was dark and before bed check we went to carry out our plan. We pulled it off without a hitch and was very careful after that to go to the pool only on our assigned times.

We all graduated with flying colors, sewed on our new sergeant's stripes and headed for a nice furlough before we were to report to a bombing range in Florida where we would meet the other men who would make up our ultimate flight crew.

Chapter 10

CHRISTMAS FURLOUGH

With my gunnery training completed, I was looking forward to a two week furlough to be back at home for Christmas. After spending almost two days on a train From Yuma, Arizona, I finally arrived at my home town, only to wait another two hours for a Greyhound bus to take me out in the country, to where my pride and joy was garaged, a nineteen hundred and forty one, Ford V/8 car. I alighted from the bus to step out into six inches of snow, but at least it was not snowing at that moment. I walked over to the house where the man, who owned the garage from whom I was renting, lived and was glad to see that he was home.

We exchanged our pleasantries and he then walked me back to the garage and unlocked it for me. I thanked him and assured him that I would be returning my car to the garage within two weeks. The car was up on blocks, to keep the weight off of the tires, so I jacked it up and removed the blocks. Then realizing that all of the tires were low, I used a hand pump, which in those days we always kept in the trunk of the car, to add enough air to each tire to get me safely to a service station, where I would have them check the car over for me.

Leaving my car at my local service station, I walked over to an appliance repair store to greet Andy, an old friend of mine. I went into his store and after visiting with Andy for a half hour or so, I asked him, "Say Andy,

48

while my car is being checked over, you wouldn't mind if I borrowed your car for a little while, just to run over to the pool room to see what is going on there, would you?'

He replied, "Sure, go ahead, the keys are in the ignition, but be very careful as there are no brakes on the car." "You never did have a car with good brakes on it" I said and walked out of the door.

The keys were in the ignition as he said they would be and I was pleasantly surprised that the engine started right away, in spite of the fact that it was so cold. I drove down the street two blocks and as I stepped on the brake pedal to slow down to make a right turn I realized that the brake pedal was already flat on the floor boards. In my mind I thought, "Boy he was right; his car really did not have any brakes on it." I made no effort to make my right turn, instead just let the car drift forward until it slowed to the point where I could make a U turn and took his car back to where I found it.

I found out later that all of the brake shoes were lying on the floorboards of the back seat, as he had removed them to get them relined, but just had not gotten around to getting that done yet. I went back into his store and said, "Thanks, but no thanks, I will just walk" as I threw his keys down on the counter. I could not imagine anyone driving a car on a regular basis on snow and ice with absolutely no brakes on it.

I walked to the pool hall but was disappointed as there was no one there that I had ever seen before, as most young men were in the service somewhere. I ordered one beer and shot one game of pool with another man there, as I was just killing time. I then walked back to the service station, found that my car was ready to go and they reassured me that my car should be trouble free during my furlough.

I then drove to see my mother, who now lived alone on a farm nearby. I had not been here since I came home for my father's funeral over a year ago. She was really glad to see me and commented on how healthy I looked. In a kidding way I said, "Oh that is from the great food that the army feeds me."

I stayed with her for a couple of more days and then told her that I would be driving to Baltimore to see my Sister Liz. She thought that would be wonderful for me to go to see her and that she would send her a couple of cakes. I responded, "You have enough to do around here without baking any cakes." She replied, "Oh no, I don't mean bake them now, when your Aunt Helen was here last month, we baked some cakes and put them in the freezer." From which she removed two cakes, boxed them up and gave them to me to give to Liz.

I took the cakes, kissed my mother goodbye, and then drove over to pick up Mike, an old schoolmate of mine who was going to keep me company on my trip to Baltimore. He suggested that we put chains on the car due to the amount of snow and ice on the road, which we did and pointed the car towards the east. We had not gone more than a couple of miles when we hit a slick spot on the road and ended up facing the direction from which we had come.

By the time we had driven twenty miles, we had spun around three hundred and sixty degrees twice and one hundred and eighty degrees four times. It did not take a rocket scientist to realize that the chains were doing us more harm than good, so at the first clear wide place in the road, we pulled over and removed the chains.

By slowing down a bit, we were able to complete the rest of the trip with only twice sliding into a snow bank on sharp curves. When I came to a sharp curve while going downhill, I would look for a bare spot on the road and head towards that spot. By applying hard brakes just as the front wheel would hit the dry spot, I could cause the rear of the car to slide in the desired direction, thus avoiding a crash.

Arriving in Baltimore, Liz, who was always ready for a party, was surprised and glad to see me. She thanked me for bringing the cakes from Mom and she knew Mike from back home. She had two other young girls staying with her to share expenses and she introduced them to Mike and me.

After we talked for a while, Mike and I went out and replenished their alcohol supply, as we were going to be spending a couple of days there.

The girls made a nice evening meal for us and after that we settled in for some serious drinking. Of course I had to tell them of some of my many army escapades. We had the radio on and we were listening to the hit parade that night. The top ten hit then was, "Don't fence me in."

Later on Mike, who did not hold his alcohol very well, decided to go upstairs and go to bed. In a few moments we heard this loud thumping noise. I walked over to the bottom of the stairs, where I saw Mike lying in a crumpled heap at the foot of them. I said, "Did you miss a step, Mike?" He replied, "Hell no, I hit them all."

We stayed with Liz until Monday morning at which time we started our trek back home. It had not snowed any more in Baltimore while we were there and the roads seemed pretty dry as we left the city, but when we got into the mountains near Cumberland, Maryland, things changed drastically.

It had been snowing daily in that area and in some areas only a single lane of the roads were cleared. It was on one of these stretches of road that we were traveling downhill and probably driving faster than we should have been under the circumstances, when we met a large dual axle truck coming up the mountain.

At that instant I had two choices and I did not like either one of them. One was to hit the truck head on and the other was to jump my car over the side of the mountain. Well, I took the latter, and just like in the movies, we went flying through the air off of the side of this mountain. We really were airborne, but were fortunate to land wheels down with the front end of the car tilted slightly forward, into a snow drift eight or nine feet deep.

We were not able to get the car doors open because of the snow, but we were able to roll the windows down and crawl out through the open windows. Once out of the car we still had to crawl and burrow our way until we got to a place where the snow was less than two feet deep.

In the distance we could see smoke rising, apparently from someone's house chimney, and started walking down the valley towards it. We had gone less than a quarter of a mile when we ran into four young lads, who appeared to be ten or twelve years old and were out of school for Christmas vacation.

They had not heard our crash, as the snow pretty well muffled the sounds from our crash landing. They were just out playing with their sleds, not the type with steel runners as city kids used, but with wide wooden runners made from two by fours. We told the boys of our plight, and upon seeing me in uniform, they clamored to see what they could do to help us. They said "You just wait right here and we will go and bring some shovels and dig you out, we will have you out of here in no time, don't leave." Yeah, like we were going to go someplace before they got back.

They did, they ran as fast as their little legs would carry them until they were out of sight and soon thereafter they reappeared with two snow shovels in hand. There was a lot of snow to move. First we had to clear a swath about eight feet wide for about forty feet that started about one foot deep graduating to eight feet deep, just to get to the front of my car.

Next we had to clear the snow away from all around the car, and even with all of that accomplished, the wheels were still not on solid ground as the underside of the vehicle was sitting on a hard pack of snow about one foot deep.

I raised the hood of the car and could not see any obvious damage to the engine compartment, so I started the engine, and with Mike and the boys pushing on the car, I put it in gear but to no avail, the rear wheels were just spinning. We were not going to go anywhere. I thought to myself, "Here in the mountains, the snow will probably be melted by March or April and then I can drive the car out of here."

One of the kids sensing my concern said, "Not to worry, my dad has a tractor; I will go get him to bring it here for you and pull you out." Two of the kids left and the other two along with Mike and I tried to scrape as much of the packed snow from under my car as we possibly could while they were gone.

About a half hour or so had passed and here came a man on an old Fordson tractor with the two kids riding on the back. This tractor was not like the modern day tractors with balloon tires that would easily spin on the snow, it had steel wheels with a ridge encircling the front wheels to ensure easy steering, while the rear wheels which were about four feet in diameter, all steel with heavy cleats welded to the wheels to give plenty of traction for good pulling power.

He introduced himself and then backed the tractor up to the front of my car, took a heavy chain and attached it from the rear of his tractor to the front axle of my car. He then put the tractor in gear, there was a little jerk and then my car started slowly sliding forward. Once my car was off of the pile of hard packed snow he stopped. I spoke with him and we agreed that it probably would be better if he would keep his tractor connected to my car, and that I would keep my car in low gear until we reached the paved road in front of his house.

Once we arrived that far, I asked him what I owed him but he would not accept any money. I guess that he thought he was helping one of his country's defenders. I thanked him profusely and gave each of the boys a one dollar bill which seemed to make them very happy.

We made the rest of the return trip home without any further problems and after dropping off Mike at his home, I drove directly to my service station to have them put my car back on the lift and check for any hidden problems. Again they assured me that no damage had occurred and that I was good to go.

The next day I went to Shanks Park, one of my old hangouts, a roadhouse known among its clientele as the bloody bucket, because of the large number of fights that had occurred there. Bert was the bartender that day. He was the son of the owner of Shanks Park. Bert was in the United

States Marines, and like myself, was just home on leave. He was about six feet two inches tall and weight about two hundred pounds and not one ounce of fat. I had a couple of beers with him there and we agreed that we would double date that night and that I would come by there around seven o'clock to pick him up, before we picked up the girls.

I arrived at the Bloody Bucket about the appointed time and he and I were having a beer before we left. By that time a small group of the regulars had started to congregate. Bert and I were just standing by the wall talking when this man of small stature, who appeared to be in his forties, walked up, interrupted what we were saying and started talking to us. It only took about two sentences out of his mouth before we realized that he had a head start on getting intoxicated. "You know" he said, "I really feel ornery tonight; I would really like to just tear this place up." To which Bert replied, "I think that you have a good idea there, and I would be willing to help you, where would you like to start?" "Well, I don't know, what do you think?" He replied "We could start by just tearing up the bar." Bert said. "Hey, man, that is a great idea" the man answered.

The front of the bar was covered with sheets of homosote, which looked like wallboard but was made of a cardboard like material. At this point, Bert just picked up the little man, carried him over to the front of the bar and threw him right through the homosote front of the bar, breaking and scattering the empty beer bottles that were stored under the bar, behind the bar front.

Bert then walked around the bar and picked the little guy up by the shirt and said to him, "Well, we did a good job on the bar now what would you like for me help you destroy next?" The man said, "Nothing, no nothing, I have had enough, I don't want to tear anything else up." "Are you sure that you have had enough?" Bert said. "Yes, I have had enough; I don't want to tear anything else up." He said. At that point, Bert drug him to the front door and threw him out of the door.

We spent a few minutes helping pick up the scattered and broken beer bottles, which fortunately, were empty, and then went out on our date. At the end of the evening and after we had taken the girls home, since we were riding in my car, I went back to Shanks Park to drop off Bert. As he was getting out of my car, he asked me to wait a couple of minutes as he wanted to check the front and back doors just to make sure that everything was secure. I watched as he walked to the front door and finding it secure, started walking around towards the back. There he was the same little guy with whom he had an altercation with earlier in the evening.

He was hiding there at the back of the bar with a blackjack in his hand and as Bert turned the corner, he got in two good licks to Bert's head with his blackjack, before Bert was able to wrestle the blackjack away from him and throw it out into the grass. Bert then settled into doing some serious pounding on the little guy. The man spoke, "Please stop, I have had enough, I have had enough, please stop." Bert's reply was, "You little son of a bitch, you said five hours ago that you had enough, but apparently you did not have, now I am going to make sure that you have had enough." He kept hitting him until the man fell unconscious on the floor of the porch. We then picked him up and put him in the back seat of my car and drove with him to the emergency room of the local hospital. Arriving there, we sat him on the floor with his back leaning against the emergency room door, so that when the door was opened, he would fall back inside. It was about one o'clock in the morning as we rang the bell at the emergency room door, and then ran like hell to get into my car and leave the premises.

The next morning, we went back to Shanks Park and found the blackjack that Bert had thrown into the grass at the rear of the bar. What we found was a piece of screen door spring about ten inches long with a nugget of lead about two inches long poured onto one end of the spring. The other end had enough friction tape wrapped around it to make a comfortable hand grip for the weapon.

The following day I took my precious car back to the rented garage and put it back up on blocks until the next time. I had to catch my train to my next military assignment in Florida, so I never heard any further information as to the outcome of the little guy. I hope that everything turned out well for him and maybe he had learned a lesson.

Sometimes silence IS golden.

Chapter 11

FINAL ARMY DAYS

With my Christmas furlough over, I boarded a train for Florida. I had a layover in Jacksonville where I transferred to another train, just long enough for me to go to a restaurant for some breakfast. I had ordered ham and eggs over easy, but when the waitress brought my plate to me there was a pile of white mushy looking stuff also on the plate. I pointed to the white pile and asked the waitress, "What is that stuff?" "Grits" she replied, "They are very good." "I don't think so, please take the plate back and scrape them off." I said. It was just that I had never seen grits before and since have eaten them and learned to like them.

My next stop was at an Air Corps base near Plant City, Florida. I spent only a few days at the camp in Plant City for processing, and then via train to Avon Park, where I was taken by bus to the Avon Park Bombing Range. There I was to meet and train with eight other men who would make up a crew for flying B-17 bombers, known in those days as a flying fortress, because it had so many guns on it that an attacking plane could find no angle of approach that was not covered by fifty caliber machine gun fire.

We were assigned to our barracks and went to the quartermaster, picked up our bedding and soon would start meeting the other men who would make up our crew. The first crew member I met was Joe, a first lieutenant, originally from Pensacola, Florida, who was to be our pilot. He was tall and slim with dark hair, a pleasant smile and easy to talk to. Next, I met Roy, a second lieutenant who was from Pennsylvania, and was to be our co-pilot. He had blond hair, was of medium height and pretty laid back. Our navigator was Jose, a first lieutenant, who was from Puerto Rico. He was small in stature with dark hair and exceptionally bright. Then there was Wade, who would be our flight engineer. He was from Indiana, was in his thirties and the only member of our crew who was married. Wade would also be our top gunner. Doug was a small blonde man from California, who would have to stay curled up in a small three foot ball, as he was to be our Ball Gunner. Angelo was from New York, was of Italian descent, medium build and dark complexioned. Angelo turned out to be the comedian in our crew. Angelo was to be our nose gunner. Blackie was from North Carolina, was really a character and was to be our tail gunner. Jack was our right side gunner and was a southern boy from Texas. I, of course, was the radio operator and left side gunner.

It was a very congenial group, and our officers asked that we not salute them, except when we were in the presence of other officers. Only Wade, our flight engineer, insisted on saluting each time that he met one of our officers.

Blackie insisted that the war would be over in six months. When pressed as to why he thought that the war would be ended in six months, he replied with, "It is only because of something that my father said to me, and he is never wrong." I asked him point blank, "Just what did your father say to you?" He answered, "My father told me that the war would be over in six months, because I never in my life had been able to keep a job for more than six months." His father was right too, as the war in Europe, where we would be heading, was over in less than six months.

Once our crew was assembled, our program consisted of going to classrooms on two days a week and flying all day for three days a week, with the weekends off. There were fifty six crews training in our group. We were listed as crew number fifty one. On class days we went to a class with other crew members in the same category, that is, all of the radio operators attended one class and all flight engineers attended another. When we flew, we always flew in the same plane, one that had returned from Europe. It had the name and picture of General Sherman painted on the nose of the aircraft. We flew in this same plane for two and a half months. Most of our flights were at twenty thousand feet, requiring us to wear oxygen masks. We made a lot of bombing runs, dropping bombs that were duds, a lot of pinpoint navigation, flying over a good portion of the southeast. I got in a lot of radio practice, using both Morse code and voice communication. On rare occasions, we actually got to fire live ammo from our fifty caliber machine guns at targets on the ground.

On this one particular day we went through our usual routine, which consisted of picking up our gun barrels and parachutes from the quartermaster. We were never allowed to leave any barrels in the guns on our planes, as there might be a chance that a live round was left in the chamber. With no barrel in the guns, there was no chance of an accidental firing. We would go to our plane, stash our gear on the plane, and then go to the front of the plane and rotate each of the engines two rotations, by physically turning the engine over by means of pulling on the propellers by hand. This would pump out any oil that may have dripped into the lower cylinders while the plane was sitting on the tarmac.

The crew would take their normal positions inside the plane for takeoff and landings. Joe our pilot, would then start the engines and prepare for takeoff, however, on this one particular morning, Joe was unable to get the number three engine started. After several unsuccessful tries with no results, Joe called the tower for instructions. The tower advised him to have us remove our gear from the General Sherman and use the plane sitting on the hard stand to our left that day. This done, we repeated our routine on our different plane and we were able to take off with no problems.

We flew in this plane for our usual eight hours or so, and Joe brought the plane down to a successful landing. In those days we considered any landing that we could walk away from as being successful. I took my gun barrel and parachute from the plane directly to the quartermaster and placed them on the counter to have them checked back in. Immediately the demeanor of the two GI's behind the counter changed and they turned white. Usually when I would come in they would say, "How many German planes did you shoot down today?" Or, "How does Berlin look from the air today?" Today, not a word, and when I spoke to them I received no reply. I finally just walked out of the building and went across the courtyard to where the officers were being debriefed.

When Joe finally walked out of the building, I said to him, "What the hell is going on here today?" "Haven't you heard?" was his reply. "Heard What?" I said. "After we took off this morning, crew number fifty six came out and got into the General Sherman. All four engines started up immediately and they took off." "What has that got to do with us?" I said. Then came the bad news, "After flying about four hours into their mission, the plane suddenly exploded in mid-air and all nine men aboard were killed."

I was so stunned at what I had just heard that I could not talk or even think. When it finally sunk in as to what had happened I mumbled out loud, "That was our plane, I should have been on it today." Then I remembered the time a couple of years before at the infantry camp when God had stepped in and saved me, and I thanked him then, and again today God had taken my life into his hands and saved me again. I knew now that nothing really bad was ever going to happen to me as I was one of his chosen.

Joe could see how shook up that I was and he put his hand on my shoulder and tried to comfort me. By that time the rest of the crew showed up. They had already heard the news and as we all walked back to our barracks, not a word was spoken.

Aside from realizing how lucky we really were, this accident affected our crew in another manner. Just as I had been associated with the same radio operators in this training program for the past eight months or more, so had the flight engineers. It turned out that Wade, our flight engineer, was the very best friend of the flight engineer that was killed in the explosion of the General Sherman, and he agreed to accompany his buddy's body back home.

That left us one crew member short, but we were lucky to pick up another excellent young man named Jake, who had gone through this training program with a previous training group, but was left behind when he ended up in the hospital for some minor surgery. He blended well into our crew and since he was single, he turned out to be my best pal.

Crew fifty one finished our training without any further major distractions. We did however end up with the highest overall training ratings of the fifty five remaining crews. As the top crew in our training group, we were entitled to a few days of holiday. All of our actual flight crew, the pilot, co-pilot, navigator, flight engineer, and myself, the radio operator, all agreed to stay together and we were able to fly our own plane to Havana, Cuba for a few days of R and R. The other crew members who were only gunners opted to take a furlough and go home.

When we landed our B-17 at the airport in Havana, and there was a bus waiting there to take us to the Hotel El Nacional, where we would be staying. While on the bus on the way from the airport to our hotel, I saw something for the very first time in my life. I saw a man plowing a field with a plow pulled by a team of oxen. The oxen had harnesses and were being worked just like I was used to seeing men work a team of horses.

After we settled in at our hotel, the bellhop there turned us on to a limousine driver who turned out to be ideal for our mini vacation. He owned his own vehicle, which was a nineteen hundred and thirty five Packard convertible, with an extra row of seats in it, which was just right for our mini crew, and since he was independent, and not affiliated with any taxi group, was free to answer to our beck and call.

On our first evening there he drove us to a dance hall that was lined with pretty young girls. Once inside the dance hall, we could go to the cashier and purchase dance tickets for ten cents each, and then, with tickets in hand, we could walk along the sidelines and select the girl with whom we would like to dance. We would hand her one ticket and we were out on the dance floor with the young lady. If we were not completely happy with our first selection, at the end of that dance, we would escort her back to her seat and make another selection.

Once we were happy with our selection, if we desired, we were then able to take the girl out to dine, or to some other party, or even to her home or a motel if that was what we had in mind. All of the young women could communicate in English pretty well, and the first thing that they would say was, "You likey me?" Of course we liked them or we would not have selected them in the first place. We partied, we drank, we ate, we danced and late that night the five of us ended up back at the El Nacional Hotel and retired.

Early the next morning we got up looking for our limo driver and found that he was already parked in the hotel parking lot awaiting his next instructions. He took us to a nice restaurant for breakfast and he took us shopping. He took us on a tour of the Morro Castle, a famous fort overlooking the entrance to the harbor at Havana. He took us to bars and another nice restaurant where we had a wonderful dinner. We really liked Havana because the cost of good meals and great booze was so reasonable.

What I thought was very unusual, was when I was in one of their retail stores, I had not enough money to purchase what I desired and I asked the manager if he would cash a check. He said "Certainly." I did not have a check with me, so he handed me a check, which I proceeded to fill in the name and address of my bank, filled out the date and amount and signed it. He cashed my check and gave me change of over thirty dollars in American money and never even asked to see any identification from me.

But time flies when you are having fun and our four nights and days in Havana, too soon came to an end. It was time to face reality again, so we loaded fifty cases of high quality booze into our plane, which was for the benefit of the officers club back on base and departed beautiful Havana. It was night time when we flew back to our base at Avon Park, and as we flew over the Florida straights, I saw the most beautiful natural picture that I have ever seen in my lifetime. The moon was just rising in a cloudless sky over the horizon, and that moonlight on the water, which was of varied depths, gave off a panorama of colors and made an awesome picture.

I can assure you that those four days spent in Havana, were never to be forgotten in one lifetime. Once back on solid ground at Avon Park, we were still given another few days furlough while awaiting the return of the rest of our gunnery crew. We then all reported to Hunter Field, an air base located near Savannah, Georgia.

While waiting for reassignment at Hunter Field, we were treated royally. We had German prisoners of war there who waited on us hand and foot. They prepared our meals, did our KP duty, cleaned our barracks and made our beds. Life there was a piece of cake. The German prisoners who were there were so happy to be in the United States that they would have done anything to stay here. While there an old girl friend of mine came to Savannah with her sister and stayed at a local hotel, which made life even a little more blissful for a few days.

By this time the war was winding down in Europe so they transferred our pilot, navigator, co-pilot, flight engineer and myself to the Air Transport command to help fly a group of new updated B-17's to Europe. That was the last time that I ever saw any of our gunnery crew or our bombardier. They then flew us to Westover Field, Massachusetts to pick up our plane. While at Westover Field I met a lady, who as a civilian, worked for the Air corps. Some two years later I met this same lady in Florida and we remained close friends for fifty eight years, until she passed away.

Upon my arrival at Westover Field, the medical department there realized that I did not have the proper medical records with me showing that I had all of the required vaccinations for overseas duty. Thus, they sent me to the infirmary and stuck a needle in my arm and then would spin me around and stick a needle in the other arm, until I felt like a walking pin cushion.

When we went to see our new plane, I found that it had all of the latest gadgets in my radio room. In addition to my normal radio equipment, I also had a radar scope, an altimeter and an IFF, (identification, friend or foe). Although there were twelve of these planes being ferried to Europe at this one time, we did not fly in formation; each navigator was responsible for the destination of his own plane.

Our first stop was at Goose Bay, Labrador, which we made without incident. I can only recall that there was snow piled up around the barracks until it reached the second story windows. Our next stop was to be Reykjavik, Iceland. As we were approaching the island, both the pilot and co-pilot were straining to try to determine which lights on the ground were of the city and which were of the airport. Fortunately, I had an altimeter in my radio room and when I saw it drop below four hundred feet, I screamed over the intercom, "Pull this damn thing up", and fortunately they did, otherwise, I might still be in the icy waters off the coast of Iceland.

When we went into the mess hall there, another young soldier came up to me as I was eating and said, "Your name is Foxx, isn't it?" It turned out that we had gone to the same high school together and although he was a couple of grades ahead of me, he remembered seeing me with my older brother. He had been stationed there for some time and I was able to update him on a few things that had gone on back home, like the tornado that a struck a nearby town to where we had lived that had destroyed most of the town.

Our next stop was Prestwick, Scotland. Although there were twelve planes that left Westover Field, only eleven planes ever reached Prestwick. Some fifty years later, I was talking to my friend in Florida, whom I had met at Westover Field, the subject of the missing airplane came up for the very first time. She remembered the circumstances surrounding the missing plane, but she had not heard how or where the plane was lost. Our final destination with the plane was Valle, Wales, where we arrived without fanfare. Our quarters while at Valle were a large building on what must have been a large estate. I recall that the shrubbery around the living quarters were well manicured into the shape of wild animals, such as Giraffes, Elephants and Lions. From Valle, we flew back to Gander, Newfoundland in the bay of a cargo plane. From there on to New York, where we had a layover for one night on the town and thence back to Hunter field.

After spending a few weeks at Hunter field, the war in Europe was winding down, and the Air Corps decided that these remaining B-17 crew members should train to fly on B-29 bombers, that we may go to the Pacific. A group of twenty eight radio operators were ordered to transfer to Nebraska for reassignment. Although we were unescorted, we were sent as a group by train with a two day layover in the windy city. Our days in Chicago were spent in bars. The first day we ended up in a neat little bar called Lipps Lower Level. It was a basement club that brought in a three piece live band in the afternoon. It was a fun place and the prices were reasonable.

The second afternoon we went to the bar in the Blackhawk Hotel, where we spent some time and money until we were evicted. My friend Handy and I were sitting at a table drinking when the subject of propaganda came up. Handy felt, with strong convictions, that all propaganda was lies. I contended that it might be a mixture of some truths embellished with some fictitious elements to present the picture that the broadcaster wished to encompass. I suppose that in our slightly inebriated condition, our voices may have gotten a little loud and boisterous and we were asked to vacate the premises.

Our two evenings there were spent at a dance hall sponsored by the USO, where there were plenty of young ladies present. The next day we caught a train for Lincoln, Nebraska, and arrived at the station about midnight. By the time that we caught our bus to the air base, checked out our bedding, it was well past two o'clock in the morning when we hit the sack. At five o'clock that morning some chicken shit corporal came into our barracks blowing a whistle and yelling, "All right, everyone rise and shine." One of our guys responded, "Come here and blow on this when you get tired of blowing that whistle." "All right, what wise guy sounded off" was his question. Of course, no one answered him.

We all got dressed and fell into a formation in front of our barracks just in time to meet our new sergeant. He introduced himself as Sergeant Lawrence Bobich, but later found out that everyone just called him Sonny, a name that fitted him to a tee. Two years later, I had a radio repair shop on U.S. highway #1 in Florida. One of the soldiers in our group was on vacation and upon driving by and seeing my name on the front of the building, stopped to see me. The very first words out of his mouth were, "Do you remember Sonny?" Of course I remembered Sonny, I could never forget him. I thought it was very nice that he bothered to stop and chat so I took a couple hours off and took him to lunch and we exchanged stories as to what we had been into for the past couple of years.

Sonny told us that first morning that since we had arrived so late last night that we would have the day off. When the daily schedule was put up on our bulletin board that afternoon we found that all twenty eight of us were on KP duty the next morning. Every afternoon when the schedule came out, we were all on the K P duty list. Near the end of our first thirty days there, we were informed that we were to be transferred to a B-29 bomber training base and were given a ten day furlough before we were to report to our new base.

I took the train to Baltimore, where my sister Liz lived. After getting off of the train I caught a street car to take me to near where Liz lived. As I was walking the last three blocks toward her house, I was passing through a Polish neighborhood, and I ran into a half dozen young men clustered around the front steps of a row house. After engaging in conversation with them for a few minutes, I found myself inside their home helping them celebrate a wedding. It was such a fun party that it took me two days in their home before that I could disengage myself from the rest of the party and proceed to see my sister.

While on the train back to Lincoln, Nebraska from my furlough I heard the news that the Japanese had surrendered to the United States on board the battleship Missouri, and that the war in the Pacific was officially over. With no war, there was no need for us to train on the B-29's so we stayed there at Lincoln. We were in limbo, just sort of left over. To try to keep us occupied in a meaningful manner, they took the twenty eight of us and divided us into pairs and assigned miscellaneous little tasks just to keep us busy. As an example, two men were assigned to go around and turn all of the front lights on, on each of our group's barracks. Two other men were assigned to turn those same lights off the next morning. That was the type of menial jobs that all twenty eight of us were assigned to do.

The twenty eight of us worked it out among ourselves in such a manner that one man would do all of those assigned tasks while working for twenty four hours straight through, and then would have twenty seven days off. Since we all had class A passes, we could come and go as we pleased. This was wonderful, we could go to Omaha or Minneapolis or any place else that we desired. But this didn't last long, as too soon we ran out of money and then we found ourselves bored and trying to make the days pass by hanging out in the recreation room or our barracks.

We decided that the answer was, "Get a job." Rob, Al and I went into town and got a job working at a grain warehouse called Gooch's Mill. Our starting job was to load six, fifty pound sacks of grain on a hand truck and wheel it from the warehouse down an incline to the loading dock by the railroad track. On one such trip, Al went down the ramp with only five bags of grain on his hand truck. They would not let him unload the grain, but rather, he had to wheel the five bags back up the incline and load on the sixth bag. We handed in our resignation that evening. One day at Gooch's Mill was enough to last a lifetime.

Next, Rob and I got a job helping build a restaurant on the outskirts of Lincoln called The Lone Oak Restaurant. The man building the restaurant was nice enough to come to the base front gate and pick us up early every morning and return us to the gate late in the afternoon. After working at the restaurant for three weeks, Rob and I decided to buy our own transportation. With our two Army pay checks, plus the money that we saved while working and a small advance from my sister Liz, we were able to assemble three hundred dollars.

With that in hand, we started checking the market for a used vehicle. We soon found out two things. One that used cars were scarce and second, that they were very expensive. We finally found one that although very old, seemed to be in good condition, at least as far as looks was concerned. It was a nineteen hundred and twenty eight Plymouth, with four cylinders and hydraulic brakes. It had wooden spoke wheels and a plush interior that seemed in excellent condition.

We made the purchase. The Cushman Motor Scooter Company had an assembly plant near Lincoln and one could see hundreds of those little scooters around town. As we were driving our new jewel back to our base we were embarrassed as we were being passed by several of those pesky little motor scooters as we were driving down the highway with our throttle wide open.

After we drove the car a couple of weeks, we decided that the car would run better if we did a valve job on the motor. Rob's father owned an auto repair shop and I presumed that Rob would have some experience doing motor repairs.

Wrong.

I knew that I had very little experience in auto repairing, and that not always with great results. I had previously owned a nineteen hundred and twenty eight Chevrolet. One cold winter day, after a light rain and a hard freeze, I got in my car and started to drive to town, however the tires were frozen to the ground and when I put my car in gear, it twisted off one of my rear axles.

I jacked the rear of my car up in the air and took the rear end of it apart. I removed the broken axle, and with the two pieces of the axle in my hands, I walked to a auto junk yard and purchased another used axle to replace my broken one. After walking back home with my used axle, I proceeded to install it and reassemble the rest of the rear end of my car. The car now drove fine except for the fact that I now had only one speed forward, but I had three speeds in reverse. I did not believe that qualified me as an expert mechanic. After taking the rear end apart and reassembling it properly, I once again had my normal three speeds forward and one in reverse.

We proceeded to pull the head from the engine, and after I ground the valves, I told Rob, "Now you can put the valve springs and clips back in the block." His reply was, "But I've never done any thing like this before." I countered with, "Well, you won't be able to say that tomorrow." Miraculously, when we got it all put back together it ran very well. It started easier, ran faster and got better gas mileage.

Almost immediately though, a new problem arose. Now that the engine would run at a higher RPM, the cylinder walls were worn so badly that sometimes when the piston fired, it slapped the bottom of the piston so hard against the cylinder wall that it would break the piston.

We temporarily solved this problem by going down to an auto salvage yard and buying a armload of used pistons, complete with connecting rods, and put them behind the back seat of the car. Then with a pair of coveralls for each of us, a can of gojo and some old towels, we were ready for any emergency. If we were driving down the road and heard the noise of a piston breaking, we would pull to the side of the road and park. Rob would pull the head from the motor from the top of the engine while I was removing the oil pan from the underside of the car, careful not to spill a drop of the oil. I would then take the bolts out of the connecting rod and remove it from the crankshaft, replace it with another piston, complete with connecting rod and then we would put the engine back together. We would then use the gojo and towels to clean up, take off our coveralls, stash everything back behind the rear seat and we would be back on the highway in just forty minutes.

This got old after a few piston changes, so we took the car to a machine shop, had them bore out the cylinder walls, we installed oversized pistons, and now had a car that not only looked good but also ran even better, with the oversized pistons. Unfortunately for us, we had spent so much time working on our new prized possession, that we lost our job at helping build the restaurant.

At least now we had a car to play with and we were no longer bored. We went to Omaha a lot as there was a large dance hall there that had an unusual policy. The only way that a girl could enter the dance hall, was on the arm of a soldier, and then she was obligated to buy the first round of drinks. Once inside, we could enjoy our first drink with the girl who we took inside and stay with her or, we could drop her like a hot potato and pick up some other girl who had been cast off and was already in the dance hall.

One night as we were on our way to Omaha we had a flat tire on our car. I don't remember why, but we had no spare tire with us. We pulled off the highway onto a large paved area and parked, and that area turned out to be the entrance to Boys Town, now known as Boys and Girls Town. Many times as the years went by I have sent contributions to Boys Town in remembrance of that night.

Fortunately for us, we had another soldier going to Omaha with us that night, so we left him in the car while Rob and I took a lug wrench and a small jack and hitched a ride into Omaha. Just before we arrived at the business section of Omaha we asked the driver to let us out. The driver gave us an inquiring look, but did as we requested.

What we had in mind was to walk the side streets in the residential area and try to locate a tire that would fit our vehicle and then we would to try to buy, rent or steal that tire. As we progressed toward town we came upon a bar and as we had not yet located a tire, so we went in and refreshed ourselves. After one drink we continued our search, but after two more blocks, no tire yet, but another bar and again we could not pass it. We continued that routine and after four bars, we just gave up on the tire idea and went on to our usual dance hall.

While in the dance hall we met another soldier from our base that had a car with a spare tire that would fit our car and he agreed to let us use it to get back to our base. We more or less stayed together the rest of the night, and when we left there in his car we stopped at an all night restaurant and I bought breakfast for all.

As we were driving back towards Boys Town, we realized how cold it had gotten. Since his car had no heater in it, we stopped and picked up one of those small kerosene flares from a roadside construction site, which we placed on the cars floor board and by leaving the windows slightly down to let the smoke be drawn out, our new heater worked pretty good. Upon arriving back at our car, we found that our little buddy had rightfully given up on us and was curled up in the back seat asleep. Our new friend stayed with us until we successfully installed his spare on our car and then convoyed back to our base.

All during the time after that we had our car in Nebraska, we supplemented our operating costs by renting our car out to other soldiers.

Whenever we went to a dance hall or a bar, we always parked our car in a secluded, dimly lit area. During the evenings, if any of our friends or acquaintances desired to do any petting in private, for a fee we would let them have the use of our car. Of course it was always stocked with a bottle of gin and a bottle of vodka, as well as a good supply of condoms and a box of Kleenex.

While we were still at the base at Lincoln, the Air Corps started cutting back on their training facilities. One of the first groups, and also one of the oldest groups there that they closed, was section "O." In closing, it meant of disposing of all of the assets that the section had accumulated over a period of three and a half years, profits from soda machines, candy and snack vendors and similar projects.

Well, let me tell you, it amounted to thousands of dollars! They did it right. They rented the mezzanine of the Lincoln Hotel to hold a party, contracted for Glenn Gray and his orchestra, for the main entertainment and a good local band as a backup, to fill in between sets. They hired a caterer to prepare and serve a lavish buffet for the remaining one hundred and fifty or so soldiers remaining in the squadron, and their wives/dates.

The bad news was that only members of section "O" would be permitted to enter the mezzanine of the Lincoln Hotel that night. The good news was that we had friends who were members and since we had shared the use of our automobile with them in the past, agreed to cooperate with us and help arrange for us to enter the mezzanine that night.

On party night, after they had entered the mezzanine with their dates, they wrapped their class a passes and dog tags in a handkerchief and threw them out of the window to us standing below. With proper dog tags and a class "A" pass we were then given permission to enter the mezzanine, no problem.

The music was fantastic and the food was fabulous with prime rib, shrimp, ribs and an array of desserts. There were also cases of the finest liquors available. After the party was over, we took a case of Old Grandad with us when we went to our car.

We had one minor problem. Rob and I looked at each other and decided that neither one of us was sober enough to successfully drive back to our base. Then a young man from section "O", who did not partake of any alcoholic beverages, volunteered to drive our vehicle to our base for us. We still had a minor problem.

He had never driven a car before. We all got aboard and with him under the wheel, we coached him how to get the car started and how to change gears. He knew basically how to steer the car since he had ridden a bicycle for many years. He put the car in low gear and with a few jerks, he had the car in a forward motion, we then instructed him as to how to get into second gear. Once we were in second and rolling along pretty smooth we decided that was fast enough for our new chauffeur so we elected not to have him get the car into high gear.

He never even stopped as we passed the guard house going onto the base; we just stuck up our class "A" passes as he drove slowly through the gate. They did not hassle us as the army was pretty lenient by that time, and they recognized the car as it had been in and out of that gate many times. When he arrived at our barracks, he did not know how to stop the car so he just ran into the side of the building. That stopped the car. At least we were back home safe and sound.

In mid November, our names came up for discharge from the Air Corps. Again, we were given an option. We could either transfer to an air base in Boca Raton, Florida with one increase in rank, or we could go to Andrews Field near Washington, DC, for our discharge. Rob elected to go to Boca Raton with an increase in rank and I elected to go to Andrews Field and get my discharge. I had had enough of army life.

I sold my interest in our Plymouth automobile to Rob, which he successfully drove to Boca Raton. I caught a flight to Andrews Field. While at the base at Andrews, I received an envelope from Rob containing the balance of money that he owed me for the car, and a letter stating that the car made the trip without any problems, but never heard from him again.

Soon after my arrival there, they started my discharge process, but some chicken shit corporal, who was typing on my papers, noticed the fact that I did not have enough points to receive my discharge at that time and alerted some officer about that. You earn points toward your discharge by how many months that you had been in the service, whether you were single or married, how many dependants you had and how many months that you had served overseas. I simply did not have enough points.

Once again I was very lucky. I have always said that would rather be lucky than good any time. A Lt. Colonel, under whose command I had previously served, was on the base and recognized my name and came to me and said, "Foxx, do you know how to type?" I replied, "Yes Sir, I took a typing course while in school, plus I had to be able to type a minimum of thirty five words per minute to graduate from radio school." He was very enthusiastic as he said, "Foxx, if you will help type the form one hundred and discharges for me, so that I can get as many of these men home for Christmas as possible, then after you return from a Christmas leave, I will see to it that you get your discharge.

I typed my fanny off until Christmas Eve and then and went and spent a week with my Sister Liz, who still lived in Baltimore. When I returned to Andrews Field after New Years, the one and only form one hundred and discharge papers that I typed were my own. I was probably the only soldier who ever typed his own way out of the United States Air Corps.

Chapter 12

Silver Lake Park

With my discharge from the Air Corps in my pocket, I left Andrews Air Corps Base located near Washington, DC, and returned to Baltimore, hoping to get a job in some industrial plant that was returning to peace time manufacturing production. I stayed with my Sister Liz, who still lived in Baltimore, while I went checking the job market. After checking various leads, both in person and via telephone for two weeks, I finally realized that those plants were merely trying to hold on to a few of their long time employees during the conversion back to civilian production and that it might be several months before additional jobs would be available in that area.

I finally gave up and decided to go back to my old home town and see just what might be going on back there. Arriving back home, it didn't take too long to find out that there was even less opportunity to find a decent job there then there had been in Baltimore. I might have been able to get a job working in the coal mines, but I had made the decision many years before that I was not going to go that route. I probably could have opened a radio repair shop there again, but I just could not see being able to make any amount of money repairing radios in that area. That was all right when I was trying to make a few dollars to have a little teen age fun, but now I was looking towards building a future.

Life seemed pretty quiet for most of us returning serviceman and since jobs were very scarce in our area, many of us belonged to the fifty two-twenty club. That was a federal program where servicemen who returned home and could not find suitable work, could collect twenty dollars per week for up to fifty two weeks, or until you were able to find suitable employment, something like the current unemployment program.

Of course twenty dollars a week would not keep a good grade of gasoline in our cars gas tank or a good grade of alcohol in our coolers, so we had to figure some way to supplement that income. Since new cars were not available for purchase, it seemed to me that there should be a good market for a good grade of used cars. A former schoolmate of mine named Arti, who was also a returned veteran, and I, both had saved some money while in the service, formed a partnership. His uncle owned some prime real estate right on a federal highway, on which a large abandoned State Road Garage was located.

The State Road Department had previously leased this property and built a large steel building on the property, where they stored snow removal equipment and sand trucks, but had since purchased property in a more central area and moved all of their equipment to the new location.

We leased the property from his uncle for one dollar per month. We then purchased our county license, our insurance and our dealer auto tags, so all we needed now was to purchase some cars and find customers for them.

We started scouring the local countryside looking for vehicles that appeared abandoned or parked out by, or in some outbuildings. Some of these vehicles had belonged to young men who were killed in the war, some others were left behind as many of the returnees left the area for work in other states. It was a lot like the old saying, "It's hard to keep the boys back on the farm once they have seen Paris"

The most desirable car in those days was a V -8 Ford with four on the floor and a fifth under the seat. The idea of the fifth under the seat was that when you kept a bottle of booze under the seat, usually an inexpensive brand like Seagram's Five. The heat from the cars exhaust pipe lying close under the cars floorboards, would make the alcohol warm, and if you were driving a long distance or late at night, when one would take a drink of the booze, it would be so nasty tasting that you could only down a couple of swallows, just enough to really wake you up but not enough to intoxicate you.

The advantage of four on the floor, was that in those days the cars did not have two bucket seats in the front of the car as they do now, but rather had what they called a bench seat that went across the entire width of the car. With a sweet young beauty nestled close to you on that bench seat while you were driving, every time that you came to a small incline in the road, even if the engine did not require it, one could shift the car into second gear and when you reached the top of the rise and one went to shift back into high gear, your right would conveniently, but accidentally, slip off of the shift lever onto the thigh of the lovely thing sitting next to you.

When we were buying those abandoned cars, we were not taking advantage of uneducated farmers; we were really doing them a favor because we were paying them top dollar for something that was just going to sit in or by a shed and rust away. By this time most of the vehicles had some sort of problems and would not run on their own power anyway. One of the cars that we had purchased would not run, so we had a friend with a truck and a chain to go with us and tow the .vehicle back to our garage. We hooked the long chain from the back of the truck to the front axle of our new vehicle, and I agreed that I would be the pilot of the towed car and do the steering and apply the brakes as necessary. When I slid into the seat I noticed that there was a five gallon bottle of water on the front floorboards. I thought, "Gee, that is nice, we can use that at our repair shop."

As we were approaching this small town, we were going down hill and I realized that I was drifting faster and getting too close to the rear of the truck, so I hit the brakes. Apparently the brakes were defective and only the left front brake grabbed, locked and immediately blew out the tire. That flipped the car over on its right side and knocked down the city limit sign.

When the truck took up the slack in the heavy chain, it flipped the car back up on its four wheels and the five gallon jug went flying through the air, landed and broke and I was inundated with about five gallons of water.

Wrong.

I was inundated with about five gallons of moonshine.

The truck driver stopped to survey the situation and I told him, "Lets get the hell out of Dodge before the local cop stops and smells all of this moonshine, then we will all be in a heap of trouble." We did not take time to try to fix the flat tire but towed the car the rest of the way back to our shop on one flat tire. We soon had a small collection of vehicles at our garage and thoroughly went over each and every one of them.

We straightened out the dents in the cars and touched up the spots or completely repainted them as necessary. If we were merely touching a small spot, we would not use our regular paint gun but rather would use a small bug spray with a hand pump as produced by Gulf Oil Company made to be used to kill flies in your home. We changed the oil and greased each vehicle, made sure that every light and horn worked and that the steering was solid, replaced brake parts as necessary, and washed, waxed and detailed each car thoroughly. Thus we could look with pride at every used vehicle we offered for resale.

We would then keep two of our best looking vehicles parked out in front of the garage with large for sale signs on them. Since the garage was located on a busy U S highway, this assured us that a large number of passing potential customers would stop and inquire about the possible purchase. In one such case, having traded cars with another happy customer, we drove to the big city to get the car title and registration in order. Arti, myself and another friend, Mike, who went along just for the ride, since none of us had a regular job, would jump at almost any opportunity to go some place hoping to see a little excitement. After we had the paperwork handled, on our way back home we stopped at a roadside beer bar called Smith's Park, to relax for a few minutes. The place was packed. The three of us were sitting at a table located against a side wall of the tavern, enjoying our first beer when suddenly somebody threw a beer bottle that crashed against the wall and splattered both beer and glass all over our table. Mike jumped up and yelled, "What son of a bitch threw that beer bottle?" Most of the patrons were returning veterans and life at home seemed pretty mundane, and they were so anxious to get into a fight that three different men at three different tables all jumped up and admitted throwing the bottle. With that many people anxious to fight, we decided just to pass on it and as soon as a waitress came over and cleaned and wiped our table, we settled back into enjoying our beer.

The bar was crowded and most of the tables were filled. We had just ordered our second round of beer when five young men walked into the tavern. They went over to the last remaining table and seated themselves. All of the while, they were looking over the bar for an extra chair. When they spotted a empty chair at our table, one of the young men walked over to our table and asked, "May I borrow this empty chair for a minute?" To which Mike replied "certainly." However, as soon as the young man carried the chair over to their table, I noticed that Mike was intensely looking at his watch. Very shortly Mike arose and walked over to their table and tapped the young man on the shoulder who had borrowed the chair and said, "I would appreciate getting our chair back now." To which the young man replied, "I asked you if I could borrow your extra chair and you readily agreed that I could borrow it." Mikes response was, "No, you asked if you could borrow that chair for a minute, and we readily agreed." "Well, the minute is up and we are expecting to receive a very important guest momentarily, and it is imperative that we have a place for him to sit at our table when he arrives."

The group of five realized that this was just a ploy and that we were just looking for trouble. After the exchange of a few more phrases the other man arose and said "I think that you are just looking for a fight." No matter how you slice it, the three of us and the five of them ended up outside of the bar and a good fist fight ensued. In those days a fight was a fist fight, no on thought about using knives or guns in a fight, although almost every young man owned a gun of some type. Fifteen minutes later, the five of them lay on the ground, not willing to arise and endure any further punishment, as the three of us brushed by the onlookers and went back inside and finished our beer. The other group did not bother coming back inside the bar to finish their drinks, but rather got into their car and quietly left. Time marches on, and three weeks later I went to visit my brother, who lived near the state line. I wanted to see my brother and sister-in-law, but mainly wanted to party with my nephew, Jerry, who was about my age. Jerry was active in the party group of the younger generation there, with a lot of contacts and that suited me to a tee. Jerry informed me that he had made arrangements to meet a couple of nice girls at Silver Lake Park, which was a summer resort just across the state line in Maryland. It not only was a summer resort but also had a large restaurant with a swinging lounge and a live band on Friday and Saturday nights. After consuming an early dinner with my brothers family, Jerry and I got into my car and drove over to Silver Lake Park. We went into the dance section and since we were early, picked out a suitable booth and settled in with a couple of beers.

About twenty minutes had passed before the two lovely young ladies came into the lounge, but there was another young man with them. I did not know what to think of that situation, but Jerry seemed concerned. After the introductions, the girl that turned out to be my date introduced us to the young man with her as being her brother Mack. That completely relieved the tension with Jerry and we settled into our booth. Of course we invited Mack to sit with us and as we ordered a round of drinks, I noticed that Mack had a bandage on his left middle finger. I inquired as to what had happened to his hand, but he just said that he did not want to talk about it. I left it at that.

Mack soon drifted off into another young group, but from time to time he would stop and chat for a few minutes in between dances. Each time that I would see him, my mind would automatically go to his left hand and kept wondering as to what had happened to him that he did not want to talk about, mainly by the way that he had responded to my original question. Near the end of the evening he came by out booth again, and by this time he had enough to drink that made him a little more talkative. Then he started telling us about the time about three weeks earlier, that he and four of his buddies had driven to the big city to do some shopping and that on their way back home they had stopped at a roadside beer bar to have a beer and while in the bar became embroiled in an argument with three other men. He then stated that the five of them went outside and got into a fight with those three other little guys and got their butts whipped so bad that they were even ashamed to talk about it. That was how he got his finger broken.

Needless to say, as I danced with my arms around the soft body of his sister, I never let on that I had any clue as to whom their adversary's might have been on that evening three weeks earlier, or even as to what area I lived in.

Sometimes silence IS golden.

Chapter 13

Saturday Night

It was seven thirty on Saturday night as I pulled into the driveway of the quiet neighborhood home where my sweetie pie, Shirley lived, and of course I always walked up to the door, not just waiting in the car and blowing my horn as most of those red necks did, and I went inside her home to meet the rest of her family.

Shirley came out directly and she sure look cute as always, I then said good evening to her mother, father and brother then and escorted her to my car, being sure to open the car door for her. Once out of sight of her home she snuggled up close to me and we petted and chatted as we were driving to a nearby town to a private club where they had a live band playing for our dancing and entertainment, and there we were to meet up with my friend Will and his girl friend.

When we arrived at the club, I was surprised to find that Will and his girl friend Wilma were already there and had a nice table reserved for us in the back. Everyone already knew each other so it was an amicable greeting and we settled in and ordered a round of drinks.

Soon the band started off with a slow number and we found ourselves out on the dance floor warming up to a expected wonderful evening. After the first dance we ordered more drinks but the girls skipped that round, we thought to protect their innocence. We talked, we drank, we danced and we thought that things were going very well when suddenly Wilma leaned over and whispered something to Shirley and they both giggled. The girls then got up from the table and asked to be excused, to which we acknowledged, assuming that they were going to the ladies room. Some time passed and we started to get concerned as to how long they were gone, when the next thing we saw of the girls were the backs of their dresses as they walked out through the front door on the arms of two other young men.

Ordinarily, we would have jumped up and ran outside and started a fight with the other guys, but this time we just sat there at the table as we were both devastated because we felt that the chic's we had brought there with us that night were our main squeeze.

After we finished our drink, we decided we would go to another club closer to home and see if maybe we could hit upon something there. Since we were driving separate cars, I suggested that he go in front and I would follow right behind him. Everything was fine until we were about half way to the other club, when the beer caught up with me and I got a severe urge to hit the bathroom. Since we were traveling on country roads, I merely pulled to the side of the road and stepped into the bushes.

Getting back into my vehicle, I realized that Will would have progressed far ahead of me so I decided to accelerate my speed a bit to try to make up some time. The last time that I remember looking at my speedometer it read somewhere around ninety miles per hour. That would have been fine on today's modern interstate, but we were traveling on a winding country two lane road. About two miles from my destination I came into a sharp right hand curve. The first time I realized that I might be having a problem was when I heard the left rear fender clicking as it was hitting the guard posts. Then the car burst through them, knocking down twenty three of them, and on down a bank and came to rest directly on top of a huge boulder, which was the only thing that kept me from plunging head first into the river below.

I must have set there for a while in a daze, not having any idea as to what had happened to me. When I finally opened the driver's side car door, the door brushed into some bushes, and I thought to myself, "I must have parked my car a little too close to the rose bushes that adorned the side of the drive by my home."

Wrong. My car door struck some brush that surrounded the boulder that stopped my forward progress, which kept my car from plunging into the river. After getting out and trying to survey the situation, I realized that I had a very serious problem, and at that point I started stumbling back up the little bank and onto the paved road.

About the time that I arrived on the hardtop, my friend Andy, who lived in a house directly above he road where I had gone through the guard rails, had heard the noise and wandered down to see what as going on. When he recognized that it was me, he just stood there and shook his head in disbelief. We spoke for a few minutes and then went down and surveyed the car situation again and soon realized how hopeless that it was. I then asked him if he would run me down to the club where I was to meet my friend Will. He obliged me, but declined to come in for a drink as he thought that perhaps enough drinking had gone on for one night.

When I entered the club I found Will sitting at a table drinking with a mutual friend of ours, by the name of George They had been talking about me and wondered what had detained me. I sat down at their table and said, "Well, I really did do it this time." George replied, "Did what?" I said, "I wrecked my car good this time, I mean I really did a number on it."

After we discussed the situation for a while, George said, "Let me fill you in on a little excitement that we had right here a little earlier this evening." It turned out that another of our buddies by the name of Frank, had been at the club a little earlier in the evening and had consumed more alcohol than he could handle. When he went outside to get in his car he got this sudden urge to go, so he whipped it out, and while standing on the sidewalk of the downtown area, and let it fly. The one local police officer just happened to be walking by and realizing what was going on, arrested Frank and hauled him off to the local small town jail. About an hour later, Frank's brother came into the club, and when told about the situation of his brother, promptly went out and located, then cornered the arresting officer. He soon became embroiled in a bitter and threatening situation with the officer, and he too ended up in the city jail.

By the time that his brother arrived, Frank had sobered up a bit and discussed the idea of him and his brother of bonding out of jail. The officer was agreeable to the bond idea and set a cash bond of seven dollars each. Unfortunately Frank and his brother did not have fourteen dollars in cash between them and when Frank offered to give a check to the officer, the officer declined the check offer and therefore both remained in the slammer.

Meantime, back at the ranch, we got back to discussing the pressing problem at the moment. That was of getting my car off of the rock and back to some safe haven. That was when George said, "Well, I guess that it is time to go down to the farm and break out old Betsy." All three of us got into Will's car and drove down the highway for a while and then turned and went down a winding gravel road. When Will pulled along side of a barn there, George pointed and said, "There is Betsy." Betsy was a large dual wheeled truck with a long flat bed, and then George went into the barn and drug out about a fifty foot heavy log chain and threw it up on the bed of the truck and said, "All aboard."

George drove Betsy back to the scene of the accident and we walked down to survey the situation and figured the best way to get Betsy near my car. He then backed Betsy down the slope until the rear of the truck was near the rear of my car. Taking the chain from the truck, he connected one end to the rear axle of my car and the other end to the rear of his truck.

My car was left in neutral and as George started the truck going forward, he was going at a pretty good clip when he took up all of the slack in the chain. At that time he jerked my car completely off of the ground, which was probably a good thing as it dislodged it from the rock that it was setting on. He continued pulling my car until he had considerable room in the front of it. He then disconnected the chain and moved the truck to the front of my car and reconnected the chain, but with a lot less slack in the chain. He then proceeded to tow my vehicle down the highway a few miles, where we disconnected it from Betsy and pushed it into Frank's garage where we closed and locked the doors.

I did realize how fortunate that I was as I did not have a bump or even a scrape as a result of my accident, and I was not wearing a seat belt, as they were not even heard of in those days, but cars were made of steel then, not just tin and plastic as the modern day cars are today.

The next morning the State Police arrived at the scene of the accident, and parked his car by the side of the road with the red light flashing. Since it was Sunday morning Andy was at home and when he saw the red light flashing, he walked down to where the officer was standing. The officer said, "Anderson, what went on here last night?" To which Andy replied, "I really don't know what happened, after I went to sleep last night, I was awakened by a loud noise and I got up and walked out on the porch and looked around but it was dark down there and I could not see any people or anything, so I went inside and went back to bed" The officer replied, "Anderson, you are lying to me."

That was the way it ended with Andy, but the State Police kept on the investigation, trying to pin the accident on to someone to try to get them to pay for the cost of replacing those twenty three guard rails plus the connecting steel cables.

It turned out that I had also destroyed Andy's mail box which was mounted on a post near to the destroyed guard rails. A fact that Andy's wife, Martha, never forgave me for as long as she lived, in spite of the fact that I did buy them a new mail box.

On Sunday morning I heard the climax of Frank's incarceration ordeal. It turned out that the local city jail was composed of sections of steel bars that were welded together in three foot sections, and were all bolted together, with similar ones making up the top of the cage. Frank had been repairing cars the day before and still had wrenches in his jeans pockets. After sitting on the edge of his cot for a while, he finally sobered up and assessed his situation. Realizing that they were incarcerated in a take-apart jail, and he had the tools to do it, he and his brother completely disassembled one section of the jail.

Once it was disassembled they stacked the sections up and had a pile about three feet high. Once that was done, he took the steel grate out of the drain in the floor, and while sitting on the pile of steel bars, he would spread his legs and raise the steel grate above his head and let it come crashing down against the pile of cell bars.

At three o'clock in the morning it must have sounded like a giant Liberty Bell making a gong like sound, that I am sure awoke most of the town folks, including the officer who had arrested them in the first place. When the officer arrived at the city jail, he was astonished to see the boys sitting on top of their jail cell and being free to walk out and go home, but not doing so. The officer then agreed to accept their check as their bond and said to them, "Get out of my jail and get out of my town." Which Frank and his brother were anxious to accommodate him on both counts.

Later, with all of the sheet metal removed from the front of my car, I replaced the radiator and a few tie rods and tie rod ends and made the car drivable. I made arrangements with a local auto body shop to repair my vehicle and then in the dead of night, I drove it to his shop while following close behind another car as my car had tail lights but no headlights.

Finally, my car was back together and repainted, and I suppose to this day the State Police are still wondering who trashed those twenty three guard rails. While the auto body man was repairing my car he reminded me that my car was exactly the same make and model as the cars used by the State Police. He gave me the name of the head mechanic, Tony, of the State Police garage and pointed out that he operated his own garage, but only on Saturday. I got the address of Tony's garage and on Saturday I went to have a talk with Tony.

Tony told me that the only difference between my car and the State police cars, was that the police cars had an engine with larger pistons and a heavier frame. He explained to me that when the engine block was cast and honed, that in the Police cars, the pistons were inserted directly into the block while in production cars, like mine, steel sleeves were pressed inside of the cylinders to reduce the piston size. Tony pointed out that he could remove those stainless steel sleeves and put in oversize pistons and I would then have an engine with horsepower similar to those of the state police. I made arrangements with Tony that I would bring my car back on next Saturday and in the meantime he would get the new pistons and would pull the sleeves for me.

On Saturday morning I was at Tony's garage early, so that the engine would have a chance to cool off before we started working on it. I helped Tony pull my engine and put it on an engine stand. He then proceeded to take the engine apart, and surprisingly enough, within an hour he had that engine stripped. He then proceeded to pull the sleeves from the block, one at a time. Everything went well until he was pulling the last sleeve, when the puller slipped and Tony did not realize it. Only after he had removed the sleeve completely did he realize that the puller had scraped a ridge all of the way down the cylinder wall.

Tony just looked at me and smiled, he said, "I guess we will have to trash this engine, unless you want to buy a new set of sleeves and put the engine back like it was." "What are my alternatives?" I asked. "I can order you a new police special motor and have it delivered to your local Ford dealer, then you can pick it up and bring it back here and I will install it for you." "That sounds good to me, "I said. "Done."

On the next Friday I picked up a complete engine at the Ford dealer, I mean complete, it even had the heads installed and spark plugs ready to go. Tony had only to transfer the generator and the starter from the old engine. On Saturday, Tony completed the installation and the surprising thing about the whole ordeal was the cost, only one hundred and ninety six dollars for the engine, plus a few shillings for Tony and I was down the road.

I was really in my glory as I now had a vehicle that would leave the Buick Roadmasters and Oldsmobile Rocket Eighty Eights in my trail of dust. I could now go completely up some of those mountains in high gear now that previously required me to shift into second gear.

From the misfortune of having an accident, something good came out of it for me.

Chapter 14

Sunday Drives

Living in an area and time where we did not have community swimming pools, bowling alleys or theme parks, it was not unusual for a young man to pick up his main squeeze on Sunday and go for a car ride. Sometimes we would have a definite destination as to where we wanted to end up and other times we just went with the flow and ended the day wherever. On one such Sunday ride we passed by a late model car that was parked by the side of the road, apparently with only a flat tire, at ten o'clock in the morning. When we passed that same location at two o'clock in the afternoon, the car was still parked there but all four wheels and tires were missing. On our way home at seven o'clock that night, the car was still in the same location, however it was now upside down, and the engine and transmission were also missing.

On another Sunday as we were traveling through the lightly rolling hills of Ohio, we came across a car lying upside down by the side of the road, naturally we stopped to see if we could be of assistance. It turned out that a young couple were driving their Terraplane automobile west at a nominal speed when all of a sudden, another car driving east suddenly veered across the center line, right in front of them. To try to avoid an accident, the Terraplane driver swerved sharply, lost control of his own vehicle and rolled over twice. Of course, that driver that caused the accident did not stop and offer to be of any assistance. Fortunately, neither of them were seriously hurt. We picked them up and took them back about twenty miles to where they were able to contact some friendly faces and make arrangements to get back to their homes, from where they would try to recover their vehicle.

That particular incident was a turning point in my automobile driving career, and probably was part of the reasons that later on in my life, I would end up having what should have been seven fatal accidents. I firmly decided on that day, that if any other driver were about to cause me to have an accident, then he was going to be involved also, I was not going to have an accident by myself, only to see the driver who caused it, drive merrily on his way without a scratch.

Another Sunday, accompanied by another couple, were driving along with my right arm firmly encircling the soft body of the young thing next to me. We were driving fairly slow as we were in no hurry, because this was a close to the girls as we were going to get. All of the car windows were rolled down, as there was no such thing as an air conditioner for an automobile at that time. As we were crossing a bridge over a river, three young hooligans were sitting on the upper railing of the bridge on our side of the road, and as we passed them by, they hurled filthy insults at us that I did not think the tender ears of these lovely's should have to endure. I drove on about a mile until I found a good place to turn around and then came back, driving even slower than before. As I was crossing the bridge I was hugging the right side of the road and then when I arrived near where the boys were sitting, I leaned on the horn and drove straight across the road toward them. The last that we saw of them was three bodies falling backwards off of the bridge and into the river.

Another Sunday found myself driving with a girl named Linda and in the back seat was the Rabbi, a neighbor of mine and an old school chum. With him was a girl named Lily, but not really a date, just a fellow student at the local college. Lily was really the girl friend of my older Brother Jack, who was still in the service. We decided that on this day, we would go to Blackwater Falls, a popular tourist resort. The drive to get to there was getting boring and as we were driving up Canaan Valley we were driving along side of a railroad track, when I came to a spot that was completely clear of trees and brush, I drove over the side of the highway and onto the railroad track. The others thought that I was completely crazy to do that, but at least it brought a little excitement to the trip. After about a mile driving on the train track, when I again saw a clearing on the left side, I whipped the car off the track and back up onto the highway.

After we returned back to our home town I dropped Linda off at her house and then the Rabbi, Lily and myself did a little serious drinking. After we had a few, the subject of my Brother Jack, who was still in the service, came up. After a short discussion as to when he was coming home or if he was ever coming back, Lily got concerned and she went on a crying jag, and the Rabbi and I just could not handle her. We drove back to the university dorm, where Lily was living, located a girl friend of hers and finally disposed of Lily in her custody.

Years later, after I was married, I bought my wife Joan, a new car for her birthday. The only place that she drove it was to go grocery shopping or to church, or a few blocks to visit with her parents and occasionally to stop by my shop to see me. After we had the car for a few months I noticed that it did not seem to run as well as it previously had and I took it back to the new car dealer and explained my concerns. The service manager asked how we drove the car and after I explained to him our situation, he suggested that what would do the car the most good would be to take it out on the highway for a little trip and run the engine up a bit.

I told my wife what the service manager had told me and I suggested to her that on Sunday next, I would drive her up to Avon Park, and show her the air base where I had met the entire crew of my B-17 bomber, and where we went through our bomber training.

Sunday morning found us driving north towards Avon Park. About half way there we saw a large billboard that read, "Lots for Sale, Avon Park lakes, Twenty Five dollars down."

I immediately exclaimed, "I am definitely interested in that, when I was stationed there about ten years ago, I had dreamed about having a lot by one of those lakes and building a little cabin on it, where I could sit on my back porch and fish all day." There was no hesitation from Joan, "We are not buying any lots at Avon Park Lakes, period." As we progressed north on US Route 27, every once in a while we would see another lots for sale sign and Joan was quick to remind me that we were buying no lots. As we were nearing Avon Park Lakes, we started seeing those large Lots for Sale billboards again. The terrain had changed from flat, to rolling hills and as we topped over a small ridge, we could see the sales office on the left of the highway and dozens and dozens of cars in the parking area on the right side of the highway, and people milling around everywhere. When Joan saw all of the frantic activities, she became excited and when we got in front of the sales office, Joan said, "Stop here and let me off, I am going in and get in line and see what this is all about, you can go ahead and park the car and come on in."

Joan went inside and went right to the front of the line and said, "I want to buy some lots." "Do you know what lot numbers you are interested in?" She said, "No". The salesman then handed her a brochure explained the numbers and asked that she go out and look at the lots, circle the lot numbers that she was interested in and then come back into the office. By the time that I parked the car and walked to the sales office, I was just in time to meet Joan walking out the front door. She was overwhelmed about the thought of owning land there, and with the excitement that was flowing there, what she did not say to me, was, "Well, if you are really interested, we might consider buying some lots." What she did say was, "We are going to buy some lots here today."

She tried to explain the situation to me and together we started walking down the gravel roads and looking at the road names and lot numbers, trying to keep them in perspective with the numbers on the brochure that he had given her. We finally decided on three lots, circled the numbers and returned to the sales office. Getting in line, we finally reached the front of the line, only to find that those three lots had just been sold. Joan was now more adamant then ever about purchasing some lots this day. We went back into the field and selected three other lots. We went back and got in line, then a sales person took us into a small office, but after we sat down at the table to draw up the sales contract, it dawned on us that we did not have enough cash money to make the down payment with us, since we did not come prepared to make a purchase. The salesman said, "That is OK, we will accept a check."

"We do not have a check with us," Joan replied. He said, "That's OK" and handed us a check, in which we had to write in the name and address of our bank as well as all of the rest of the necessary information.

We drove back south the proud owners of three lots at Avon Park Lakes, which we kept for thirty six years, but I never did get to build my little cabin on that lake.

It turned out to be just another Sunday drive.

Chapter 15

Fair Time

Every morning around seven thirty you would find Arti and me in our garage working in some manner, on one the used cars that we owned and hoped to make presentable in order to make a sale to someone. Soon thereafter three or four other local boys would be sitting on nail kegs watching us work. Mostly they were just killing time watching us work, but a few times we would actually pay them real American dollars for helping us make some repairs. Like removing bumpers or fenders from cars that needed major repairs, or just putting a car on the lift and doing a grease job and oil change for us, or maybe sanding a car in preparation for painting. Almost every day that we worked at the garage, we had some work for outside help.

Some just came to share our drinking activities. We had very strict time limits on drinking alcohol at our garage. Before ten o'clock in the morning, we permitted only wine on our premises. Usually the wine was ninety nine cent port wine, but once in a while we would splurge and buy some sherry at one dollar and forty nine cents per bottle. From ten o'clock in the morning until five o'clock in the afternoon, only beer was permitted and at five o'clock we went right to the hard liquor, which usually was Old Grandad or Jack Daniels.

Others would just hang around to listen to customer haggling over trading a car or one trying to sell us a piece of junk, purportedly as a cream puff. One such car that we owned was a blue nineteen hundred and thirty six Chevrolet with knee action, we had bought this car for hard cash and although old, really looked very good. The car started right up and ran decent, the brakes seemed all right and the steering was sound.

We detailed the car so that it looked really clean and then we put it on the lift and did our usual grease job and oil change. That was our big mistake. Once we greased the front end of that car, the steering was so loose that one could hardly keep it between the ditches when driving it. After replacing several front end parts, we just sort of gave up on it and parked it along side of our garage near the back. It had a new paint job on it and really looked good from a distance.

Many times when a customer would stop by and check on our autos and were unable to find one that they liked or could afford would then ask, "How about that old blue Chevrolet sitting back there. After a minor inspection and a test drive they all ended up saying the same thing. "Thanks, but no thanks."

The car had too many little problems.

We were finally able to sell the car to a young man who worked in the coal mines, he liked it because it was a four door model, and had some fellow workers who would pay him to ride back and forth to work. But in just a couple of days, it was back. He told us that he had not had a decent days sleep since he bought the car. He said that they worked on the night shift at the mines and the first night he drove it, it ran pretty good, just a little hard to steer, but the next morning he could not get it started on his own and had to get a push from a fellow worker. It ran home all right but he had to work on it most of the day to have it ready for the nightly run. No sleep. The second night was a repeat of the same, working all night again in the mines and again all day on the car, as his fellow workers were depending on his means of transportation to get to work.

Of course we bought the car back from him. He bought another car and we even reimbursed him for the cost of the title transfer. We worked on the front end again and resold the Chevrolet, but alas, in another few days it was back again. Once again we spent some more time and money on the front end of that Chevrolet and the third time we made the sale, it stayed sold.

We learned our lesson from that Chevrolet though, that was the last time that we ever greased the front end of any of our cars. We would change the oil and oil filter and grease the rest of the car, but not the front end steering parts. From then on, we would merely take a rag and wipe off the grease fittings on the front end parts and smear fresh grease around the fittings and bushings, just as though we had greased those fittings. But no grease was ever forced into the tie rod ends or other front end fittings.

We once had a nice clean, late model Studebaker for sale and were asking eight hundred dollars for it. We had a lot of prospects that were interested in buying it but none could come up with the money to make the purchase. One afternoon we had a serious minded prospect look at the car for some time and was haggling with Arti to get him to come down on the price. Finally the customer took out his wallet and pulled out six one hundred dollar bills and laid them on the hood of the car and said, "Now why don't you give me the title to this car and let me take it off of your hands?" To which Arti responded, "No, I will come out here every morning and pee on the car and watch it rust up before I will sell this car for six hundred dollars." No sale was made at that time.

Once we had a customer for a vehicle, we would have to go to the big city to get the title and registration transferred and in many cases had to arrange for financing. On one such occasion we took a friend of ours by the name of George with us, as he had nothing to do and was just going along for the ride. We were concerned that by the time we had all of our paperwork resolved that the local liquor stores might be closed, so we stopped on the way to the city and bought a fifth of Old Grandad for our nightly escapade. In those days there, all of the liquor stores were state owned and were never open in the evenings. We were right about the time situation because it did take longer than usual to complete our business transactions, and when we returned to our car we found that George, whom we had left baby sitting our car while we were inside, had gone fast asleep in the back seat.

We did not think too much about that and went ahead and drove him back to his home, which was on a winding gravel road off of the main highway. Only when we tried to awaken him did we realize that while we were working on the paperwork in the city, George sat in the car and drank our nightly supply of alcohol, until he had almost completely emptied the bottle. George was totally passed out.

We went and knocked on his door but no one was at home, fortunately in those days, no one ever locked their doors, so we carried him into his house and stretched him out on his sofa and left him there, sound asleep.

After dropping off George, we returned to our respective homes to prepare for an evening of excitement as this was the opening night of our county fair. The fair is the major civic festival of the year in small towns like this. The fair, in most places is held at the county fairgrounds, but not in our case, here the fair was being held right in the middle of downtown, on Main Street with the booths and rides lined up on both sides of the street and about half way down each of he side streets.

All automobile traffic was detoured completely around the fair. When we arrived at the fair, there seemed to be a lot of confusion going on. Barricades were destroyed, some booths were in shambles and the few people that were there in the area just stood there shaking their heads in disbelief. It took about twenty four hours to get the whole story, but it unfolded something like this. Apparently, about one hour after we had dropped George off at his home, he awoke from his drunken stupor and still with no one at home besides himself, went outside and got into his own car, which was a nineteen hundred and thirty four Lafayette.

Keep in mind that his home was down a winding gravel road about one quarter of a mile from the main highway, however today there were no gates or winding roads for Gorge this time. Once he had his car started he drove straight through one closed gate and two barbed wire fences to get to the main highway and thence on into town.

Not realizing what was going on, he drove straight into town and only when he knocked down the first set of barricades, did he realize there was a detour. He then took the detour, but his encounter with the barricade had attracted the attention of the fair goers, one of which was a middle aged man named Adolph, who took it upon himself to do something about this driver who seemed so reckless.

Adolph immediately deputized himself, jumped on his Harley Davidson motorcycle and started following George. He followed him completely around the detour and back onto the main highway, which then went up a steep hill and out of town. By this time George realized that Adolph was chasing him so he speeded up a bit and as soon as he got out of sight from Adolph, he quick did a "U" turn and headed back towards town. When Adolph realized the direction that George was going, did his own "U" turn and realizing that he was not going to catch him, pulled a pistol from under his belt and started shooting at George.

The gunshots only inspired George to go faster and since he was now going down a steep grade anyhow, at the speed he was going, there was no way that he was going to be able to make a ninety degree detour turn, so he again crashed through the barricades and through everything else that was set up in the middle of the street, all through the set up for the fair. At the north end of town there was a sharp curve in the road and although he was able to navigate the turn, he was not able to keep his vehicle under control after making the curve and he ended up flipping his car over twice.

His Lafayette was a total loss but he did not even have a scratch on his body. I guess that was only because that he was totally inebriated and relaxed. And believe it or not, no one where the fair was set up was killed or even injured. I guess that was just the luck of a drunk.

He was promptly arrested and spent the night sleeping off his hangover in the slammer. Since he was the son of the ex-county Sheriff, who still had considerable clout in the local legal field, was able to walk away from the whole ordeal with just the one night in jail, and only a small fine to pay. I did not even make him make restitution for the bottle of Old Grandad that he drank, as I felt that I owed him one for his use of his truck at a previous accident of mine.

Chapter 16

FAREWELL PARTY

All good things must come to an end and now the time had come for me to move on to bigger and better things. I tired of buying and selling used cars, working with dirty used engines, ending up in the evening with my arms sore from sanding cars preparing to paint them, and I ended up with myself and my clothes filthy dirty. All of this to barely eke out a meager living.

One day as I was working on a greasy transmission on one of our used cars, our long time rural mail carrier, Cullen Bryant, stopped and talked with me. Remembering that I had a radio repair shop back when I was sixteen years old, he said, "Sly, you are too smart to be doing this kind of work," and as I looked at my greasy hands and greasy clothes, I finally made the connection. He convinced me that it just not worth the effort.

Before leaving my present environment, I was determined to do something that would that would make an impact on the area that I was leaving, that would not be forgotten for years. I set a date for a party on a Saturday night at my mother's home, down on the farm, and I invited about thirty of my friends in my age group, both boys and girls, for my going away party. All of those were invited, could come alone or bring a friend, with only one stipulation, that was, that if they were married that may not bring their own spouse to my party.

On the night of the party, about twenty five cars showed up with about forty people in them. I had a record changer with most of the latest hit tunes, a keg of beer on ice, plenty of soft drinks as well as a decent assortment of hard liquor. I had a volunteer bartender on hand and the first hour of our get together was spent letting everyone get acquainted. I did not have name tags for the guests then as I would now, because those were young minds and could still remember other people's names. This was a rural area surrounded by small towns and most knew each other anyhow.

The guests were arriving and I was greeting and mixing with my guests when an old school chum, and former business partner, Arti, said to me, "Foxx, why is it that when anything wild or unusual is going on, you are always right in the center of it. Why are you always out somewhere raising hell?" My response was, "If you don't raise a little hell when you are young, what in the world are you going to talk about when you get old?" "Foxx, getting old is not anything that YOU will have to be concerned about," he replied.

After I felt that everyone was settled in, we started playing some serious adult games. One such game was to have the girls standing up in a line, and then bring the men into the room, one at a time blindfolded, and to try to identify the individual girls by feeling their legs, but only from the knees down. I had my date, Louise, who, with a small rubber baseball bat in her hand, would stand by each girl as she was being checked, and if a man's hand started to get a little too high, she would give a good rap to the hand of the offender. Some of the girls even exchanged shoes with other girls to help confuse the men. Of course men are easily confused anyhow, particularly when it comes to ladies legs.

Another game we played was something like playing pin the tail on the donkey, except instead of having a picture of a donkey pinned on the wall, we had an almost life sized picture of a nude woman pinned on the wall. The way we played that game was, we did not pin anything on the picture, instead we would have the men place their index finger onto a red ink pad, and then see who could put their red fingerprint closest to the most important body part of the girl's picture.

We would then bring the men into the room one at a time, let them look at the picture and then blindfold them and then lead them down until they were about one foot from the picture, so that they would have to extend their arm to reach the vital spot on the picture. As the men would thrust their arm forward with their forefinger protruding, another person would quick slide a deep jar of Vaseline up to the picture, so that their finger would go into the jar of Vaseline. I can assure that their reactions were both varied and funny, somewhere between surprise and glee, as we snapped pictures of the men with their finger in the jar of Vaseline.

We also had a game that included the local bully, who just happened to be present, and the young man most bullied by him. We then had them lie down on the floor, head to head. We had them hold each others left hand and we placed a small rubber ball bat in the right hand of each man. We then blindfolded both men, and we would have each take turns trying to hit the other one in the head, by telling where their head was from the position of the left hand. After a couple turns, we then removed the blindfold from the young man who had been bullied and let him get in a few free shots, to the pleasure of his audience. When we finally took the blindfold away from the bully, we pretended to also have just removed the blindfold from the other young man, so the bully never really knew the truth, but was never quite sure as to why his opponent seemed so much more successful than was he.

After we finished our games we settled in some serious partying, eating, drinking, dancing, etc. All during this time there were some other scenarios going on. In one such instance, Arti had brought a girl to the party, but Don, who had not brought anyone, but had just gotten a new Chevrolet automobile, and had enticed Arti's girl to get into his new car, and she was prepared to leave the party with him, until Arti appeared on the scene. As Arti approached Don's car, Don quick rolled up the windows and locked the doors. At this point, Arti took off his right boot and with his hand firmly around the toe of the boot asked Don, "Which window do you want me to break out first, the windshield of the driver's side window?" Don apparently did not want anything to happen to his new car and reluctantly released his captured prize.

In another instance, Ralph had brought a young woman by the name of Carrie to the party. Carrie was known in the community as being promiscuous. Bruce, a newly married young man, had come to the party without his wife, as per instructions. Bruce got Carrie cornered in the house alone with a drink in her hand, and eventually into his car and they both left the party. Well, this did not set too well with Ralph and another young man who was there, because they felt that Bruce was trying to make personal property out of something that belonged in the public domain. They then got into their own car and after chasing Bruce down the road for four or five miles, finally caught up with him, pulled along side of him and forced his car into the ditch. They then got out of their car and gave

Bruce a pretty good beating, returned Carrie to their car and went back to the party, leaving a battered Bruce standing by his car, which was stuck in the ditch, at 11 o'clock at night and with no cell phone.

By three o'clock in the morning all of my guests had departed, except for my date Louise, who just happened to have been the salutatorian from my high school graduating class five years earlier, who was home on vacation from California. When I went out to take her home, I found one strange car left in the parking area. We looked all over the place for a dead or passed out body, to no avail. We then figured that someone either could not get their car started or had lost their car keys. We found out later that the car belonged to the son of a local prosecuting attorney and he felt that he was too intoxicated to drive and caught another ride home, as he did not want to cause his father any embarrassment.

Sunday was a day of R and R for me, and I spent the day visiting with my mother because once that I left, I knew that it may be some time, if ever, that I would be back again. Monday I gathered up everything that I expected to take with me on my next expedition, which to go to Florida and start a new business repairing radios.

With everything loaded and in place, early Monday evening I went back to the garage where we previously did the repairs on the used cars we bought and sold. I had made arrangements with a few of my friends who used to hang out there, setting on nail kegs while watching us work, at my party Saturday night, that I had planned a little surprise for a certain nosey neighbor before I left.

Right across the highway from the garage where we worked, was a house that sat on a little rise and a man named Rowdy lived there. He was retired and anytime that we were working there, you would find Rowdy sitting on his porch with a pair of field glasses in his hand, watching our every move. That was the reason that I stopped by the garage early, to make sure that he might be aware that something might be going on there that night.

As soon as it got good and dark about a dozen of us boys gathered there, and started a good roaring bonfire. We then gathered up our usual nail kegs and all sat on them around the fire while drinking beer. We were talking about my upcoming excursion to Florida and they were betting on how long it would be before I returned home. At a predetermined time, two of the fellows got into a loud verbal argument and the rest of us created enough of a ruckus to be sure that Rowdy would be watching.

One of the fellows shouted, "I am going to settle this once and for all." He then ran to his car and returned with a twelve gauge shotgun, walked right up to the other fellow and blasted him, point blank. He went down like a ton of bricks, let out one loud moan and then all was quiet. One of our fellows bent over our fallen comrade and yelled out, very loudly, "He is still breathing, let's take him to the hospital." I yelled back, "You are not putting him in my car and get blood all over it." Someone else yelled, "I will take him in my car," as he ran and brought up his vehicle. I helped throw the victim into the back seat of the car and it headed off towards the hospital with the rear tires screaming on the asphalt. Only the group around the fire knew that the shotgun was loaded with a blank.

Feeling that we had accomplished what we set out to do, we all got up, whipped out our things and let it fly onto the fire. After making sure that the fire was out, we put the nail kegs away and went home. The next morning I found myself in my car headed south towards Florida and feeling very good about my going away parties.

That same day Rowdy went over to our local convenience store and asked, "Did you hear about that man getting shot down at the Lohr's garage last night?" The convenience store owner said, "No, this is the first that I have heard anything about it. What can you tell me about it?" Rowdy then went into detail about the group sitting around the fire, the argument that followed and the shooting that he actually saw. Rowdy said, "I even called both hospitals this morning and neither one had any record of anyone being admitted with a gunshot wound. I really do not understand this."

The store owner assured Rowdy that if he heard anything at all about the shooting, that he would fill Rowdy in on the details. For the next few weeks Rowdy asked every person he met if they knew anything about the shooting, and it appears that only Rowdy knew anything about it. Rowdy could not understand why no one else knew about the shooting, after all he had heard the argument, and through his field glasses, saw the shooting and saw the man crumple to the ground, saw him loaded up allegedly taken to a hospital. It did not seem possible that no one else had seen or heard anything about it.

The shooting was such an obsession with Rowdy he could speak of nothing else, until the state stepped in. The state was very good to Rowdy, however, as they provided him with free room and board as well as counseling, at the state insane asylum at Weston, for the next six months. I guess by that time, the counselors had convinced him that the shooting had never really happened, just something that happened in his mind.

Success for the little people.

Chapter 17

New Business

I had been stationed in Florida while serving in the Army Air Corps and liked the climate there. At least, if I was only able to eke out a meager living, I would be eking it out in a warm climate. This time when going to a new location to try to make a living, I owned a car that was paid for, had a reasonable plan for a business and enough money in my pocket and enough determination in my mind to make it work.

Arriving in Florida, I rented a small, inexpensive apartment and then a small section of a busy gas station as my base of operations. While my only advertising was a hand painted paper sign pasted to the front glass of the gas station, I busied myself building a work bench and a couple of shelves; One to hold the radios (hopefully) waiting to be repaired and the other to hold the repaired radios waiting for the customer to pick them up.

Fortunately the station was very busy and after a few days a customer brought in my first radio for repair at this location. That was followed by a straggling few other radios, but I could see that was not going to be adequate, so I instituted a new program. I would go to the shop at seven o'clock in the morning and work on repairing the radios I had on hand. Then I posted my sign that stated "Will return at 1:00 p.m." Then I would get in my little sedan delivery vehicle and go door to door soliciting radios to be repaired. I approached every appliance retail business, furniture and department stores.

Within just a few days my little telephone with only four digits started ringing on a regular basis. I would pick up and deliver the radios and record players for repair, from the business addresses at no charge. I would make house calls to their customer's home for only a charge of one dollar and fifty cents, and that included pick up and delivery, if necessary. I soon had all of the major appliance retailers as well as furniture stores calling me on a regular basis. Macy's Department Store, formerly known as Burdines Department Store and Sears Roebuck were solidly on my customer list.

I soon found myself contacting the local unemployment bureau searching for anyone who had previous experience in radio repair. Some of the applicants only experience seemed to have been merely turning a radio on and off, and of some of them I even questioned whether they had ever seen a radio before. I then contacted a private employment agency and requested that if they had any prospects with any type of prior electronic experience to give me a call.

Soon after opening the repair business, the first local AM radio station came on the air. In those times, a promoter would be able to buy one half hour or one hour segments of radio broadcast air time, and then would go out and sell his own advertising along with his own programming. I bought an ad on a program known as Drive with Wild Bill, a drive time show that played country music records and aired five days a week from four o'clock in the afternoon until six o'clock. This was a perfect way to reach the locals in our community as almost all of the locals were either farmers or cattle ranchers. At that time Florida was the second largest cattle producing state in the union, following only Montana. The farmers raised beans and peppers as a mainstay and hired a lot of migrant workers.

Since I was trying to build a reputation as being representative of all of the people, I also bought advertising on a show known as The Progressive Serenade. This was a program that ran from five o'clock in the morning until seven o'clock and played gospel records and reached almost one hundred percent of the households in the black and migrant community.

While working out of the service station, I became acquainted with one of the fellows who worked at the service station. He was an ex-GI who had been in the Military Police and at one time had the task of guarding German prisoners of war. After a few trying escapades with them, he started calling them mules. When one of the prisoners struck him with his fist, he used the expression, "That one of those mules kicked me."

As my business started to grow and I had the task of weeding through a long list of inadequate employees, I realized more and more that my service station friend was right and I adopted the phrase and referred to my employees as mules, as mule number one or mule number seven.

A typical comment from a new employee at the end of his first day on the job was, "How am I doing, boss?" My typical answer was, "Well, so-so, but I would not recommend that you start reading any continued stories in the local newspaper." When I used to sit and enjoy a cocktail with my friends, Joe and Vera, I recall telling them of my trials and tribulations with prospective new employees, but I never gave up on my faith and I told them, "Just as sure as the sun rises in the east tomorrow morning, one day I WILL have a twenty mule team working for me repairing radios." And I did, too.

The radio advertising, plus word of mouth and my personal solicitations was working and soon I had my shop full of radios. By this time I had even taken over one side of their office to my little paper work. I had contacted a company called, "Mail Me Monday" to do my bookkeeping, in which I would go into the office on Monday morning and fill out a relatively easy form, and drop it in the mail. Everything else they handled for me. Every month they would send me a form filled with figures and all I had to do was write a check and mail it to the IRS.

It soon became obvious that I would have to move to larger quarters, as I had borrowed, begged and stole all of the available space from the service station and there was not even enough room for me to build another service bench. I located another new building going up and they agreed to add a store front for me, which at the time seemed more than adequate. In our new quarters, we built enough service benches, to accommodate eight service technicians at a time, three large sections of shelves to hold radios for repair and two large sections to hold the repaired radios. We still had a lot of room for console radios and record players as well as for parts storage. We certainly thought that we were well situated as far as work area was concerned for some time to come.

Wrong.

Within two months, all of the shelves for incoming radios were filled and we were forced to place them on one of the repaired sections shelves. It even got worse, until we finally would hang repair tags on a nail by the entrance door along with a pencil, and when a customer would come in with a broken down radio, we would ask them to fill out the repair tag, place it on the radio, walk forward as far as they could and then set the radio on the floor and then back out of the our shop. At that point we would call our radio station and ask them to stop running our ads until further notice. We agreed to keep paying for the ads, but just not run them.

We continued our search for competent repair men and delivery men. We were getting more responses for help and fortunately we were able to sort out a few good ones from the culls. One such person was a young man named Mark, who came to us working under a government training program, in which the government supplemented his income above our training salary to give him a livable income. He was an ex-sailor who had worked as a radio operator in the navy. Although he had some knowledge of parts names and nomenclatures, he had no prior radio experience, prior to going into the navy, and absolutely no training on how to repair them.

He showed a lot of ability for learning the tricks of repairing, and exhibited a natural acceptance for learning the trade. I was very excited to have him working with me. His only drawback was that he had a knack for making what we called stupid mistakes, sometimes doing damage to our test equipment or even the radio which he was on working itself.

My brother, Harvey was working with me at that time, and when Mark would pull off one of his bad boners, Harvey would say to him, "I am going to castrate you the next time you screw up like that." Mark had worked for us for about three months, and about once a week Harvey would have to repeat his threat, but Mark was starting to get better and the threats were getting farther apart.

By this time we had signed up with a security company, who had taped our windows and had alarms on our windows and doors, and should there be a break in, the alarm would ring directly in their office. They also had a security guard that would stop by our building twice every night, at various times to make sure that everything was secure and that no one was prowling around our building.

One morning Mark came into work and came up to me and said, "Boss, today will be my last day working here." I said to Mark, "What is your problem, you seem to be making great progress in your training program here?" "It is about the nightmares, I have been having nightmares lately, and after the one I had last night, I just can't take it any more." He said. "Tell me about it, Mark." I said. "Last night I dreamed that I was working here and really screwed up bad, and Harvey grabbed me, castrated me, and threw my balls in the garbage." "After the store was closed, and it turned dark, I came back to the store and I went around to the back, and was going through the garbage looking for my seeds. During the time I was in the back looking through the garbage, your security guard came by, and when he came to the rear of the building he saw me. He then handcuffed me and arrested me for attempting to break and enter into your building." "I would not take that serious Mark, besides I have not heard Harvey make that threat for some time now." "I know," he said, "But the thought is so embedded in my mind and I just can't concentrate. It will be better if I just move on."

And he did.

Chapter 18

DELIVERY SERVICE

This town was really a wonderful place to live. In those days we had single family residences, with well kept lawns, two lane highways, and no condominiums or high rise apartments with hundreds of people living on the same block. Most motels and restaurants had a sign clearly posted that stated "Restricted clientele." There were basically four groups of people who lived in this area at that time.

First, you had, what we then called, the old rich. This was a group of very genteel people, who had inherited money, who, when one would do a service for them, and then present them with a bill, would always ask, "Are you sure that is enough?" They clipped coupons. That was the expression that described that group of people who lived from the dividends of their stocks and bonds. They would almost always invite you into their home, offer you a soft drink, coffee or tea, and usually tip you well when you left.

Second, there was a group that was called the new rich, they were an entirely different breed. The people of this group generally were course, greedy, haute and difficult. These were people who had come into some money lately, either through gambling, an invention, just luck, as in the stock market, a good real estate investment or a criminal operation. These people would never invite you into their home, offer you a beverage or give you a tip, and whatever you charged them, they thought it was too much.

Third, we had the working middle class. These were the barbers and the beauticians, the bartenders and barmaids, the carpenters, the service people, who repaired your radios, your car or the roof of your house. They were the ones who ran all of those small Mom and Pop businesses. They were really the backbone of our community. They were kind, considerate and compassionate, and would usually say, "Keep the change" when they paid their bill.

Fourth, we had the itinerant workers. These were mostly black people who lived in government housing, or in small rickety shacks, with no electricity and that had no windows, only solid wooden hinged shutters, that they could swing open to let in some light. Some were saving and diligent and had managed to move into small houses of their own. These were largely built on unpaved streets with no electricity available.

We would buy what was called "Farm Pack" batteries, forty eight at a time to sell to those families on easy payments, to run their battery operated radios. I had a radio repairman working for me in that area and I recall him saying, "I am sick and tired of working on those old rat eaten radios." He was, of course, referring to the battery operated radios that would come in with the cones eaten out of the speakers and the wax eaten from the coils by mice.

Once, when I was on holiday in the Bahamas with my wife, Joan, we were taking a sightseeing trip in a carriage. In the course of our trip I had the opportunity to converse with the driver, who was black, when suddenly he exclaimed, "Man, I remember you, you fixed my radio when I was picking beans over in Pompano, and it sho worked good too." At one time there were two separate towns in the area, one was called Pompano, as for a popular fish that flourished off the beaches there, and the other was a narrow strip along the ocean front was called Pompano Beach. The two towns eventually combined into a single city, called Pompano Beach. The high school in Pompano Beach did not call their athletic teams a name like the Tigers or the Lions, they were called the Pompano Beanpickers.

Whether you lived in the high rent district or the slums, we offered the same free pick up and delivery services on radios that we repaired, just as I had ever since my first repair shop when I was sixteen years old.

I had a man working for me by the name of Olen Roberts. He was able to handle minor repairs and parts replacements. He had just arrived in South Florida, down from Massachusetts, and thought that the people here were terrible, operating segregated schools, segregated hospitals, and having almost all black people living in their own area, with even separate churches, restaurants and hospitals.

At one time two black men were injured in a car accident on the federal highway on the south side of town. A black ambulance was summoned and the driver drove right by the all white hospitals on the way to Provident Hospital, which was an all black facility. As the driver was weaving along the side of New River to get to the designated hospital, the speeding ambulance driver lost control of his vehicle and plunged into New River. In the confusion that followed, one of the injured patients drowned. A white police officer reassured the other patient, "Do not worry, I have already called for another ambulance to take you on to the hospital." To which the man replied, "No suh boss, do not call me no am-bu-lance, call me a Negro taxi, I wants to get there alive."

The white folks here had the general agreement, "That the black folks here were entitled to the same civil rights and same civil liberties as the white folks, provided, that they accepted the same civil responsibilities that the white folks did."

After making pickups and deliveries in the black area for two months, and understanding their attitudes, he began to realize why they were treated the way they were. At that point he started taking up a collection to try to raise enough money to go to Washington, DC and blow up the Lincoln Memorial. Mr. Roberts made most of our pickups and deliveries into the black area.

It was one such a delivery that he was making on a Tuesday morning. He had delivered a large Zenith console radio that we had repaired, to a Mrs. Williams. When he first brought the radio into the room, Mrs. Williams said to one of her sons, "Leroy, move dat table for de man, dat is where de radio goes.

When Olen was finished, he handed Mrs. Williams the repair bill for nineteen dollars and fifty six cents. She said to him, "Can youse wait til Saturday.? I get paid then and I will bring the money in to your shop."

I guess that Olen felt sorry for her, with five kids to feed, and he did not see any signs of a man being around the house, besides, the radio was big and heavy, and probably did not want to lug it back to the truck. Olen said to her, "Now, you are sure that you will bring the money in on Saturday?" "Oh yes suh, ah sho will" she said.

With that, Olen left and returned to our shop. When he came in, he explained to me that he had let her charge the bill, and said, "Don't you worry none about your money boss, I know that she will come in and pay you, but, if she don't, I will pay the bill for her." Saturday came and went. Mrs. Williams was a no show. On Monday, I gave Olen the bad news.

He said, "Not to worry, I WILL collect that money for you." I know that Olen was concerned, because nineteen dollars and fifty six cents was almost half of a weeks pay for him.

At ten o'clock on Monday night, Olen called Mrs. Williams and reminded her that she had failed to come in and pay her bill. She said to Olen, "Don't worry, I will be in tomorrow and pay youse." Tuesday came and went. Mrs. Williams was a no show Tuesday night at eleven o'clock, Olen called Mrs. Williams. Same comment from Olen. Same answer from Mrs. Williams. Wednesday, Mrs. Williams was a no show. Wednesday Night at twelve o'clock, Olen called Mrs. Williams. Same comment from Olen, same answer from Mrs. Williams. Thursday, Mrs. Williams again failed to show up with the money. Thursday night at one o'clock in the morning, Olen called Mrs. Williams. Same comment from Olen, same response from Mrs. Williams. Friday was no different, no appearance from Mrs. Williams. Friday night at two o'clock in the morning, Olen called Mrs. Williams. Same comment from Olen, same answer from Mrs. Williams.

I was working in my shop on Saturday morning, when a woman came in that I had never seen before, and said, "I am Ms. Williams, I wants to pay my bill that I owes you" With that she handed me nineteen dollars and fifty six cents. I thanked her and gave her a receipt. Then as she turned to leave, she said "Now I hope you will get thatt mad dog off my back. To this day Olen Roberts is known to the world as Mad Dog Roberts.

Chapter 19

INDIANAPOLIS

Having lived most of my life up north, I loved car races and went to see them wherever they were held in my general area, and had always dreamed of going to watch the BIG race at Indianapolis, but just never made it.

Now that I was living in Florida and had enough money to afford the trip, I was determined to see the big one. I planned my vacation to coincide with the thirtieth of May and had been in touch with two of my old school mates, Arti, and the one we all called the Rabbi, both of whom still lived up north, and were excited at the thought of attending the race with me.

My game plan was to drive back to my old home town, visit for a few days and the three of us would go to the race together. I had taken my car to my local mechanic and left it with him for a couple of days to have him check it over and do any preventative repairs that he may deem necessary, as this would be a grueling trip during the upcoming two weeks.

I was not too concerned about the engine itself, as it was a new Police Special engine, as produced by Ford for the West Virginia highway patrol. I had left my home in South Florida right after noon and intended to drive straight through, which at that time, with no interstates, would have been about twelve hundred miles. I did not have cruise control on my car at that time, but tried to keep my speed around sixty five miles per hour. That seemed to be a safe speed and the local bears usually would not harass you driving like that.

I had gone out of Florida and through Georgia and was driving on Highway US #1 around eleven o'clock at night, driving North through South Carolina. At that point, a Rocket Eighty Eight Oldsmobile pulled alongside of me and stayed right next to me for about a mile. Concerned about the fact that they were staying by my side for so long, I kept glancing over to take a look at them from time to time. I recognized the fact that there were two black men in the front seat of the Oldsmobile, when they realized that I had been eying them, they suddenly they pulled away from me and I soon lost sight of their tail lights.

They must have slowed down considerably, because I caught up to them after driving only about five miles, and passed them right on by with no problem. As I passed them by, I thought that it was odd that I would catch up with them so soon, so I reached under my seat and pulled out my Smith and Wesson Thirty Eight Special, took it out of the holster and laid it on the seat beside my right leg. I drove a couple of more miles, when all at once there it was again, that same Oldsmobile was driving right along side of my car. I noticed that it was there, but pretended not to know, but when, after another mile, the vehicle was still right beside my car, I reached down to my seat, picked up my thirty eight special, laid the barrel across my left arm, which was resting on the rolled down window of the drivers side door, pointed the barrel directly at the passenger in the Oldsmobile and pulled back the hammer. Instantly, the passenger realized that he was under the gun, he must have told the driver, "Get the hell out of here" and the Oldsmobile accelerated at full bore and I never saw the vehicle again.

I arrived back at my home town early the next afternoon, went immediately to see my mother, who still lived back on the farm. After visiting with her for a while and depositing my traveling bags in her house, I went out and contacted both the Rabbi and Arti. Both assured that they were ready and able to accompany me to Indianapolis.

I discussed with Arti the idea of the two of us going out and hitting a few of the old road houses that we used to frequent, to see if we could find anything worth picking up. He was agreeable. Apparently, since I had left the territory, he did not have a lot of fellows who wanted go out and party like I did. I picked him up about seven thirty and we went first to a place called the Red Onion. This place was really dead. We sat there and drank a couple of beers and only a half dozen fellows came and went and no girls, we could see no future there so we split. Next, we drove down to Shanks

Park, a place known in the community as the Bloody Bucket, because of all of the fights that went on there.

It, however, did live up to its name, although there was only one couple sitting at a table, there was a goodly number of young men around. While we were there, we saw two minor altercations. During the second fight, one of the contenders pulled out what appeared to be a long barreled thirty two revolver. I got up and told Arti, "Lets get the hell out of here before someone shows him how to put the cartridges in the chamber."

Adios, Shanks Park.

We next went to Smiths Park, which was a little less wild than the others and found that there were some girls there. We danced with some of the girls, but really did not hook up with any. Since I had been away for less than one year, I still knew many of the young men who were there, and I spent most of the evening telling them stories of my experiences down in Florida, with the bugs, the beaches loaded with girls in bikinis, and the Water Moccasins.

When the place closed, we drove back down the road and started to cross the bridge into town. Standing there, right in the middle of the covered bridge, was a local policeman, waving a flashlight. I saw him standing there, but did not stop, I merely flashed my lights and blew my horn, and as the officer stepped back out of the middle of the bridge, I kept right on going.

This particular bridge has a history.

First, it is the only covered bridge in the United States, through which a federal highway travels.

Second, it was the scene of the first land battle of the Civil War, as Union and Confederate troops fought for control of this of this bridge, as it was an important crossing of a major river for their troops.

Third, forty years later, at a gas station up the hill from the bridge, a tanker truck driver, who was delivering gas into the stations tanks, had the filler hose running unattended, as the driver was inside the station, trying to make out with the lady attendant who worked there. The tank overflowed and before the driver realized it, gasoline had run all of the way down the hill and onto the bridge. He did finally realize what was going on and shut off the flow of gas. Soon thereafter a small car going through the bridge backfired, setting the gas on fire and the bridge burned and was severely damaged. When the highway department started to evaluate the repairs, they had to go back to the highway department at Richmond, Virginia.

There, they found that the bridge was built in 1856, while Virginia and West Virginia were still one state, and they still had the complete architectural sketches intact, on file, in Richmond. Now the highway department would be able to completely rebuild the bridge back to the original specifications.

The day after the bridge incident, I was visiting at our local gas station-convenience store when another officer stopped in. When he saw me, he recognized me, and started talking to me, and told that the other officer was considering having charges brought against me of assault with a deadly weapon (my car). I went on to explain to him just exactly what had happened. I told him, "As we were approaching the bridge last night, we saw a Greyhound Bus parked along side of the road, near the bridge. "When we entered the dark covered bridge, I did see someone in the road, in some sort of uniform, but at that moment we figured that it was the driver from the Greyhound Bus, that he probably had a flat tire and I was in no mood to help change a tire on a bus at that hour of the night." "Besides, it is just his word against mine and I have an eyewitness that can corroborate what I am telling you," I must have sold him a convincing story, as I never heard anything more about it.

When we were through discussing the bridge activity, he started telling me about an incident with Clyde. Clyde was a local alcoholic, who was well known to the local gendarmes, as he had spent several nights in the slammer, as a result drunkenness or disorderly conduct. He said, "I was walking down the sidewalk one night last week and I met Clyde, who was walking with one leg on the sidewalk and the other one in the gutter of the street." "I watched him for a few moments, then I approached him and said, "Clyde, you are drunk again. When I said that, Clyde threw his arms around me, hugged me and kissed me and exclaimed, Oh, thank God, thank God, I thought that I was crippled, thank you."

I spent the next day and night at home with my mother.

The following morning I packed one change of clothes, not that I expected to use it, but just in case, as we were driving straight through to Indianapolis, watch the races, and drive straight back home. The change of clothes was just in case of a minor tragedy. I also took a raincoat.

I picked up the Rabbi and Arti and we were off to the races. I was driving and a few miles before we reached Parkersburg, West Virginia, I noticed that one of the red lights on my dash had come on, indicating that my generator had stopped charging. I knew that I would have to get it repaired before we got to the races, because there would be much too much traffic around Indianapolis to depend on keeping on getting my battery charged, or getting anything repaired.

Once I hit Parkersburg, I stopped at a service station and he steered me to a garage who he said would be able to repair my generator on the spot. We lost about two and a half hours getting the generator repaired, but still had plenty of time to make the starting time of the race. We walked to a local restaurant and had a good meal, while the generator was being repaired.

We all checked the map and with Arti driving and the Rabbi sitting up front to keep him awake, we got him headed west on route fifty, as I curled up in the back seat to catch a little sleep. I was awakened from a deep sleep by the bumpity bump, bumpity bump of the tires crossing a bridge. Still half asleep and not knowing how long I had been sleeping, I thought, "Oh no, he went too far, we must be crossing the Mississippi River." Wrong. We were crossing the Ohio River. With Arti driving for over two hours, we were now fifteen miles further from Indianapolis, than we were when Arti started driving. It appears that he was driving west on route fifty until he hit Athens, Ohio, he then got on route fifty A and ended up going back east.

Now, we were getting pressed for time to make the race, so we decided that had to be the end of driving for Arti. With Arti safely in the back seat, me driving and the Rabbi being the keep awake man, this time we really were off to the races. We arrived at the race track too late to get seats in the grandstand, as there was limited seating at that time, but were able to get a good location on a rise in the infield. Where we were situated, we could see the start-finish line and the first turn.

With our field glasses, we were able to keep track of the few cars that we were really interested in following, and with our stop watch and a scratch pad, we were able to keep track on who was driving the track a little faster and who was slowing down. During the race there was a wreck on the first turn, in which the driver, who was driving a car with a sixteen cylinder engine, was killed, and we had a bird's eye view of all the action. That was the last sixteen cylinder car to ever enter the Memorial Day races at Indianapolis.

All in all, it was a very exciting race, and we were all very happy that we were able to be there in person and watch Mauri Rose win the race. After the race was over, it did not take too long to get all of the cars out of the infield, and back on the highway. I was driving, and when we got about fifty miles away from Indianapolis, we stopped at a roadside restaurant and had a good meal. We only had snack food all day, since that nice meal in Parkersburg the evening before while we were waiting to get my generator repaired.

After we finished our meal, we put Arti back behind the wheel, and I retired to the back seat again. After he drove for three or four hours, he got lost again, and ended up at the end of a dead end street.

I don't know where we were, but I do know that it was really dark, there were several street people around a fifty five gallon drum, that had a fire burning in it, and that was the only light in the area. I would really have panicked, except for the comfort of knowing that I had my thirty eight special, loaded with hollow point bullets, under my seat.

I had Arti back the car out of the alley and drove to a service station that was open, where we fueled up, looked at our map, and asked directions to get back on the main east-west highway. We changed drivers with me under the wheel and put Arti in the back seat and I told the Rabbi to knock him in the head with a hammer, if he even suggested driving any more on this trip. We made the rest of the trip back home without incident. I stayed and visited with my mother for a few more days.

I had no steady girl friend there, and I did not have a great interest in getting a date, as there was too much of a chance of getting into trouble or a fight at the local clubs or bars.

I had no problems as I drove back to Florida, but will admit that I was a little apprehensive as I drove through South Carolina.

Chapter 20

Bridge Over Troubled Waters

As the volume of radios being brought into my shop for repair was increasing by leaps and bounds, so was the need for additional repairmen. I had standing requests for prospects at all local private employment agency's as well at the federal unemployment agency. Every few days a prospect would show up for an interview.

By this time I had made up and printed a one page questionnaire, which included their name, address and telephone number, and a few basic electronic questions. I also had a tray which contained various parts of the then current radios such as a vacuum tube, a condenser, a transformer, a resistor, of which they were requested to identify the size of the resistor by the color code on the side of the item and, and to identify by names all parts included.

I was surprised to find that the only thing that many of the potential employees knew about a radio was how to turn it on and off. Some prospects could not even read the printed words on the questionnaire. When the prospect completed the paper, I could take one glance at it and determine whether he had any experience at all in repairing radios. If there was any indication of any kind that he any knowledge of making repairs, then I would take him to work bench and hand him a radio which previously had been working perfectly and I had replaced a good part with a defective one.

I had three such radios made up on hand and would have the prospective employee check the one with the simplest of problem first. If they were able to diagnose that one, then I would give them one a little more difficult. Only the prospect that could diagnose all three radios in a reasonable amount of time got any consideration as far a getting a job doing the actual repairs.

Later on, I would hire men with only limited knowledge of repairs to take radios in and out of their cabinets and to do the actual parts replacement once a qualified serviceman had diagnosed the trouble. Also to drive our service vehicle to pick up and deliver the customers radios. One such prospect was Harold, who came to me from the federal unemployment agency, and handed me a form, which I was to fill out and return it to the agency, advising them as to whether I hired him or was willing to hire him.

Upon filling out the application, one glance convinced me that he had some knowledge of radio repair. I then handed him the three doctored radios and he completed the diagnosis of all three in a reasonable length of time. I was pleased to announce to Harold that he was hired and after stating what his starting wages would be, asked when could he start? He himmed and hawed and finally came right out and stated what he really wanted. That was, he wanted me to fill out the paper that I was to return to the unemployment agency stating that I was not willing to hire him. He said that he had been away from home for almost three years and had a lot of things that he wanted to catch up on. He wanted me to state on the paper that he was not qualified and I would not hire him, so that he could collect the unemployment benefit of twenty dollars a week, offered to returning veterans until such a time that they could find suitable jobs.

I told him I was not willing to do that, because I was so badly in need of employees myself. He then came up with another proposition, he said, "My sisters boyfriend is also into radio repair, if I bring him in here to you and you hire him, then will you fill out my papers as I requested?" I could see that he really did not want to come to work for me and probably would not make a very loyal employee, so I agreed to hold the papers to give him a chance to return with his prospective, future brother in law.

The very next day he reappeared on the scene with another young man that he introduced to me as Mr. Waters, Muddy Waters to be exact.

I had Muddy fill out the application, and then gave him the first radio to repair. He obviously was nowhere near the qualified repairman that Harold was, but I figured that something was better than nothing, so I agreed to the hiring of Muddy, but at a lower pay scale than I had offered Harold. Since he was about my age and unencumbered, often we would go to some bars after work together. In those days, Ft. Lauderdale had only a limited number of cocktail bars and lounges, since most of the people living in the county were either cattle ranchers, or farmers, most of the bars were road houses that served only beer and wine.

As we were spending more and more evenings together, we were exchanging some of the stories about what we had engaged in while in the service. I had been in the Air Corps, while he had been in the Coast Guard and had spent most of his time in the service on a cutter patrolling the Caribbean. He was telling me that after a long period at sea, his cutter finally docked at San Juan, Puerto Rico for a few days of rest and recreation. On the second night there, while at a local bar, and since there were almost no girls present, he became listless and took off his little white sailors hat and put on the head of another sailor sitting at a different table. A few minutes later came back to that same table and accosted the sailor, inquiring, "What do you think you are doing wearing my hat?" Well naturally, that led to a fight and soon almost all of the sailors in the bar were involved. During the heat of the battle, someone kicked Muddy in the groin and he ended up in the hospital, where as a result of the blow, due to the extreme swelling of the organ, had to have his left testicle removed.

At that point I exclaimed that it must of been the worst fight that he had ever been engaged in his life. He replied, "Oh no, the worst fight that I have ever been in, was after I returned home. It happened right down here on state road seven at Greg's Bar and Grill." It was on last Halloween Night. I was in the bar with several of my friends, including some girls and when closing time came, the bartender announced, "You don't have to go home, you just have to get the hell out of here" Muddy said, "There was another large group of boys and girls, that I did not know, still in the bar and together, we all agreed to stay and make this a private club party, with each patron paying a one dollar membership fee, for which we would receive our first drink free". He continued, "After about an hour, with the juke box blaring and the beer and wine flowing, everyone appeared to be having a great time, when suddenly an uproar started. It apparently started out as a war of words about someone trying to steal another's girl and soon escalated into the worst fight that I have ever seen, I mean it was a real knock 'em down and drag 'em out fight." As he finished his dissertation, I just sat there in silence for a few minutes until Muddy said, "What is the matter with you."

With that, I stuck out my hand to shake his hand and said, "Meet a key member of that other group, you see I was a part on that other group there on Halloween Night, but I do not recall seeing you there." He replied, "There were so many people involved in the brawl that you and I may have been slugging it out with each other." You never know just whom you might meet in the dark of night, particularly if it was in the worst fight of your lifetime.

Muddy had two brothers, an older one called Rippling Waters and a younger one called Dripping Waters. He also had a younger sister named Bubbles. Muddy invited me to attend a bachelor party for Rippling as he was getting married. The Waters boys had lived all of their lives in Hollywood, Florida and had a lot of local friends, and when I arrived at the party, I was really surprised to find there were dozens of young men in attendance. At the party they took up a collection and collected enough money to pay for the first two months rent on the one bedroom part of a duplex for the newlyweds to live in to start their life together. After Muddy rented the apartment, he kept one of the keys and had access to the duplex.

The wedding was to be on Saturday afternoon, with what Rippling thought was to be a dinner party to follow, and he did not realize that what we had planned was a real chivaree, which was to last all night Saturday night and all day on Sunday. A party which was to be wild and raucous, where the bride, although a part of the party, was to be kept isolated from her husband until late Sunday night. If this had been held in West Virginia, the bride would have been abducted from the party and kept in the company of one of her girl friends for a couple of days. At this party, at least Rippling could see his bride on occasion, but not allowed to dance with her or even talk to her. Late Sunday evening Rippling took his new bride to their new quarters. What he did not know was that Muddy had mounted a floodlight in their bedroom that was hooked up to a timer that was set to turn on the light at one o'clock early Monday morning. By that time, a group of our friends had collected outside of their bedroom window. At one o'clock when the light flashed on, Rippling, with no clothes on, jumped up out of bed and hit the wall switch for the ceiling light. That only made the room brighter, much to the delight of the roaring crowd outside of their window. Rippling then jumped back into the bed and tried to cover both nude bodies with a sheet, which was the only bedding present on the bed.

Muddy worked for me mainly as a parts replacement guy and also was used as a pick up and delivery man. In those days many of the city streets, as well as those in the county were not paved and of course had no street signs. If Muddy was out on the road and when he called in for instructions as to what his next assignment would be, and I would give an address of a call to be made, if he did not immediately recognize just where that family lived, his first question was always, "What bar is it near?" He did know the exact location of every bar in the county.

One evening as it was quitting time I asked Muddy, "Would you be so kind as to drop off this repaired radio for me, the customer lives on Ravenswood road and is only a few blocks out of your way, on your way home?" Muddy agreed to deliver the radio and told me later, "That when he went to the door of the mans house and knocked on the door, a man came to the door and when I said, 'I have a repaired radio here for you," the man replied, "Oh, that must belong to my father." Muddy said that he thought, "The man who answered the door looked old enough to be God's grandfather." "When the elderly gentlemen who owned the radio came to the door to retrieve his prized possession I thought that he must have been the last remaining live veteran of the civil war."

A couple of years later, Muddy himself got married and bought a two bedroom home in Wilton Manors. Later, I was walking along the street with Muddy one evening when we met a young lady who was dressed only in a skimpy bikini, a common sight in Ft. Lauderdale. As she passed us by, Muddy turned his head and let his eyes follow her down the sidewalk for a time. I spoke to him, "You are a married man now, you are not supposed to look at things like that." He responded, "Just because that I spent my last fifty dollars to buy a new suit does not mean that I can't look in the store windows on the way back home with it."

As time passed, they sold their home and the last that I heard from them they were living on a small farm in Virginia and were raising Pygmy Goats.

Chapter 21

THE FLOOD

It was a beautiful morning on the fifteenth day of May. We had a very dry spring that year, but about two o'clock that afternoon, it started to rain, and we had a very hard rain. The next afternoon, it started to rain again. In fact, it rained every afternoon, from then on, through the first week in October. Earlier in this century, when Lake Okeechobee was at a very high level, a hurricane struck that area and the eye of the storm passed directly over them, and hundreds of people drowned as the eye passed, when the wind suddenly changed direction, driving the waters of the lake back at the opposite direction, flooding the entire area. Ever since that time, whenever the water in Lake Okeechobee would rise to a certain unsafe level, they would open the flood gates to try to reduce the water level to a safe condition during hurricane season.

In the meantime, a businessman had bought ten thousand acres of low lying property, west of Ft. Lauderdale, lying just west of, and adjacent to highway U S 441. When they would open the flood gates, it would tend to flood the eastern section of the everglades, which included the ten thousand acres that had been purchased for development.

Knowing this, the developer built a large, secure dyke from highway U S 441, around the northern and western edge and back to 441 on the south. This was one of those years that the flood gates had been opened early in the season at Lake Okeechobee to keep the lake waters at a reasonable level.

There was a small beer bar, called the Cracker Box, located just north of the property being developed, but on the east side of US 441. I had stopped in the Cracker Box a few times. The owner, Joe was very congenial and I liked him a lot. It got to be my regular hang out. I would even pitch in and help him, if he got jammed up. As a matter of fact, when his wife Vera, came to Florida for the very first time, I took Joe in my car to the train station to pick up Vera and his daughter, Myrna. After talking with Vera, I realized that I had casually met her, while she had been working as a civilian employee at the Air Corps base at Westover Field in Massachusetts, when I had gone there more than two years earlier to pick up our new B-17 bomber which we were to fly to Europe.

By spending a lot of my off duty hours at the Cracker Box, I got to know most of the farmers and ranchers that lived and worked in the surrounding area. At that time, Florida was the second largest cattle producing state in the nation, second only to Montana. Central and South Florida had a large contingent of those cattle ranchers.

After the big hurricane in September, the ranchers were really hard pressed. The water was backed up from the dyke all of the way up to Lake Okeechobee, about three feet deep. These ranchers had gone to the county commissioners and even to the governor to try to get some relief from the flooding. Their complaint was, that their cattle were walking around in water up to their bellies, they could no longer graze, and that the ranchers had to deliver food to their hundreds of cattle daily, in swamp buggies and air boats.

At the end of a hard day, many of the ranchers would end up at the Cracker Box for a little relaxation. I would hear them talking among themselves, but not whispering, that if they did not get some relief soon, that they would take matters into their own hands. Now comes October. There is a hurricane rolling around in the Atlantic about two hundred miles off of the coast of St. Augustine.

General Electric had been considering dropping a large load of dry ice into a hurricane to see if that would cool the hurricane down enough to make it break up and disband. That is just what they did on this hurricane. They vehemently denied any such participation for almost twenty years, but did finally admit to the experiment. The next evening as a few of the ranchers came to the bar, one of them told me, "Tonight is the night." I did not have to ask him what he meant.

I knew.

The ranchers took about fifty cases of dynamite, inserted the individual sticks into the dyke, tied them all together with fuses, and let it blow. The resulting explosion leveled about one quarter of a mile of the northern part of the surrounding dyke. Almost instantly, a flood of water more than knee deep, swept through the development and all of the way to the Atlantic Ocean. At that exact time the hurricane which had been loitering off the coast of St. Augustine, now energized by the dry ice, had turned south and crossed over land, dropping approximately sixteen inches of rain in the Ft. Lauderdale area that night.

Water in some of the downtown Ft. Lauderdale area was five feet deep. New river normally merged into the Intracoastal Waterway and flowed south, but now it was so flooded and moving with such force that it washed away the land barrier and flowed directly into the Atlantic Ocean.

There was one residential section near downtown, which was now jokingly called Folsom's Lake, since all of the homes were surrounded by water. The developer of the projects name was Folsom. To counter all of the criticism that he was receiving about the flooded conditions surrounding the homes that he had built, Mr. Folsom ran a full page advertisement in the local newspaper, offering to buy back the home from any dissatisfied owner, returning full purchase price plus ten per cent profit for their inconvenience. The property had doubled in retail value since the original sale, and Mr. Folsom therefore had no takers, but it did quiet the naysayers.

After the hurricane passed, I drove out to U S 441 to see how the Cracker Box survived, to find that it was open, and undamaged, with only splotches of shallow water standing around it. One could look west from U S 441, and you would think you might be looking at the Atlantic Ocean, except for an occasional tree sticking up out of the water. Water was all there was, as far as you could see.

The next night I went with Fred and Dusty, hunting for frog legs. We took a three cell flashlight, a palm frond and a couple of gunny sacks, got in Fred's flat bed pickup and drove a couple of miles north on U S 441. When we came to a dirt road that led out into some ranch land, we pulled down into it off of the main highway. The truck was now standing in about ten inches of water. Fred took the flashlight and Dusty took the palm frond, both of whom were wearing hip boots, and stepped out into the water.

I was wearing regular shoes, so I took the two gunny sacks and jumped up on the flat bed of the truck. With the flashlight, Fred could see the bull frog's eyes flashing through the water and grass, the light would mesmerize the frog, Dusty's eyes would follow the beam of light, and whack the frog with the palm frond, grab the frog by the leg and throw him up on the flat bed truck. I would grab the frog and throw him into the gunny sack. Dusty was good too, as he never seemed to miss that frog.

Standing up on the flat bed of the truck, I could look down in the water and see dozens of water moccasins swimming all around in the water. Once dusty pretended to whack a frog, then reached down and grabbed a water moccasin by the tail, and threw it up on to the truck bed. I took one quick look at that moccasin and immediately jumped into the water. I did not take time to think, because there was only one moccasin on the truck bed and dozens of them swimming around in the water. The moccasin on the truck bed then slithered off into the water and I then slithered back up on the truck bed.

Ten years later, Myrna, the daughter of the owner of the old Cracker Box was married and living on a ranch on that same dirt road with her husband John, and it was still a dirt road. On the Fourth of July, Myrna and her husband, John, invited me, my wife Joan, and our two small sons to their house for dinner. Once we arrived there, John said to me, "I have a new colt out in the barn, would you like to ride him?"

I said, "Sure, why not, I was raised on a farm, I am used to being around horses." John put on a saddle and a halter, not a bridle, on the colt. I climbed aboard and the colt started trotting away from the barn. I was paying more attention to the saddle that I was sitting on, than I was on riding the colt, and the next thing I knew, I was laying on the grass and the colt was walking away. I was not that easily discouraged. I got up, caught the colt, climbed back aboard and away we went. That colt tried everything he could to get me off of his back, he would buck, he would run fast and then slow down quick, he would rub along the fences, run under low hanging tree limbs, anything that he could do to try to get me off of his back. I was determined; I stayed on his back until he was just worn down. He finally just walked back to the barn where I dismounted, feeling a certain degree of satisfaction.

On Labor Day next, John and Myrna invited us back again. As soon as we arrived there this time, I noticed that John had on a full leg cast from his hip down, on his left leg. I asked, "John, what in the world happened to you?" He replied, "You know that colt you were riding when you were here on the Fourth of July, well, about a month later, I decided to take a crack at it." "This is the results" he said.

That same road is still there today, although not as a dirt road anymore, but the paved main entrance of a town of over one hundred and twenty thousand people, plus another high rent district, harboring another ten thousand more.

Chapter 22

New Security

As the flood waters were receding, the customer base out at the Cracker Box resumed back to a normal flow. The county sheriff stopped by to see if everything there was all right and if they needed any help of any kind. That was the kind of a sheriff that he was. Joe told the sheriff that he did not need any assistance, but that a nearby resident, who just happened to be in the bar at that time, had lost everything in the flood and was really destitute. The sheriff walked over to the man and introduced himself and after talking with the gentleman for a few minutes, reached in and pulled out his wallet and handed the man sixty dollars, no questions asked. The sheriff was well known for this type of generosity and his loyal constituents were able to reward him with reelection to his job as sheriff, after the governor had previously removed him from his sheriff's office for malfeasance in office.

The sheriff and his brother ran a company that furnished juke boxes, and pin ball machines, for a percentage of the gross take, in such places as the Cracker Box, clubs and even drug stores. That was also the company that were supplying the slot machines (although not legally) to these same group of customers. The fact that the sheriff permitted these machines to operate in his county was the main reason that the governor removed him from office in the first place.

The Cracker Box was a recipient of the full package, a juke box, a pinball machine and of course a one armed bandit. We had heard that some of the bars in the area had been broken into and the coins removed from the machines. And in some cases, the slot machines were stolen completely. Since I was in the electronic business, I devised an alarm system for the Cracker Box. It was rigged up in such a manner so that if any door was opened, any window was opened or broken, or any wires were cut, the alarm would sound. The alarm itself was located in the Quonset hut where Joe and Vera lived and was connected by wires to the Cracker Box. At that time, I was living in a second Quonset hut located on the premises, near to where Joe and Vera lived.

Only one time did the alarm ever sound. When the alarm started ringing, Joe immediately cut it off and came and awakened me. With my thirty two caliber revolver in my hand the two of us were slinking through the wide open space between the Quonset huts and the Cracker Box. As Vera was watching this unfold, she was laughing her ass off at us as we were trying to be inconspicuous as we crept toward the Cracker Box, but it was a bright moonlit night and there was nothing for us to conceal ourselves with as we moved forward. Anyone within one quarter of a mile could easily have seen us as we made the trip. Fortunately, we found nothing or nobody in or around the Cracker box once we arrived there. Apparently a mouse probably had crawled over one of the sensors that I had placed inside the premises.

A few years later, this same sheriff, was called to testify before the United States Senate Keefaufer Committee, investigating crime and corruption. He never did get to testify though, as he died of a heart attack as a result of stress at the very thought of having to testify before that Senate Committee, before his turn came to appear before the committee.

Stress will get you every time.

Live Pure.

Chapter 23

CHARITY DRIVE

My radio repair shop was located on a main highway in a business district, and thus was exposed not only to a lot of automobile traffic but to a lot of foot traffic also. As a result, I had the opportunity to meet a variety of business personnel, as well as a broad spectrum of consumers.

One of the people I had the opportunity to get to know was a young delivery man by the name of Dean. He was in his mid twenties, good looking with a very nice personality.

He would deliver packages to my shop two or three times a week, as well as to other merchants in the area. I had even invited him to go fishing with me on my boat, which he had accepted on two different occasions.

We never partied together at night though, as he was married to a very pretty girl from Tampa, and was out of the night life loop. I had met his wife, as I had repaired and delivered a console radio and phonograph to their apartment

Then came the time for a local civic club to have its annual charity drive. The charity would have members collect money on the street corners all week long and then close out the fund raising with a giant party at a local night club on Saturday night.

Being in business, I felt obligated to purchase tickets, and I did purchase two tickets, but would have wanted to attend anyway.

Knowing that this particular club had risqué shows, I elected not to invite a girl friend.

Since I had an extra ticket and did not want to go alone, I invited Dean to attend with me.

He told me that he really had intended to purchase a ticket, but hand not had the opportunity to do so. He thanked me for the ticket and agreed to meet me there at the club.

I arrived at the club at a time that I thought was a little early, but already the parking lot was nearly full. Fortunately, there were several off duty deputy sheriffs who were there, volunteering their time parking cars, and directed me to a vacant parking spot.

When I went inside, I was glad to see Dean was already there. I bought him a drink and we shared two or three others during the evening. The management had put together a great entertainment package for us. They had a live band there, a great male and a fabulous female singer. Interspersed by songs, were several strip tease girls appearing on stage.

Let me tell you, they were built for comfort and were not bashful!

At about one o'clock in the morning, when the last girl finished her act, she removed her last little tidbit of clothing, and put out an open invitation for some young man to come forward onto the stage.

By this time, Dean had consumed enough alcohol, and he ended up on the stage with this nude woman.

To put it mildly, I would say that Dean had his hands full, and certainly got his money's worth, for the price he paid for his admission ticket.

When I saw him the following week, making deliveries, I asked him, "How did you like the show last Saturday night?"

He replied, with a sheepish look on his face, "It certainly was different anyway."

A few weeks later, his wife heard of his escapade on stage with a nude woman. I don't know how much she knew, but it was enough for her to pack her bags, tell Dean goodbye, and go back home to her parents in Tampa.

Dean was devastated, because he really and truly loved that woman, but had just screwed up.

He started trying to call her, but she would not talk to him on the phone. After about two weeks of the unsuccessful phone calls, he started letter writing. He would write her a letter every day, and then try to call her every night. After a month of letter writing, she finally agreed to talk to him on the phone.

After two more months of pleading, apologizing, begging and promising, she finally agreed to come back home to him, if he would come over and pick her up.

Early on Saturday morning Dean got in his car and headed for Tampa. When he was about half way across the state, on Route 60, a dump truck driver, driving in the opposite direction, fell asleep at the wheel, struck his car head on, and Dean was killed instantly.

Every time I think about Dean, I think about a morality joke that I had heard years before. It went something like this:

A little doggie fell asleep alongside of a railroad track, with his tail laying up on the track. When the train came along, the first set of wheels cut off a little piece of his tail. That woke the little doggie up, and he stuck his head up to see what had happened. The next set of wheels then cut off the little doggies head.

The moral of this story is: "Never lose your head over a little piece of tail.

Chapter 24

PORKY'S

Many people have had the opportunity to go to Blockbusters and rent the movie called Porky's, but only a few realize that this was NOT a story dreamed up by some one strung out on drugs, but there actually was a person who was nicknamed Porky. He was a man of large bulk and easily fit the vision of someone who might be nicknamed Porky.

He was known to drive around in a Cadillac convertible which had a hood ornament that consisted of real steer horns that were actually wider than the width of the Cadillac itself. I had the opportunity to know him when he brought that Cadillac to my service shop to have the radio in it repaired.

There really was also, a night club known as Porky's. It was well known for attracting unescorted young women, for serving watered down drinks and had a large, well respected bouncer. Porky's lounge sat well back from a well known federal highway, and was considered large for the time of its existence. It had a man made lake with a sailboat sitting in it between the front of the building and the main highway.

It was known for many other activities as well, including one time there had been a burglary at a five star furrier known, as Adrian Thal's, located on Las Olas Boulevard. Some time later when local authorities entered the premises of Porky's night club with a search warrant, they found the stolen furs stuffed up the chimney when one of the officers asked Porky, "How do you suppose these stolen furs ended up in the chimney of your place of business?" Porky responded, "Santa Claus probably brought them down the chimney." I do not believe he convinced the officers, that was how the furs ended up in the chimney of his place of business.

The time of the year came when a local civic club had their annual charity drive, and of course I felt obligated to purchase two tickets to attend. All week long members of the club were on street corners collecting funds and this year the big grand finale party was to be held at Porky's.

This year they had added a little different twist for use of the tickets also, because not only did the tickets get you into the club for the party but they were then put into a hopper for a drawing of the grand prize.

This time I kept both of my tickets, to enable me to double my chances of winning the grand prize.

The grand prize was a prepaid weekend getaway, at a well known resort in the Florida Keys, with your choice of the strippers at the show as your hostess.

The party at the club went well, as usual, until about half way through the evening. Apparently some ticket holder's wife found out about the drawing and the grand prize. The word must have spread among the women and some one of them had enough clout to have the governor send in the state police and the FSLE officers. I mean that club and the parking lot was flooded with state officers!

That brought the strip tease part of the club's attractions to a complete halt, and of course, no drawing, no grand prize, no weekend in the keys with your choice of the strippers, which brought great disappointment to most of the young single men there and to probably a lot of the married men also, who were in attendance.

Chapter 25

Happy Halloween

After I had been in business for a couple of years, I instituted a health insurance plan for the employees, but then wanted to do something for their children. I talked it over with the employees and we decided that it would be nice to have a Halloween party for all of their kids. For the first couple of years we would hold the party in someone's backyard, with food, soft drinks, games and prizes. We would give a prize for the best and second best costume, for the worst and for the most creative costume for the girls and the same awards for the boys. We tried to make it so that most of the kids could take home a toy that they could remember and cherish.

As time went on we would end up renting a hall or reserving a spot in a county park to have these events. One of the best ones that we ever had was one we held at a private horse ranch west of Boca Raton. At that party we spent almost two months working out the details to make sure that it would be a party for the kids to remember for a long long time. Of course the children were expected to come in costume, and they did. After all were assembled we took them on a genuine hay ride in a wagon filled with hay and pulled by a team of horses. While they were on the ride, we were building a nice bonfire in a pit that we had built earlier, so that when they returned, and after the costume judging, we had a wiener and marshmallow roast for them. With bar-b-que spare ribs available for those who still needed more food.

Then, after about an hour of playing games, we had them all assemble around the camp fire for the story telling finale. I had a PA system in my car with a microphone attached and I had Paul, one of my older employees, who had a deep voice and could put real meaning into words, to do the commentary. We had taken a scary Halloween story and changed the words a bit to make them fit our particular plans. We had previously cut out from plywood, a witch riding a broom, with arms outstretched as though to grab some kids. I had a local sign painter do the painting on the witch and he was able to make her look real. We ran a zip line, which was a long twisted cable, similar to the ones used to stabilize electric poles from the top of one tall tree, swooping down over the campfire and on back up to a much shorter pine tree. The Witch was secured to the cable through the use of eye hooks, and was pulled to the top and held there with a release latch that was activated by a rope that ran from the latch, down through the tree limbs to the ground.

Paul was telling his story over the PA system, and when he came to the part where the witch was coming to see how many kids she could grab and take them with her, back to her den and boil them in oil. He stopped for a moment, and then screamed, "Oh my gosh, here she comes, run for your lives." At that moment another person pulled the release rope on the witch, and I flashed the spot light from my car on the Witch. The eye hooks from the Witch made a screaming sound as it came down the steep twisted cable. I was able to follow the brightly painted Witch with her black pointed hat and black cape, with my spot light, only because I had practiced it for two nights before. By the time that Witch actually went over the camp fire, there was not a kid within fifty feet of the fire. I later felt bad about the little trick that I pulled on them, but I spoke with every one of their parents later and none of them had noticed any nightmares or bad reactions from their children. Most thought it was fun.

In the years before the kids program at the horse ranch, we were very rapidly expanding our radio repair business, television had not reared its ugly head yet, and we were well known and respected in the business world. We were getting letters from all over the United States inquiring as to whether we needed additional employees.

One such letter came from Cecil who lived in Mississippi. When I replied to him I asked if he had a telephone where I could reach him, I also included our business number. After a couple of phone conversations with him I assured him that he would have permanent job with me, if he were ever in my area, providing he could perform as he claimed. But if he could not produce the repair work, it would be adios, Cecil.

Two days later, in walked Cecil, but he certainly did not look like I had pictured him. He was about five feet and six inches tall and not pleasingly plump, but disgustingly obese. As a result of that, plus his mannerisms and dress code, he became known as the big fat slob. I put him right to work and he was as good a radio repairman as he said he was. Our normal work schedule in those days was from eight o'clock in the morning until five o'clock in the afternoon.

We were ahead of the curve on many fronts. Long before there were any commercial telephone answering services available, we had made arrangements with the telephone company and a lady who lived about two blocks from our shop, to have our phone line run into her house with a separate telephone. Any time between 5:00 p.m. and 8:00 a.m. that our phone rang and we did not pick it up within two or three rings, this lady would answer it and it would sound just as though she were right in our shop.

After Cecil had worked for me for only about a week, he noticed that many times that I did not walk out of the shop right at five as the other employees did. He said that if I wanted him to, that he would and stay and work with me for an extra hour or two. I said that sounds great to me, as we had so many radios waiting to be repaired that they were setting on the floor until there was hardly any the place that you could walk in the shop. "If you want to, we can plan on staying tonight until seven, if that is all right with you. I will pay you for your time." Cecil agreed that it was all right with him too.

Enter: One problem.

Since he and his wife were only renting a room temporarily, they had no telephone and he could not call his wife and let her know that he would be working late. Instead of getting home around five thirty, Cecil arrived home about seven thirty. When Cecil arrived at work the next morning he had a black eye and a large bandage of the side of his head. I said to him, "What in the world happened to you last night?" He replied, "When I got home last night my wife did not know that I was working late and about six o'clock, she went to the landlord and asked if she could borrow their phone to call and see where I was. I spoke up and told her that I was working late."

"You lying ---, she said, you weren't working, you were having a party, and without me. I called your shop about six o'clock and some girl answered the phone and I could hear music playing and girls giggling in the background. With that she smashed me on the side of the head with a cast iron skillet."

Apparently the woman who answers our phone had a radio playing in the background and that was the background noises that Cecil's wife had heard when she phoned the shop. It had never dawned on me that I needed to tell all of my employees that we had a woman who answered our telephone after we were closed. Now I knew.

Cecil healed and continued working for me. As Halloween time approached, I decided to have a separate costume party, but this was to be only for employees and their spouse or companion. I needed to know who was coming and what type of drinks they preferred. As I made my list of people who would be in attendance, along with their preference of drinks, so that I would be able to accommodate every ones choice of beverage. I had Cecil and his wife's name down, but at the last moment he informed me that his wife would not be attending.

Since the party was to be held at a private residence, I gave to Cecil the address and directions, including the easy way to find the house. I told him that he would not be able to miss the place as it would be surrounded by a lot of parked cars.

By 8:30 p.m., everyone had shown up in full costume, everyone except Cecil, that is. About 10:00 p.m. Cecil walked into the party, wearing the same clothes that he wore to work that day, the only thing different was, that he had on a small mask covering only his eyes. When I asked him why he was late, he explained that he was driving along looking for the address I had given him and when he saw all of the cars parked at a house a block before this one, he never even looked at the address, assumed that was our party and went on in and joined their Halloween Party.

It was only after he won fifty dollars as the best costume at the party and everyone else took off their masks, did he realize that he was at the wrong party. He said he put the fifty dollars in his pocket and without taking off his mask, slipped out of the front door and came on down to here. We had an adult Halloween Party every year after that.

One year I went as a robot. The next year, after shaving off my mustache and shaving my legs, wearing a slinky dress and an abundance of costume jewelry, I went as a lady of the night. The employees did not know who I was until I unmasked.

At that party Willie and Andy were in attendance with their wives. Andy spent almost the entire evening trying to make out with the unmarried sister of the man who hosted the party, totally ignoring his wife. Apparently almost everyone drank more than they should have, and when they were going home, Willie was driving with Andy up front, with their wives sitting in the rear seat. On the way home a local police officer pulled them over because the car seemed to be weaving all over the road. When Willie stopped the car, both he and Andy got out of the car. After the officer spoke to Willie for a couple of minutes, he determined that Willie was not capable of driving, was very considerate and asked that he let the other man drive the rest of the way home. The other man was Andy, who was standing in front of the car with the headlights on him, wearing only Indian moccasins, a loin cloth, a headband with feathers in it and circles of targets painted in red, on his chest and on his back. This was the character that the officer felt was suitable to drive the car the rest of the way home. Once Andy got home he became sick and went into the bathroom. As he was down on his knees throwing up his guts, his wife was standing behind him beating him over the head with a very sizeable purse, yelling at him, "Are you having a good time yet!"

The next year we rented the DAV hall in which to have our Halloween Party. That year my wife Joan went to the party as a bowling ball. The ball was three feet in diameter. I had cut a series of different sized circles out of plywood, bracing them together with lengths of one by three wood. I made it in two parts, with the bottom section having a flat bottom and a seat built in, along with a 45 RPM record player, which I had reconstructed to play on self contained batteries The top half was perfectly round with three holes in it as for finger holes in a bowling ball, so that she could get fresh air. The whole thing was covered with papier-mâché, and spray painted black.

About an hour before anyone was due to arrive at the hall, I carried the ball into the hall and placed it on the floor at what I knew would be the proper location. Once located there, Joan climbed inside the ball and sat down. I then placed the top half of the ball over her head and she was reasonably comfortable inside the bowling ball.

My costume was that of a purple people eater. It was all purple material with a pair of wings and a cornucopia used to form the horn on my head. Inside of that horn, there was a speaker which was connected through a wire running down through my outfit to a phone plug that I could plug into the side of the bowling ball, thus broadcasting the song, "One eyed, one horned, flying purple eater" which was playing continually. Naturally I was seated on a chair located directly next to the bowling ball.

We had a real Judge, a small claims court Judge who came as a favor to me, and select the most original costume. He finally declared that the bowling ball was the best costume at the party, providing that there was someone inside of it. At that point I removed the top of the ball and Joan stepped out on the floor.

Chapter 26

OPEN RANGE

Prior to 1948, Florida had what they called the open range law. That was, that all domestic animals, including cows, horses, sheep, pigs, etc. had the right of way on all public highways. This meant that if you were driving down any public highway in Florida and you came across a cow or a pig in the middle of the road, it was your responsibility to either stop your vehicle or otherwise avoid hitting the animal. If you failed to do so and struck any domestic animal, then you were responsible for any and all damages, including the cost of replacing such animal.

I had vaguely heard of such cases but my first close up contact with anyone having such an experience was when my drinking buddy Fred, struck and killed a cow while driving north on US Highway 441, on his way north to his Friday night poker game. Fred immediately replaced the front bumper, grill and radiator on his pickup truck and was never served any papers and thus was never required to make restitution for the deceased cow.

I had recently traded in my 1941 Ford for a 1942 Lincoln. My friend Joe, the owner of the Cracker Box Bar, then purchased my previously owned Ford from the dealer. Although I had been living and working in Florida for over a year, and always desired to go to Key West, but just never had the courage to drive my Ford that far on that lonely highway. The first weekend that Joe owned his new ride, he and his Wife Vera and Daughter Myrna, drove to Key West and had no problems at all.

In those days if we wanted to enjoy a pizza we had to drive to Miami to make the purchase as there were no pizza parlors in our area. One evening Joe and Vera were going to Miami for pizza and asked Fred and myself if we would like to come along. Of course, we had nothing better to do so we agreed and all piled in the old dependable Ford and headed for Miami, down US Highway 441, which was right in the middle of the cattle country in South Florida.

About one third of the way south to Miami, while driving this deserted highway with the old, dim headlights of yesteryear, there it was, a cow standing right in the middle of the southbound lane. Joe was able to stop the old ford, but about three feet too late. The cow was well imbedded into the engine compartment of his car.

As we were trying to get the cow and the car out of the traffic lane, fearing another vehicle might strike us and compound the damages, another car load of young men stopped and helped us drag the cow to the side of the road and then push the car safely to the berm.

That done, they then drove me back to the Cracker Box Bar where I retrieved my own vehicle and drove back to the scene of the accident to pick up my compatriots. I assured the young men that if they were ever in our area at a time that the bar was open, that free beer was theirs for the taking. Joe, Vera, Fred and myself continued on to Miami in my car for our pizza. Every evening after work for the next two weeks, I would go straight to the Cracker Box and check about doing any shopping that they may need while their car was being repaired. Incidentally, it cost Joe eighty dollars to cover the cost of the dead cow.

The next incident was about ten o'clock on a Friday night and I was on my way to Coral Gables to see my main squeeze, a nurse who worked in a hospital there and got off duty at eleven o'clock. I was cruising down US Highway 441 at my usual one hundred miles per hour when I noticed a long string of vehicles coming toward me at a very reasonable, if not slow pace, considering the time of the day. I immediately figured that there probably was a Florida State Trooper at the head of the line so I promptly applied my brakes and by the time I reached the first of the oncoming vehicles I had lowered my speed to about 55 per hour while driving in a 45 mph zone. I felt that would be a safe speed, against a police officer going in the opposite direction.

Wrong.

As I passed the first few of the vehicles I noticed that none of them were police cars. I was amazed by that fact but not nearly as amazed as I was when I neared the last of the oncoming cars and there it was, standing right in the middle of my lane, not a cow, but a horse!

I instantly realized that I had three choices, but less than two seconds to make that choice. One, I could hit the fifteen hundred pound horse directly, or two, I could hit the oncoming car head on, or three, I could dive my vehicle into a twenty eight foot deep canal, with little chance of escaping my vehicle. I chose the horse and as I struck the horse, the hood of my three ton Lincoln went directly under the body of the horse and the horse then rolled right over the top of my vehicle onto the ground behind me.

As soon as I had seen the horse standing in the middle of my lane of traffic I applied my brakes, but a three ton vehicle does not stop instantly. By the time I got my vehicle stopped I was about forty feet past where the horse landed after rolling over my car. By the time I walked back to where the horse was, amazingly, the horse had struggled to get back on his feet and was limping off to the side of the pavement.

Only the last of the oncoming cars bothered to stop to see what was going on. It turned out to be a man and wife and they only wanted to see if I was all right or if they could be of any assistance. I said no, and thanked them for stopping and as they got back into their car I noticed that they had not taken an interest as to who I was or had not even looked at my cars license plate.

As the horse was still limping along side of the road, I walked back to my car and inspected the front of my car. Surprisingly enough, there was no damage to the front end of my car, I had only a cracked windshield and the top of my vehicle now dipped down instead of bulging up in a rounded fashion.

I continued on to Coral Gables and was only a couple of minutes late in picking up my date. The incident certainly gave us a lot to talk about that night and for some time to come. I was very fortunate, that in those days the car bodies were made of steel instead of tin and plastic as they are today, otherwise my car would have been flattened by the weight of that horse.

I had my windshield replaced and the top popped right back with only a minimal amount of body work required. I never heard anything about the horse but deep in my heart I prayed that it did not have to be put down.

Chapter 27

TV Time

When television came along, I surely wanted to get in on the ground floor and I jumped into television repairing with both feet. Some of the manufacturers offered service bulletins and Du Mont had a three day service seminar in our area, which I attended. Since I had practically learned to repair radios on my own, TV repairing came easy to me.

We were already doing all of the radio and phonograph repairing for Macy's, formerly Burdines, and Sears Roebuck, Jordon Marsh and all of the furniture and appliance stores in the area. It was only natural that we would continue with their television repairs and installations. We handled the service and installations also for RCA, Admiral, Emerson, Magnavox, Philco and Motorola.

In those days delivery of a television did not just consist of carrying a television set physically into a customers home, but also involved the furnishing and installing an outside television antenna, along with a minimum of a thirty foot mast pole or tower, plus running the lead in wires as well as guy wires to keep our gusty winds from blowing the antenna down. RCA Service Company had not yet originated.

We soon had over twenty five employees, with fourteen service vehicles on the road, with our own two way radio communications in them. In the early days of television in Florida, with the high humidity, one could expect a new set to break down once within the first ninety days of ownership and every six months thereafter so long as you owned the set. Once we repaired an out of warranty television for a customer, we could almost make out our bank deposit slips in advance. You can see that the television repair business was an excellent business to be in at that time.

It was not unusual to have well over two hundred television sets in our shop for repair at one time, and if a customer would call up the next day after their set came in for repair, we would say to the customer, "Yes, Mrs. Jones, we have your pride and joy in our shop for repairs, but we had two hundred other sets on hand to repair and as soon as we fix all of those other sets, we will check yours." I don't think so.

We had to concoct a lot of little white lies to keep our customer base happy. I finally built a "U" shaped service area, and late in the afternoon each day, I would have a less talented repair man remove the cabinets and set up about twenty television sets ready to be plugged in and checked on this work area. I would then go to work at four o'clock in the morning and by the time that the regular repairmen came to work at eight o'clock, I would have sixteen or eighteen of those sets ready for someone to permanently solder in a few parts and reassemble the sets for delivery.

Appliance sales stores were always trying to attract some of our better servicemen to come to work for them and I tried to devise many ways to keep our employees with me. We offered benefits that were unheard of for our class of employees at that time. We offered paid holidays, paid vacations, paid sick leave, free medical and hospitalization, for the employee and their families, annual beach picnics, Christmas dinner parties at restaurants or golf courses, Halloween parties for the employee's children and separate Halloween parties for the adults.

I had one young man named Eric working for me who epitomized an industrious person. He always seemed extremely busy, but never seemed to accomplish very much. One day a customer of mine came by and told me that he had just seen Eric cavorting on the beach in a bathing suit, at a time when he was supposed to be working.

When he checked out that evening, I told him, "Starting tomorrow morning, I am going to start every day with a bathing suit inspection." "What does that mean?" he said. "That means that every morning, when the men report here to work, I am going to ask them to drop their drawers, so that I may see if they have a bathing suit on under their work clothes." The very next morning when Eric came to work, he came to me and said, "Boss man, I believe that it is time for me to move on to bigger and better things, but so that I do not leave you stranded, I am now giving you a two weeks notice so that you may have the opportunity to hire two men to do all of the work that I have been doing."

"That is very nice of you Eric, but it will not be necessary," as I led him into the office and had the bookkeeper draw him a check for time performed to date, and then escorted him out of the building, never to see him again. On different occasions, some unions would try to organize our employees into a union, but found that the union could not duplicate the benefits that we were already giving to our employees.

Customers can be aggravating sometimes though and on occasion would really get to me. One time I had a customer that really irritated me, as I had sent a repairman to this ladies home at her request and when our repairman went into the home, upon checking the television found that the only reason that it would not perform was because the electric cord was not plugged into the wall outlet.

Since our serviceman had really not done anything in the way of repairs, the lady refused to pay for the house call. She gave my man a hard time and he called me on the phone, and after listening to his side of the story, I said, "Put the lady on the phone." After listening to her story I finally said to her, "I will tell our man to just forget the service charge this time, providing, that as long as you live, you promise me that you will never call me again." She said, "I promise."

A few months passed and one evening after I had normally gone home, the telephone rang, and when I answered the phone, I recognized the voice of this same lady asking us to come to her home and make a service call on her television. I said to her, "The last time that I spoke with you on the phone, madam, you promised me that as long as you lived, you would never call me again, and here you are calling me again and you are not even dead yet."

She begged and pleaded, "There is no one else in the television repair business that I can trust to fix my set, won't you please, please send your man out to my home." After listening to her for a while I told her, "I will send a man to your home on the condition that when he pulls into your driveway, you walk out and hand him twenty dollars, in cash, and if you have any change coming after the repairs are completed, then he will give you your change." She agreed and was a good customer forever after that time.

Another time I had a gentleman as a customer who felt the charges to repair his television were unreasonable, and after haggling with him for some time, I finally became disgusted with him and told him, "You may take the television home with you without any charges, providing you promise me that you will never darken my doorway again." He promised. Several months later, this same man stood out in the street, not wanting to enter our door, and kept yelling at our store until he got the attention of one of my employees, to see if he may please bring in his television for us to repair it.

Sometimes on Friday evenings some of the boys, after getting their checks, would hang and we would have a couple of cold ones and maybe play a few hands of poker. On one such evening a customer by the name Custer came by, and seeing that we were still there, asked if he may be able to pick a small portable television that we had repaired for him. We said, "Certainly." "Is it possible for me to charge this repair?" he said. "If I had a name like Custer, charge is one word that I would never use in my lifetime." I replied. Of course, I did let him charge the repair.

We truly were one of the largest electronic service organizations in the Southeast United States.

Chapter 28

KOREA

Things were starting to heat up on the Korean Peninsula and when Toby, Charlie, Willie, and I stopped at our favorite neighborhood bar after work on this Tuesday evening, for our usual one drink, one of the first topics that came up was when Toby asked "Did any of you get an invitation to join back up, to sign up for the reserves?" Charlie replied right away, "Yes, but I don't think that I will volunteer for anything at this point in my life." Willie's response was, "I really don't know if I received anything or not, I was not expecting an income tax refund check in the mail and I usually only check my mail a couple of times a week, how about you Sly?" I replied, "Yes, I received such a letter but when I opened it and no bonus check fell out I lost all interest in it, I really did not even read the letter, tell me about it, Toby." Toby says, "The government has been talking a lot about increasing the size of the armed forces for fear that Korea was poised to march south across the Yalu River and would go all the way to the south tip of the Korean Peninsula, and are considering reinstating the draft to build the size of the army back up. This letter was just a reminder that if any of the young veterans were to sign up for the reserves, then they would not be subject to the draft again." Charlie pointed out, "I don't like the sound of that reserve business, how do you fellows feel about just joining the National Guard? That reserve business sounds too easy to get your number called."

Willie responded , "I would be willing to give the National Guard some thought, lets all look into it and discuss this again next week. All agreed we would consider it for a week and discuss it again. I really never thought much about it, but I did realize that the television news talking heads were spending a lot of time discussing the Korean situation, particularly in those days, as television was very new and there were not a lot of programs available to fill the time slots.

During the ensuing week I did try to listen to as much of the news as possible, to try to be in a better position to continue our conversation on the following Tuesday. The next Tuesday the four of us met again and by that time, Toby, Charlie and Willie had all pretty much made up their minds that they would all join the National Guard. Toby says, "How do you feel about it Sly?" My reply was, "Once was enough for me, I have been there and done that, and it would take a Recruiting Sergeant in a Jeep and a lasso to corral me to get me to sign up for anything in the military! I have worked too hard to get my business built up to where it is now to jeopardize that."

Toby, Charlie and Willie all signed for the National Guard. Within the first month all three had gone to camp for a weekend of training. After only three months of training for one weekend a month. Charlie got a call. Goodbye Charlie, goodbye South Florida, hello Seoul, South Korea. Another month and another weekend at the National Guard training camp, and then Toby and Willie got their call also.

Since Willie was working for me at that time, I volunteered to take him to the National Guard Armory where a bus would be waiting at six o'clock in the morning to take them off to camp. When we arrived at the armory early the next morning, a reporter from our local newspaper was on hand to capture a picture and a few words from the departing volunteers.

The next day the picture on the front page of our daily paper showed Willie waiting to step into the National Guard bus with the reporters question below "Willie, how do you feel about shipping out to serve your country again?" Willie replied, "I don't think we ought to have to go."

Chapter 29

ROAD TO RAIFORD

Television was in its infancy, and good repairmen in that field were very hard come by, so when I was able to hire one who was competent, sometimes I would have to put up some of their idiosyncrasies to keep them on the payroll. One such person was Steve. At that time we were handling all of the repair service in our area for Sears Roebuck, for Macy's, (formerly known as Burdines), and all of the local appliance and furniture stores.

We were receiving letters, inquiring the possibility of employment from places as far away as New Orleans, Las Angeles, Hong Kong and Spekholzenheide, Holland. Steve was from Akron, Ohio and we corresponded first by letter and then by telephone. I did not promise him any permanent job but did say that if he were in our area, that I would guarantee him the opportunity to show his ability. He said that since his mother owned a cottage in the Florida Keys the next time he came to visit her he would stop by and see if we could get together.

When he arrived in the Ft. Lauderdale area, he came almost immediately to my shop and I gave him the opportunity to show me his skills. He obviously was no Einstein, but did have a good general knowledge of how a television worked, and seemed to me that he would be a productive addition to our work force. Steve worked for us for about nine months, doing mostly service calls to our customer's homes and was well received and well liked. Once after he had made service calls a couple of times to the home of a prominent lawyer, the lawyers wife later telephoned me and told me they were very satisfied with the repairman I had been sending to their home, that he fit right in and she felt as comfortable with him as an old shoe.

He did have some down sides. For one thing, when we would give him his first calls in the morning, no matter if we gave him one service call or four, he would not call back for additional service calls until after noon, and the same thing in the afternoon. We realized we would have to give him at least four or five service calls the first thing in the morning, and the same thing again in the afternoon, because we would not hear from him again that day. He was one of the main reasons that we later installed two way radios in all of our service vehicles.

Another of his little quirks was that he would never return to the repair shop before closing time, rather he would always bring the service truck back late and park it in its assigned spot, lock it up and leave, taking the keys with him. After a while we began to realize that many times he would come back later, take the truck and use it for his personal transportation, and that sometime late at night or early the next morning would again return it to its assigned parking spot. I finally would go back to the shop in the early evening, check the odometer on his service truck, and then check it again when he would return to work the next morning. This was the convincing factor that he was in fact, using our vehicle after hours for his own pleasure, and probably driving while intoxicated. My greatest fear was that he would get into an accident with our vehicle and kill someone while driving intoxicated.

On another front, we had a policy of paying a small commission to dealers who would send us business, but we set aside four service stations located in the four quadrants of the city. We did not pay them commissions, however, in return for their business we authorized our drivers to stop as they needed fuel at any of those four stations, get gas and oil as necessary and sign the ticket. At the end of the month those stations would bill us for our purchases.

One day when Steve was off I was using his service truck to run some errands, then realizing that I was low on fuel, I pulled into one of the designated service stations for gas. In those days, the station attendant pumped the gas for you and checked your oil and water. The attendant was talking to me as he was putting the gas in the vehicle and asked, "Where was Steve?" I told him that he had the day off. He did not ask me my name nor did I volunteer that information. When we went inside to write up the bill for me to sign, the attendant asked "Do you want to add a couple of packs of cigarettes to this bill like the other drivers do?" I said, "No, but thank you anyway, you have been very helpful to me."

A local gasoline company had been bugging me for over a year to install a gasoline tank and pump at my shop for use in all of our vehicles, that I would have better control of the gas usage. That little incident convinced me that putting in my own pump would be the right thing to do.

Done.

That turned out to be one of my better moves, because in those days, when the gas tanker truck pulled out of Port Everglades full of gasoline, the driver would make his daily round of deliveries, and at the end of the day, if there was any fuel still in the tanker, the driver would merely pull to a side road someplace and dump the remaining fuel on the ground, and return back to the port completely empty. When one of those drivers told me of what was going on, I convinced him, and he in turn got several other drivers to participate, that if they were returning from my end of the county, they would stop and dump their excess fuel into my tank. Since I was buying regular grade of gas, I did not care whether they dumped in regular or high test gas into my tank. On an average, the drivers would dump from twenty gallons of fuel, up to one hundred and fifty gallons at a drop.

I would reward them by replacing an antenna on their car, or repairing a car radio or television for them. In some cases I rewarded them with cash. In the end, everyone was happy, and I am sure that the environmentalists would have been extremely happy with our arrangements.

Steve had one particular bar that he would frequent at an almost daily basis, and it was located in downtown Ft. Lauderdale. After he had worked for us for a few weeks, he started paying his bar tab with a personal check. A few months later, when he would pay his bar tab, he would ask if he could write the check for a larger amount and get ten or twenty dollars cash back. As the months went on, he kept getting larger and larger amounts of cash back. His mother owned a cottage down in the Keys and sometimes he would go down there on weekends. When he went there, it turns out, he would request a cash back amount from the bar there, also. Finally on a day that he was scheduled to work, Steve was a no show. Later in the morning he called and said that he had a little personal business to take care of and that he would probably be off for a few days. Later that day a customer of mine who worked as a jailer at the county courthouse, called me and asked, "Do you realize that one of your employees is in the slammer here?" "No," I said, "Do you know his name?" "No, but I will check and call you back," he replied.

In those days it was not unusual for one of my young employees to get in a bar fight and end up in jail for a day or two and this customer of mine knew that. A few minutes later he called me back and told me that it was Steve and that he was being held on some bad check charges. He was unable to bail himself out and although his mother could well afford to do so, she refused to do it because of his lifestyle. It turned out that he had written three bad checks to the local bar and total amount of those was in excess of seven hundred dollars. Apparently while visiting in the keys to see his mother he had some serious bad check problems there, too.

A few months passed and when he came to trial, the judge threw the book at him and gave him the maximum, which was five years in the Florida State Penitentiary, at Raiford. Less the time he had already served.

He did leave behind something of value though, a saying that became a cornerstone of my philosophy ever since those days and that was, "The road to hell is paved with good intentions." So was the road to Raiford.

Chapter 30

BLACK CAT SUPERSTITIONS

We were sitting at the bar in a Big Daddy's Lounge where we had been meeting for a couple of drinks, once a week for a while. There was Sonny, a slight blond haired kid in his early twenties, who worked for a dealer customer of mine, and I got to know him when his boss would keep sending him over to my warehouse to pick up parts. Then there was Ralph, who was a tall thin dark haired man from New York, who was in his mid thirties and worked for me as a television repairman, and mainly made house calls to my customer's home. Mark, I did not know much about, he was a drinking buddy of Ralph's and he appeared to be in his early thirties, and seemed to have a bit of a temper, if aroused. He did however, as many of my acquaintances did, leave behind a famous quote, and that was, once when he called his wife at the end of a poker game, saying, "Honey, you can go ahead and sell the s--- house, I just lost my ass."

After we had ordered our second round of drinks that evening, Mark made the comment, "Don't you have any lounge's here that have a little action going down?" "Not really, this is a pretty small town. We would have to go to Miami if you want to see some real action." "Do you know of any such places down there?" He inquired. "Oh yes, I know of several such places there, I used to go down there every week when I first came to this area, heck, there was not even a pizza parlor in this hick town then, if you wanted a pizza, you drove to Miami." "Well, let's make arrangements to go there for the evening next week," Mark said. "Fine by me, if it is all right with all of you, instead of coming here directly from work, let's all go home and clean up and meet at my shop around six thirty. Since I am familiar with the area, you can leave your vehicles parked at my shop and all can ride with me in my car."

Agreed.

The next week we met at my shop, all got into my Lincoln and I drove directly to Polly's Parrot Club in Coral Gables. The club was well known for its good, inexpensive drinks, always a bevy of unescorted females and a parrot that would amuse the patrons. The club had a long straight bar and the bartender had a parrot that he put on the bar and the parrot would make a round trip from one end of the bar to the other. It took about twenty minutes for the parrot to complete trip and it was rewarded upon its return with one sip of a special drink that was flavored to appeal to the taste of the parrot, but was also spiked with alcohol. After a couple of trips, it became more intoxicated, and then it would stop in front of a bar patron and say something like, "Hi Fatso," or "Hi Shorty," sometimes it would blurt out "Tip, Tip." As its trips progressed, the demeanor of the parrot would change, and the quality of it's walk deteriorated and it became noticeably unstable as it walked up and down the bar, until at one point it fell on the bar and unable to rise again. That seemed to appeal to the humorous side of the bar patrons.

At that point the bartender gathered the bird up and put it in its cage, which was hanging right behind the bar. After the demise of the parrot, we had to make a decision, stay there and stare at the bartender, or try to make a move on somewhere to look for greener pastures. With the four of us traveling in one car, and away from our home base, it seemed improbable that we would be able to hook up with a group of girls, so we decided to move on to another bar that would have a live band, and a dance floor. I knew of just such a lounge. Our next stop was the Black Cat Lounge, right in the middle of downtown Miami. As we entered, I noticed that a decent three piece band was playing and that there was a good sized dance floor. The tables all seemed to be occupied but the waiter escorted us to an unoccupied one and we settled in for what we thought was the rest of the evening.

Wrong!!

We sat down at the table and shortly thereafter the waiter came by again to take our order. I ordered Old Grand Dad and water, Ralph and

Mark ordered Chivas Regal and soda and Sonny ordered Crown Royal on the rocks. When the waiter returned with our drinks, we paid him and gave him a substantial tip to be sure that we would see him again that night. As soon as Sonny took a sip from his glass, he exclaimed, "This is not Crown Royal". The rest of us then took a drink from our own glass and all decided that we had not received the drink that we had ordered. We all sat there taking very small sips from our glass as we listened to a couple of numbers by the band.

By that time the waiter returned and we all ordered another round of the same, not yet wanting to make a scene over the first round of drinks. He returned to the bar and gave his order to the bartender. In the meantime I had gotten up from our table and was leaning against the other end of the bar. I watched as the bartender prepared all four glasses and then poured the contents of one bottle of alcohol into all four drinks. The bottle that he poured the drinks from had a label on it that read, "Landsdowne Reserve" a label that I had never heard of before and have never seen since.

I went back and was seated at our table with the others, and told them as to what I had witnessed at the bar, before the waiter returned with our drinks. When the waiter put our drinks on the table, he also put the check down and was waiting for payment. Sonny, Mark and Ralph all picked up their drinks and sampled them before they paid for them. I knew what was in mine and did not have to taste it to make up my mind. When the waiter insisted on payment for our drinks, an argument ensued between our group and the waiter. I am sure that under the circumstances, since we had already been drinking for a couple of hours, we were probably a bit loud and unruly, but when I let it loudly be known that we were paying for prime drinks and were being served inexpensive well drinks, that brought out the ire in some of the other patrons. Someone yelled, "I knew there was something wrong with my F------ drink." By that time most of the patrons had joined in the verbal assault. The band, fearing the worst, stopped playing and exited the band stand to a back room.

Some one, not from our group, threw a chair which broke the large mirror behind the bar. From that point on it was not so much of a fight, as it was just a barmaid, the bartender and two waiters, against a room full of angry patrons, but just a matter of a shoving match and seeing who could destroy the most of the bar.

We continued the destruction of the bar for about fifteen minutes before six Miami policemen arrived on the scene. One of the officers said that such outbursts were getting to be a weekly affair, but that it seemed much worse tonight Our group walked right out the front door as the officers were talking to the bartender trying to find out what had started the ruckus. It did not look as though anyone was going to get arrested that night, but we did not want to stick around and find out. We decided that we had enough excitement for one evening and got into my car and returned to Ft. Lauderdale and called it a night.

After about a month passed and I had not seen Mark any more. I asked his buddy Ralph, "Where has Mark been, I have not seen him for the past few weeks". Ralph replied, "Oh, he got in a bar fight a couple of days after were went to Miami and since he was out on bond, the police threw him in the slammer, where he is awaiting trial on a second degree murder charge." I thought, "Hmmm, nice company".

Another few months passed and Ralph left my employment and went back to New York State. When income tax time rolled around I received a letter from Ralph posted from the Sing Sing Prison in New York. He asked that I send his W-2 form to him at that address as he was paying a small debt to society there that he owed.

That got me to thinking about that time at the Black Cat Lounge, with Ralph in Sing Sing prison in New York, doing time for God only knows what and Mark in jail in Florida awaiting to go to trial for murder, as to how lucky I was to just walk away from the Black Cat Lounge incident in Miami without being involved in some more serious crime. Incidentally, they closed Black Cat Lounge on that night and it never reopened again.

Chapter 31

FISHING TRIP

It was hot in the summer of 1961 and as the phone rang again, I nervously lit another cigarette as I waited for the inevitable voice of a harried secretary stating, "Mrs. Jackson was on the phone again inquiring as to the whereabouts of the TV serviceman, for whom she was impatiently waiting." As I reached the phone station I realized that I already had one cigarette burning in the ash tray by the phone, I picked up the phone and courteously greeted Mrs. Jackson, "Yes Ma'am, I will get on our two way radio and find out the exact location of your repairman, hold on a moment, please."

I picked up the microphone of our two way radio and blurted out, "7AO249 calling truck number eleven, come in number eleven, over." "Ten four" came the reply from the driver of truck number eleven, and after a short discussion with the driver, I was able to reassure Mrs. Jackson that the repairman that she was awaiting was only two blocks away and would be at her door in just seconds. She did seem pleased as she hung up the phone.

This is the way that the days were going, since this was only the second day back to work after the long Labor Day weekend, and many of the locals with children had returned from up north in time to put their children back in school. Up to one half of the television sets of the

returning customers would not operate properly after sitting idle for up to
three months in the high humidity that we had here.

With the thought that televised football games were only days away
and/or with kids under foot, those parents could not cope with the thought
of not having a working television on hand. One older customer said to
me, "What in the world am I going to do without a working television?"
I replied, "You could spend the evening having a pleasant conversation
with your wife, as you did before television came along," at which point
he became very belligerent.

By the end of the week I was beside myself, so I called for a special
meeting on Saturday morning of all of the servicemen who made house
calls for me. At that meeting I gave every person there an opportunity to
try to explain why they thought that it took so long to travel from one
customers home to another. After all, our normal routine was to give each
serviceman only initially three service calls to start each day and they were
usually in the same general neighborhood.

After those three calls were completed, they would contact base via
our own two way radio system and we would try to give them one call at
a time near to where they were at that time, in order to handle any special
customer requests. After all of the discussions and the pro's and con's, it
mostly boiled down to the fear of getting a traffic ticket.

Most traffic fines at that time were only fifteen dollars, but there was
not a lot of crime going on in our little city, and police officers were giving
out a lot of tickets for little mickey mouse offences, like following too close,
(in the city), failing to come to a dead stop before making a right hand
turn, or one of your left wheels touching a yellow painted center line, not
to even mention a speeding ticket for exceeding the speed limit by five or
six miles per hour.

Once we had clarified what seemed to be the biggest sticking point,
the traffic fine, I proposed a plan that was unanimously agreed upon and
the plan was to work like this: We would form a traffic fine club, for which
I would contribute twenty five dollars to start the fund, and each driver
that wished to participate would sign up to have twenty five cents deducted
from their pay check each week and that money added directly into the
fund. The fund then, in turn, would pay for any and all traffic fines that
each member may get, with no limits, both on duty and off duty, for up
to thirty five dollars for each ticket. However, if any participant were to
receive a ticket for reckless driving or DUI, then the club would pay up to

thirty five dollars towards their ticket and that driver would be expelled from the club, no ifs, ands or buts.

Well, not only did every driver sign up to join, but every employee, except one secretary, who had neither a drivers license or a car, signed up to join the club. We now had thirty members which added $7.50 to the fund each week. Needless to say, the club was a smashing success and after three months not only had the customer service calls speeded up to a more satisfactory level, but we had not had a single traffic ticket.

I then had another meeting with all of the employees present and we agreed that once the cash pool exceeded two hundred and fifty dollars, then we would have a special beach party. We always had one beach party around the first week of May, but this would be a second one. The members were so enthusiastic about the extra party that they voted to increase the weekly contribution from twenty five cents per week to fifty cents per week, so now we could be increasing the fund by fifteen dollars per week and would be able to have that extra party much sooner.

Time passed quickly and the funds in out traffic fine club increased steadily and, believe it or not, after a year of operation not a single traffic ticket had been turned in. There may have been one or two tickets issued, but if there were any, the guilty party was too embarrassed to turn in the receipt for collection.

The next meeting we held was one evening after work, most of the employees stayed around and we brought in some Kentucky Fried Chicken and some beer, and we discussed how we would spend our excess money over a few hands of poker. It was decided that we would get our biggest bang for our buck if we had our party the weekend after Labor Day. By that time all of the summer visitors had returned north to put their kids back in school and it was still too warm for the flocks of hard core snow birds to arrive. We decided at that meeting that we would have a deluxe party right after Labor Day in Key West and to go all out to have a really special party.

Right then we set up three committees, one to arrange for our transportation to and from the Keys, one to arrange for a place to stay while there and one to arrange for some special entertainment while there. After kicking it around for a couple of weeks, it was decided that the best way to resolve this would be to actually make a trip to Key West in advance to find out what was available there at that time of the year.

I had an outside salesman who went to Key West regularly on a monthly basis, so to minimize the cost, I agreed that the next time he was scheduled to go there, that provided he was a member of one of the committees, that six of the men, two from each committee would make the trek there and work out a report. I had given them three checks made out and signed in the amount of two hundred and fifty dollars each but with no payee's name on them, for the committee to use to make deposits as necessary for our trip.

After the committees return, we had another evening meeting at which we were all filled in on the general details as to how the program would work. It was concluded that we would drive down in one of our vans and two of our station wagons, and that one of our employees, who owned his own plane, would fly down with two more of our people, and we would pick them up at the airport in Key West.

We had made a deposit and rented the entire Cactus Joe's motel for the weekend, as well as the sixty five foot drift fishing boat, named the Greyhound, for our fishing pleasures. The evening entertainment was easily handled, as at that time the adult entertainment in the private clubs was anything that you could have wanted, and without any special requirements. No deposits were used for the transportation, only for the drift fishing boat and the motel.

Finally, as summer was drawing to a close, we were making our final preparations for our big event. The showcase of our caravan was a Chevrolet Corvan, which had the engine in the rear and on the inside there was a flat place at the front of the interior and a flat place at the rear, over the engine compartment, with a lower flat area in the center of the van. This worked out perfect, as we built a small table for the center of the van, covered it with felt and suspended a twelve volt light from overhead, to make a nice poker table. Then we purchased two pads as were intended for use on lawn furniture to make for comfortable seating for six, three at the front of the van and three at the rear of the van.

We were scheduled to leave our shop right after five o'clock in the afternoon on Friday, drive to Key West and get settled in there on Friday night.

We were to go fishing on Saturday, and do our partying at local clubs on Saturday night. Sunday was to be another day of fishing and around four o'clock we would check out and drive back home. I had made a commitment to the members that if we over spent our budget, that I personally would advance what ever funds as might be necessary to make the trip a complete success, with the funds to repaid at a later date as they accumulated.

Labor Day came and went and some of the employees brought in a good supply of ice chests, in which to transport our food and beer. By Friday evening we had our beer iced down and had purchased a goodly supply of various hoagies from Dan's Submarine Shop in Ft. Lauderdale as well as a large bucket of Kentucky Fried Chicken, so we really were good to go.

I was one of the participating poker players in our Corvan, and to tell you how my luck was going to be for the weekend, although I played in every poker hand from Ft. Lauderdale to Key West, I did not win a single pot, I lost them all. One of the players at our table was a man named Dom, and he sure won a lot of the big pots. He was about half in the bag when we started our trip and just seemed to stay at that level. Typically, if someone would say, "I raise" Dom would come back with, "That's my bet." And if someone would say, "You don't even know what game we are playing." Dom would respond with, "Well, what game are we playing?" If someone answered, "Deuces wild," he typically would lay two nines and three two's and say, "In that case, I guess that I have five nines." That is about how the poker game went en route to Key West.

Once we arrived at Cactus Joe's, we checked in with the manager where he gave us access to the keys to all of the rooms. We set aside two of the larger rooms to be used for storage and poker rooms. Everyone then selected their own private room from what rooms were left. Once everyone got settled in, we went to the two poker rooms and started a game in each room. By two thirty in the morning we had dwindled that down to just one poker game in one room as some had lost all that they felt comfortable in losing or just tired and went to bed.

Five of us were still at it, come morning, including Dom, until it was time to change and get ready for our day on the boat. We rounded up everybody early and went to a local restaurant for breakfast. Two of the fellows took one of the station wagons to the local airport to pick up those flying in and brought them to the restaurant. With breakfast over, everyone was excited as we went to the docks and boarded the Greyhound for our day of fishing.

Those of us who needed it had a cold beer as the captain pulled away from the docks. We all put two dollars into a pot to be won by the person catching the biggest fish. On the way out to sea the first mate was issuing everyone a deep sea rod and reel that was already baited for the first drop into the water. Every one that is, except Dom, who was still half blown out of his mind and stretched out on top of one of the motor hatches.

156

Once the captain reached what he considered a good fishing spot he cut the engines and we were told that we could drop our lines into the water, which we did with high expectations. Everyone, except Dom of course, as he had no pole. So Dom complained loudly, "How can I catch a fish, I don't even have a fishing pole?" To which the first mate replied "I am not going to give that drunk a three hundred dollar fishing rod and reel, as he would probably lose it overboard, anyhow."

I agreed with the mate, but after a little discussion, I convinced him to rig up a nice hand line for Dom. With that he baited a hook on a heavy line and threw it over the side then I securely attached the line to the right arm of Dom, who was still lying flat on his back on top of the motor hatch.

As time went by almost everyone had caught two or three fish in the eighteen to thirty inch category, everyone except Dom, that is. Suddenly Dom, with his right arm flailing wildly, yelled, "I think I got a bite, I think I got a bite." With the help of the first mate, using a net on a long pole, they finally landed a fifty inch Wahoo, which of course turned out to be the biggest catch of the day. That was the way our fishing day went.

When we returned to the docks, we gave the edible part of our catch to some of the happy onlookers who always hung around the docks as the fishing boats returned. In no way were we going back to the motel and prepare a fish dinner. At the motel we showered and had a couple of beers as we played a few hands of poker and relaxed before hitting the night clubs of town. That done, we went to a nice restaurant where we enjoyed a great meal that included green turtle soup. The waitress there directed us to a club that she said had a nice lineup of girl entertainers. We took her word for it and upon completion of our meal, proceeded on over to the aforementioned club.

We spent about half an hour there and were not really impressed, but we did run into another patron there who turned us on to what turned out to be the club that we were really looking for. As we exited the club we noticed something unusual, there was a police paddy wagon parked right in front of the club entrance, and as we walked the two blocks to the next club, the paddy wagon followed right behind us.

The decor of this new club seemed a little more luxurious, and the greeters and waitresses were all hot looking chics. As it turned out, our waitresses were also our entertainers, as they were serving double duty.

After we were settled in and listening to a good band playing one of our fellows excused himself and went to the men's room. He was gone so long that we were getting concerned as to his whereabouts. When he finally returned he was really excited. "You know in the men's bathroom there is a little hole in the wall, and you can see right into the ladies dressing room." "I watched as the waitresses came in and changed their clothes into other costumes, and they took off everything except their bra's and panties, I was really excited." We then broke him the news that while he was gone we had witnessed our first strip tease show, and that the two girls who were putting on the show took off everything right down to their birthday suits. You could just see the disappointment creep over his face.

It turned out that these girls were not only our waitresses and our entertainers but were also available as our companions. Whether you wanted to dance a few dances or just have some female companionship at your table to share a few drinks, they were available for anything that you wanted to do, that your wallet could afford, and I do mean anything.

In the early morning hours we finally exited the club, and sure enough, there it was, the paddy wagon was still waiting for us. We were good boys though, we were not rowdy and did not give the locals an excuse to use their paddy wagon, but we returned quietly to our motel rooms at Cactus Joe's.

We did not play poker once we returned to the motel but a few of us did stay up the rest of the night listening to some tunes and just talking about everything that had been happening. Two of the men, who were catholic and felt obligated to attend church services, arose early on Sunday morning, got dressed and started out of the lobby to attend services, when the motel manager remarked to one of the men that although he was dressed with a shirt and tie, was walking out in his shorts, as he had neglected to put on his trousers. He was directed back to his room and completed the project. He must have had a bad night.

After breakfast we finally arrived at the Greyhound just before noon. The captain was beginning to wonder if we were going to show up at all, but he really did not care as the day was already paid for anyway. The enthusiasm for fishing was just not there, there was no mention of a pot for the largest fish, perhaps one day of fishing was really enough, particularly after a big night at the club. We discussed this with the captain and he had us back at the docks well before four o'clock schedule, as we were anxious to move on. We went back to the motel, loaded up our gear and soon were on US 1 headed north. About four hours later, one of the passengers in the front of our van said, "Well, there it is, the Hollywood City limit sign." To which Dom, who had never passed out, never sobered up, never slept, but just stayed in that state of limbo replied, "I sure will be glad when we get to Key West, you know that I have lived down here for seven years and have never even been to Key West." Dom had been in Key West for two days and was so far out of touch with reality that he did not realize that he had even been there at all.

A few months later as we were preparing for another traffic fine club party, some of the members suggested that we make a return trip to Key West, but I adamantly resisted, because I knew that we could never, ever duplicate the wonderful memories of the previous trip.

Chapter 32

D U I

My business had been good, so I ordered a new Dodge Lancer station wagon. I was excited on the day that I actually took delivery of my new vehicle. As was the case of many evenings, I had to stay late at work, to finish up this days work, and to lay out the schedule for the next day.

At this time the county was very small, and due to the fact that I had a very large service business, I probably knew, as customers, half of the county's population and many knew me. As I was driving home that evening, at about the half way mark home, I came to a traffic light, which was red at the time. There was a large Buick stopped in front of me, and he had stopped almost under the traffic light. Realizing where he was located, I stopped well behind him.

Apparently he had gone well out into the intersection, stopped and backed up, to get out of the way of crossing traffic. He then forgot and left the automatic transmission in reverse. When the light turned green, he stepped on the gas and really accelerated, full bore. Not forward, but in reverse, smashing into the front end of my brand new vehicle. As the Buick finally pulled away from me, I took a pen and business card from my shirt pocked and jotted down the license plate number from the car.

It turned out that the second car behind me was driven by a local policeman, who was driving a police car and on duty. He immediately pulled along side of me, and upon recognizing me, called out to me, "Foxx, who are you running over now?" "You are not going to believe this, but that Buick that just pulled out of here, backed into my brand new vehicle" I answered. I handed him the card with the license number on it and said, "This is the license number of the Buick that just hit me." With that, he turned on his flashing red lights and took off after the Buick. I followed after him, but at a much slower pace.

About two miles further up the road, he had caught up with the Buick and had him pull into the parking lot of a local restaurant. When I arrived on the scene, the officer was trying to get the driver out of his car. As I watched, the officer finally got him to exit his car. The officer tried to see if he could walk in a straight line, but he was unable to, as he could hardly walk at all. The officer then called for a wrecker, and put the man in the rear seat of the police car.

When the wrecker left with the car, so did the police car, on the way to let his victim sleep it off in jail. I went on home, very upset about the damage to my new vehicle, but feeling good about not being hurt in the accident. The next day I took my new car back to the dealership from whom I had purchased it, for repairs. When I got my vehicle back from the dealers and it looked like new, I tried to move on and forgot the whole incident.

About three months passed, and from out of nowhere, I get a subpoena to appear in court, as a witness in a Driving Under the Influence case. When I got to court, I find that I am facing the same man who was driving the Buick that smashed my new car. The Prosecuting Attorney called the arresting officer and he testified about how he pulled the man over and the problems he had in getting the man to get out of the car. He continued with all of the ramifications of the arrest.

The Prosecuting Attorney then called me to the stand. I told of how I was stopped, and this man had driven out into the intersection, put the car in reverse and backed up to clear the lanes and left the car in reverse. I said "When the light turned green, he floored the gas and slammed into my new car, and then after causing the accident, he put it in drive and left the scene." "He never came back to see if I was injured or not, and he left the scene. When I got to where the officer had him stopped, I parked my car and observed what was going on. The way the man staggered around when he exited his car, he was obviously intoxicated."

At that point the man's Public Defense Attorney jumped up and said to me, "Just what training do you have that would qualify you as an expert, to declare that this man was intoxicated?" "Well, my dad was the biggest drunk in West Virginia. I lived with him night and day for sixteen years, and I certainly am in a position to positively identify an intoxicated person when I see one." I replied.

With that reply, the defense attorney had no further questions for me. I continued with my observations, pointing out that the man could hardly stand, let alone walk in a straight line. The judge went on and levied a hefty fine against the man, plus lifted his driver's license for only one year, since this was his first DUI offence.

Chapter 33

The Raid

I was a Lieutenant Governor of the Optimist Clubs for the state of Florida, and was at a convention in St. Petersburg, when my business office received an emergency call for some electronic parts, that had to be delivered in a rush, and since our regular delivery people had already been dispatched for the day, my secretary called my wife, Joan, and asked her if she would make this emergency delivery for this customer. Joan was familiar with the place of delivery, as she had made several deliveries to that area before. After some mumbling and grumbling, Joan finally agreed to make the delivery, provided that when she arrived at our office, the order would be in the truck and all of the paperwork ready, so that she would not have to wait around, once she arrived at our office.

When she arrived at our office, the truck and paper work were ready to roll, but they had one more little favor to ask of her. On her way back home from downtown Miami, would she please stop and pick up a television set from a distributor. It was only three blocks out of her way, so she agreed to do it.

Joan had been making deliveries on and off to the Miami area for three years and knew most of the short cuts and parking places. The down town traffic was unusually heavy this day and she could not park in her usual loading zone space, so she had to go to a different area to park her van.

She was very concerned, as she had all she could carry of electronic parts, and struggled to get them to the place of business. When she entered the premises, the owner of Rodriquez Exports asked her to take them straight on back to the shipping room, as they were going out of town at three o'clock that afternoon. When she got back to the shipping area, she was overwhelmed, for there she saw thousands of rounds of ammunition, and guns stacked everywhere. The owner of course, paid her in cash, and it was well over one thousand dollars.

By the time she got outside, she was so shook up by what she had seen in the shipping department, plus walking around with all of that cash money, surrounded only by Spanish speaking people, as no one there spoke English, that she could not remember where she had parked the truck. After walking around for a bit, looking for her van, she finally saw a policeman. She explained to him that she could not find her truck. His response was, "You probably parked it in a no parking zone and it has been towed away." He was absolutely no help. She stepped back onto the sidewalk, standing there in despair, when she saw another officer coming down the street from the other direction. She walked out to the policeman's car and started to speak to him, but she was so shook up that nothing came out of her mouth.

Sensing that something was wrong, the officer said to her, "Please get in the front seat of my car." When she sat down in the car, he asked, "What is the matter?" Joan replied, "I parked my truck and delivered some parts to Rodriquez Exports, and since I could not park in my usual loading zone, I had to park somewhere else, and now I can't find my truck. I don't understand it has my name written on both sides and the back of the van. When I took my parts order back to his shipping room, I saw thousands of rounds of ammunition and guns lined up everywhere." The officer then asked her, "Was there anything special about your delivery?" "Yes, that it had to be delivered before two o'clock, as the shipment was going out of the country at three p.m."

He started driving around slowly, looking for her truck, and in the meantime he continued pumping her for as much information as possible about this export company. Suddenly she exclaimed, "There it is, that is my truck." He stopped the car and as she started to get out, the officer said, "Wait." With that said, he walked around his car, and said "May I have your keys, please?"

He took her keys, went to her van and opened the door, then checked inside to be sure that no one was in her vehicle. When she pulled out of downtown Miami, she thought that the officer was following her, but she soon lost sight of him.

When she stopped at the wholesaler to pick up the TV, the man at the loading dock said, "What kind of trouble have you been into, I saw that police car follow you into our parking lot, and he is still there?" She was too scared to reply, and merely pretended that she did not hear what he had said. After she had the TV loaded into her van, she noticed that the policeman was still following her, and he followed her to the entrance to the turnpike, where he turned around.

She continued on to our store and was telling my secretary, "I don't know just what is going on, but the Miami Police followed me all the way from downtown Miami until I got on the turnpike." She then went on to tell her about the problem that she had finding her van.

She stopped by a Farm Store and picked up a gallon of grape drink, went on home, filled a glass full of ice and grape drink, went into the TV room, turned on the TV and sat down on the sofa to relax. She kept sitting there and relaxing for a while with the TV on, until finally, the news came on.

She soon noticed that a police officer was leading a man with his hands handcuffed behind his back, out to a police car. Joan had to do a double take on that picture, because the man that they were leading to the car in handcuffs, was the same man who had given her all of that cash money only a few hours earlier.

She watched the scene for a few minutes and then the spokesperson for the City of Miami Police Department came on and said, "We had heard on the street that a large cache of weapons was going to be illegally shipped out of the country, but we did not know from where or when." "Today, we received an anonymous tip as to where the cache was kept and also the time the shipment was to take place."

When Joan heard that, a chill ran down her back and stark fear came to her eyes. We had outside flood lights all around our house, that would illuminate our entire yard. That night, not only did she turn on all of the outside lights but also every light inside the house. The next morning, our neighbor from across the street, walked over and inquired, "What was that light show all about last night?" After Joan explained to him what had happened, he replied, "You were only attracting more attention to yourself, you should have merely kept the whole place dark and you would have been more secure."

For the next month, she would not deliver back to Miami, and never, ever would she deliver in the area of Rodriquez Exports.

Chapter 34

EXPANSION TIME

During these years our type of business was very seasonal because as soon as Easter passed, most of our northern visitors had gone home, and the locals who may have television problems requiring repairs usually would not have the repairs made at that time because if they were gone during the summer, the would probably have to have the TV repaired again when they returned in the fall.

My problem was to how to keep my workers gainfully employed during those slow summer months, because if we let them go in the spring, they very likely would not be willing to return to work for me in the fall. Fortunately for us, general motors came out at that time with air conditioners available on their new models of Chevrolet and Cadillac automobiles. Since we were already doing warranty and other service work on car radios and automatic headlight dimmers, plus repairing electric door locks and radio antennas for most of the new and used car dealers in the county and some adjacent areas, it was obvious that was a wonderful opportunity for us to increase our business.

I had no previous exposure or experience with any type of refrigeration, but I did have two older men working for me at the time, both of whom had some experience repairing water coolers, ice makers and room air conditioners. When they realized that I was serious about getting involved with auto air, they gathered up what literature each had, and I had a few evening meetings with them going over the basics of how the refrigerant system worked.

It soon became obvious that more research was needed, and I was able to obtain a copy of a small publication as put out by a well known state university, on auto air conditioning. I realized that there was going to be a demand for a lot of after market air conditioners in our warm climate and decided to try to get in on the ground floor of auto air conditioner business, and the parts necessary to repair them, and I wanted to be the first local distributor for these items.

There was a fledgling manufacturing company in our area that was buying such auto air conditioner parts from the original manufacturers, and assembling a complete unit under their own name. Their management was receptive to the idea of other dealers wanting to get involved in this new industry and were able to supply me with quite a lot of literature. They sold me a complete after market unit that was probably already obsolete, for a very reasonable price.

I took each of those parts to a local machine shop and had a section cut out of each piece, so that anyone interested could see the inner workings of each of the individual parts. I took pictures of a mechanic actually installing an after market auto air conditioner and also of someone servicing an air unit. From these pictures I made slides and made a series of audio tapes explaining to a novice as to what was involved in selling a customer on having an air conditioner installed in their car and the advantages of the same.

We would show them that a car with a large V-8 engine would get better gas mileage on a trip, having his air conditioner on and his windows rolled up than he would with no air conditioner and his car windows open. We explained how to install the units, how to service them and even how to arrange financing for them.

If a garage or service station operator called and ordered a set of gauges and a case of Freon to be delivered, our parts manager would check our records to see if this was a new customer, and if so, would not have our regular delivery personnel make the delivery, but either I would deliver the items or someone who was knowledgeable would show the new customer exactly how to hook up the gauges and what to look for in installing the Freon.

In those days many small garages and service stations had large "A" frame signs standing by their drive that stated, "Tune ups, 6 cylinder

$6.95, 8 cylinder $8.95." However, if you pulled in there and when they opened the hood on your car and saw an air conditioner installed in your car, they would not touch it with a ten foot pole. We aggressively held regional training seminars to encourage dealers to get involved in the sales and service of auto air conditioners. When we were running the slides at our seminars, after about thirty minutes we would slip in a slide of a nude woman just to be sure that everyone stayed awake. We worked with dealers both large and small to increase our share of the business.

We had a man on our payroll whom had spent much of his life as a itinerant sign painter, and we would have him paint signs at their place of business promoting the sales and service of auto air conditioners, at no cost to them. Once I had my training program in place and with my large base in the automotive field already, and with a large fleet of trucks available for delivery, it was not at all difficult to convince the local after market manufacturer that we were in a position to distribute their products to the dealers better than they were.

That was to be our first of many products that we distributed. When Motorola realized what a large dealer base we had established, they came to me and asked that we distribute the Motorola line of auto radio products for them. That was followed by Delco, having us distribute their products as applied to auto radio and auto air conditioners. ThermoKing, a large company involved in truck air conditioning and refrigeration, had decided to go into the manufacture of after market air conditioning units for cars and light trucks. Prior to our involvement with them, their largest distributor sold 25 units during a year. In our first year with them, we took delivery of, and sold 1,440 units.

At one point, we were installing so many radios and air conditioners in Toyota cars, that with our skilled four man crew, we could complete the installation of a radio and air conditioner every hour. I mean, down the road the most air conditioners that we ever installed in one month was 451 units. We became a factor in the business and one of the largest distributors east of the Mississippi River, if not the largest.

By this time our employee payroll roster had increased to over forty employees.

Chapter 35

SAGA OF THE FIREBIRD

My wife Joan was delivering some new car radios to the Pontiac dealer in Miami when she noticed a different looking car sitting atop a car carrier on the Pontiac lot. The car was a small red two door coupe with a white vinyl top and a tachometer on the hood. Joan was impressed. The Pontiac dealership was operated by a man who had previously operated a Studebaker dealership in Ft. Lauderdale, and had been one of my better customers. Joan was in the parts department delivering the radios, the owner walked in and recognizing Joan as my wife, and started talking to her. She asked him, "What kind of car is that red and white car outside on the car carrier?"

"That is a Firebird, a new line of vehicles that they are adding to the line of Pontiacs in the middle of the model year. That is the very first one to be delivered to my dealership." Without any hesitation and asking no questions about the price, Joan said "I will take it, what time can I pick it up?" "After one o'clock tomorrow," the dealer replied. At one o'clock sharp the next day Joan was sitting in front of his showroom waiting to pick up her new car. She did not realize it, but she probably originated the term "sign and drive" on that very day, as that was all that she did, signed her name and drove the car home, not even asking the cost of the vehicle. She drove the new Firebird directly to my office, anxious to show off her new acquisition.

She said she loved the car but that she had a hard time starting up from a traffic light. I said to her, "Let me drive it and check it out." "Fine was her reply, but I am going with you." With me driving, we went for a ride around town and soon realized that the problem was, with a big 400 cubic inch engine in a little light car like that, when you really accelerated starting up at a traffic light the rear end would just jump up and down and it was hard to get any real traction. I ultimately solved that problem by putting two pieces of railroad track three feet long and three burlap sacks filled with sand into the trunk of the car.

Anytime that we were driving the car we had to be very cautious, because it attracted a lot of attention and was very fast and easily caught the attention of the local police. I must admit though, all during the time that we owned the Firebird, neither of us received a traffic citation while driving it.

We had owned the vehicle for only a few months when Joan had gone shopping with a girl friend and after dropping her friend off at her home, returned to our home. She did not realize that a plastic trim strip had fallen loose from the car, leaving very sharp barbed steel projections sticking out from the car that were now unprotected.

As she reached into the rear seat area to retrieve some packages that she had purchased she cut a deep gash into her left arm that bled profusely. She immediately went to the emergency room of our local hospital for medical treatment which included some stitches. Shortly thereafter she returned the Firebird to our local Pontiac dealer who reinstalled and secured the plastic trim strip but did nothing as in regards to the cut on her arm.

At a dinner party at our home a few weeks later I told a group of my friends that I was going to write a letter to Pontiac concerning her injury. They all laughed at me and said that I should just forget about it and save the cost of my postage stamp. A neighbor of ours, who lived right across the street from us had formerly been a design artist for Lindy toys and really knew how to make colors talk. I discussed this situation with him and he agreed to work with Joan on her arm. After painting up the area of her wounded arm to make it look at least as bad as it was originally, if not worse, we took several close-up pictures of her arm.

I do not recall the exact wording of my letter to Pontiac, but I recall that I started it by complimenting them on the wonderful car that we had purchased and that I was sorry that I had to even write this letter. I pointed out that I did not seek a legal solution to our problem and that I was sure that they would not seek a legal confrontation either. I included in the letter a copy of the title to the car, a copy of the work order in which the plastic strip was replaced by a Pontiac dealer, a copy of Joan's medical bills and two of the more gruesome pictures we had taken of her arm. Of course I included her pain and suffering and my loss of companionship in the letter. I then inserted a dollar amount that I thought would be fair to all parties concerned.

This done, I dropped the letter in the mail box and our mailman whisked it away. One week passed, two weeks passed, three weeks passed and finally an envelope arrived from Pontiac. Inside was a letter of apology from Pontiac and a check for the exact amount that I had suggested as being fair to all parties, which was eighteen hundred dollars.

Who says that the little guy never has a chance!

A couple of more months passed and the holiday season was upon us. Joan and I were meeting another couple for dinner at a local popular bistro, the Friday night before Christmas. Of course we were driving our Firebird. We were in the restaurant for a couple of hours and when we came outside there were a lot of flashing lights on police cars and policemen milling all over the parking lot. Joan right away yelled out, "What is going on out here?" One of the officers replied, "Two cars have been stolen from the parking lot." Joan said, "I hope one of them was not my Pontiac." We soon found out that one of the cars was a Cadillac and the other one was our Firebird.

Joan walked up to one of the policemen standing there and said, "Don't just stand there, do something!" To which the officer replied, "What is the license plate number on your Pontiac?" Joan answered "I don't know." After that she was a little less verbal.

Unfortunately, we had just picked up the car from the Pontiac dealer where it had been for routine servicing that evening, and inside the car was a copy of the repair order which included our name, address and phone number. Also in the car was a garage door remote, keys to the front door of our house and a card that listed a private telephone number that was not listed, and known only to my immediate family. As a direct result of that theft, we had to have the locks on the doors of our house changed, we bought a German Shepard guard dog, we had to buy a new garage door mechanism and remote and our longtime maid quit because the phone would ring and no one on the other end of the phone. She was scared.

171

On Tuesday evening following the theft, I received a phone call on my private line. To my surprise, it was operator of the valet parking service from the bistro from which our car was stolen. I wrote down his name to be sure as to whom I was talking, and he inquired as to whether I had heard anything further about our stolen car. I assured him that I had not but thanked him anyway for his interest on our behalf. I knew instantly that he was in on the theft, as the only possible way for him to have obtained my private phone number was from the card inside of our stolen car.

I immediately gave all of the pertinent information that I had to the local police and to the FBI. I do not know what follow up action was taken by either party, if any, as I never heard a single word from either group. No inquires, no depositions, or even an inquiry to see if I had retrieved my stolen vehicle.

The Cadillac was recovered in Rochester, Minnesota ten days after the theft and our Firebird was recovered in Scottsdale, Arizona some three months after the theft. It was left there by a man who wanted to road test a Ford Bronco, which he ultimately stole, leaving behind a Firebird with bullet holes in one side of the car.

In the meantime we had already settled with the insurance company and we never took possession or saw the Firebird again.

Chapter 36

REAR END ACCIDENT

My wife, Joan, had gone to Miami to pick up some parts for me and when she stopped by my office on the way back home, I convinced her to take my newer station wagon through the state inspection station to get a new inspection sticker put on the windshield. In those days, all vehicles in Florida, even newer ones, were required to pass state inspections every six months. This Pontiac station wagon was just six months old. The inspection station was only a few blocks out of her way on her way home.

Joan was not too happy about going to the inspection station and waiting in line, but finally agreed. She was driving up Dixie Highway and was stopped at a traffic light, one stop light before her turn off to the inspection station. Then from behind her came a lady in a car who made no effort to stop, as there were no skid marks, and struck her solidly in the rear.

After the police came and made their report, in which the other lady was given a ticket for failing to keep her vehicle under control, Joan continued on to the inspection station. When they finally inspected the Pontiac, it failed to pass, even though it was only six months old, as one of the headlights failed to burn.

Two days later, with a different driver driving, that same Pontiac Station wagon just stopped running. After having it towed to a service garage, the mechanic found that the pinion shaft had snapped into two pieces. The pinion shaft was about one foot long and two inches in diameter, made of solid steel.

One week later Joan was in the hospital having an operation on her back.

Weeks later, we found that the lady who had struck our Pontiac station wagon, had only the minimum required insurance, ten thousand dollars. Another few weeks passed and an adjuster from her insurance company called me at work and asked, "Would it be possible for us to meet with me and discuss the accident in which your Pontiac was involved." "Certainly, you can come by at any time, and within a few minutes I would be able to give you time to discuss the situation with you." "No he replied, "I mean, I need to meet you at your house, as your wife will have to be present. I replied, "Very well, how about eleven o'clock tomorrow morning? As soon as I get the days work organized tomorrow, I will go right back home." "Great, I will meet you at your house at eleven o'clock tomorrow morning, with your wife present." he said. I went back home early the following morning, eagerly waiting to hear what the insurance adjuster would have to say. He arrived at almost exactly eleven o'clock, and had another adjuster with him. I complimented them on their timely appearance. He responded, "Yes, we try to be prompt, as some customers become very upset, if we are even a few minutes late."

We all went into our living room and sat down. The main man rifled through a few papers and then spoke, "I understand that you have a late model Pontiac that sustained some minor damage in an alleged accident." "I would not call it minor," I said. "According to the police report, the vehicle had only a bent rear bumper," he replied "That and a broken headlamp" I said, showing him the failed inspection report of later that same day. "And this," I said, as I showed them the pinion shaft that was broken it two pieces, "The car was struck hard enough to break this. That and the fact that a week later, my wife had to have an operation on her back" I continued.

He came back with, "She may have fallen off of a ladder and hurt her back." I could now see where this conversation was going. I said, "She might have, but she didn't. She got her back damaged in a car accident the week before." I continued, "If we go to trial, there is not a jury in this land that would not agree to award her triple her hospital bill, which incidentally, was over seven thousand dollars."

He countered with, "My client has a policy with a maximum of ten thousand dollars. By the time you hire an attorney, a private investigator and lose time off from work, you will be very lucky to end up with half of that." He then pulled out of his brief case, and handed to me a check made out to my wife and me in the amount of six thousand dollars. "Ordinarily you would probably be right. But this is no ordinary case, and I am not just your ordinary client. In the first place, I have an attorney on retainer and there will be no difference to me in my cost, whether he is in court two hours or twenty four hours per year. Second, since I own my own business, there will be no loss of salary to me, to be in court for two or three hours. Also, due to the severity of my wife's injuries, I continued, I should have no trouble getting a judgment as requested, even though your client may have a policy for only ten thousand dollars, if I show my willingness to accept it, and make it interest free, I should be able to get an assessment for payment of five dollars a week until the balance is paid in full," I said.

"Now," I said, as I handed him back his check made out in the amount of six thousand dollars, "I know why they call you insurance adjusters. If you were called insurance settlers, you would have come in here with a check made out to us for ten thousand dollars. Due to the type of business that I am in, I mingle socially with many doctors and lawyers, and have discussed this case with different ones over the past few months. They all seem to be in a general agreement that for you to defend a solid case like mine, it would require your company to hire two high priced lawyers with a minimum cost of twenty thousand dollars. So, I will tell you what I will do, if you can come back here to my home within the next fifteen minutes with a check made out to us for nine thousand, nine hundred dollars, we will accept it and sign off on our claim. We are willing to adjust the amount of our claim so that you can live up to your name. I will wait here by my phone for fifteen minutes, if I do not hear from you by that time, do not call, write or otherwise try to contact me, as I will see you in court."

With that last statement, the two adjusters got up and exited our home. Ten minutes later, my phone rang. It was one of the adjusters on the phone saying, "Please wait right there, we are coming right back with a check for you." Sure enough, in another five minutes they were back with a check made out to us, in the amount of nine thousand nine hundred dollars. We signed all of their release papers and they were gone.

The next morning Joan was there waiting, and as soon as the bank opened, cashed her check and was off with her nine thousand nine hundred dollars, on her one day shopping spree. Soon after I arrived home that evening a package arrived for her, with a balance due C.O.D. for something that she had bought and did not have enough cash left to pay for it.

Chapter 37

BONDED

As my business grew, we were now handling money by the millions; many times the cash was handled by people in whom I had little confidence. I finally got to the place that I preferred getting a check even from a new customer, rather than cash, because the losses from bad checks was so minimal that even one loss from one large cash transaction would exceed our bad check losses for the year. As an example of the times, the local Rolls Royce Dealer would not accept cash for payments for cars, parts or service. Only checks, cashier checks or credit cards. Their bills were so high that they were not comfortable in having some of their employees handling fifteen hundred dollars to five thousand dollars in cash, or more.

In our case, many times when our serviceman was making a service call to one of our customers, a next door neighbor would ask our man to come next door and check their television. If our man had a temptation to be dishonest, then he would go next door, put in a couple of vacuum tubes into their set, put the old tubes back into the original tube carton, collect from the customer, put the money in his own pocket, and be on his way. Since there was no record in our office of a call being made on that customer, I had no way of knowing that, and it was just like it never happened.

As time wore on, I became more and more suspicious that things like this were happening, so many times as I stayed in the office later at night. I would take the service caddies used by our outside servicemen and go through and check every vacuum tube carton, to be sure that a new tube was in each package. It turned out that two particular service caddies always had discrepancies. At that point I decided to have all of my employees bonded and insured. I felt that if the employee knew that he was bonded and insured, they would be less likely to be dishonest.

I even had a professional lie detector company come in and give all of our employees a test. I promised the employees that I would not read their answers, but that I would, if I had a second examination. The examiner would have each of the employees write on a sheet of paper any and all dishonesty that they had previously engaged in, that included everything from taking gasoline from our own pump, money, tools, parts and even time. The final question that he would ask was, "Was there anything that you have done while working here, aside from what you have written down on that paper that might be considered dishonest?" That way the employee could say, "Absolutely none" and pass the test. I only requested the examiner to make me aware of any individuals that I should watch for. The two names that the examiner gave to me to look out for matched exactly with the two whom I had previously found discrepancies. Those sheets of admissions were put in a Manila envelope and kept in my office safe. I then contacted a bonding company and had all of my employees bonded.

Only after I closed the business, did I open that Manila envelope and read all of the admissions of dishonesty. I previously had catalogued thirteen ways that my employees were taking advantage of me. After reading those sheets, I discovered nine more ways of being dishonest that I never dreamed of.

One Sunday I made a service call to a customer's home, and after repairing the television I made out the bill and gave it to the customer. At that point, the customer said, "Oh no, this set is still under warranty." I said, "From whom did you purchase this set?" "Your company." he said. "Do you have a receipt?" I asked. "No." he answered. "How did you pay for this set?" He said, "By check." I asked, "Do you have the check? "No, but as soon as I get the returned check from my bank I will call you," he responded.

About a week later the customer called me and I went back to his house and he presented me with a check made out to "Hank ----" for $650.00.

I asked if I may have the check and he agreed to let me keep the check. It turned out that "Hank" was the husband of my wife's best friend whom she had known and worked with in Chicago years before. That was the reason that he came to work for me. I took the check and went to the bonding company with it. They told me to call "Hank" into my office and discuss the situation with him, but not to stand between him and the door, in case he wanted to just get up and leave. I did just that and explained the situation to him. He neither admitted to the act nor denied it, he just got up and left. I never fired him and he never quit, he just never returned to work for me again. The bonding company reimbursed me and I understand that he did reimburse the bonding company.

Chapter 38

FATHER AND SON CAMPOUT

Business was good, and since I was making a good living from the community, I felt that I should contribute something back to the community. I had been a member of the local Optimist Club for some years and was currently serving as a Lieutenant Governor for our district. I had helped run the local Soap Box Derby for the past few years and through my business, sponsored a team in a Colt League and a group in Junior Achievement from our local high school.

Our church was attempting to start a Boy Scout troop. Even though I had no sons of Boy Scout age, since my wife was a Den Mother and I had two boys in the Cub Scouts, I wanted the Scout Troop to be a success and I volunteered to serve as their Scoutmaster. With the advent of my scouting programs, along with my other civic activities, I found myself away from home on the average of four evenings every week, not to mention the times during the days when I would have to pick up certain items, or referee a ball game.

I held our weekly meetings on Tuesday evenings and with the help of another dedicated church member, once each month we would take all of our scouts on a local camp out. I found out that the secret to keeping the boys interested and out of mischief, was to always have a program in

179

place for every event that took more time to complete then the time that would be available.

After several months of these camp outs, we decided to have a father and son camp out. At this camping trip, the only way that a scout could attend was, if he was accompanied by his father. I made one exception to that rule, as we had one young scout whose father was a WW II Veteran and had recently passed away and I treated him as though he was my son, since neither of my sons was old enough to be Boy Scouts. We all convoyed to our campsite right after lunch on Saturday afternoon, and spent the next couple of hours setting up our tents. We had a good turnout, with thirty one fathers in attendance. I then divided them into four different squads so that we could have various competitions.

We played some games, including volley ball and horse shoes, until time to prepare our evening meal. We let everyone get involved in that, each squad led by the attendant fathers. After we finished our meal, it was then time to start our campfire. I had gone to great effort to be sure that the campfire would be a complete success. A couple of weeks earlier, I had gone to a local appliance retail store and asked them to save me the wooden frames that come attached to the bottoms of various appliances. Early on Saturday I collected those wooden squares and took them to our projected camp site, dug a nice round pit and placed those squares, one on top of the other in the pit, with the larger ones toward the bottom to form a nice cone.

To start the fire, I had brought my youngest son Ross, who was a cub scout, to do the honors. He took a small handful of dry wood shavings and placed them inside of the fire pit. He then took a piece of hardwood about one foot square, with a small indent carved in the center, a wooden rod of soft pine about eight inches long and one half inch in diameter, and a small hardwood hand held piece, with another indent carved in the center and filled with grease, so that part of it would turn with a minimum of friction.

With the large board placed in the pit by the kindling, Ross placed the rod into the indent in the bottom board and placed the small board at the top of the rod, then using a bow with a string wrapped around the rod, as he pulled the bow back and forth, it would spin the rod. By putting pressure on the rod, it created friction at the bottom and thus produced heat. Ross then pulled the bow back and forth for a few minutes, when suddenly the kindling burst into fire and within a couple of minutes, the whole cone was ablaze.

One of the fathers then spoke, "All of my life I have heard about someone starting a fire by rubbing two sticks together, but this the first time in my life that I have actually seen it done."

Almost.

What he did not see, was that after Ross tired of pulling the bow back and forth, spinning the stick, he placed his left knee onto a electric sewing machine foot switch, which I had buried in the sand earlier in the day.

The wires from that switch connected a six volt battery, which I also had buried earlier, connected to two terminals mounted on a small board with a tungsten steel wire between them. I had the heads of six strike anywhere matches carefully taped against the tungsten wire, and when the wire got hot it immediately ignited those matches, which in turn set fire to a large bundle of rags, which had been inundated with mineral spirits, and instantly burst into flames.

Now that the campfire was burning, our scouts proceeded to put on a program to entertain the fathers, a program that we had been working on in our weekly meetings for several weeks. After a listless night in which a lot of conversation was taking place, as well as watching to see a balloon which was circumnavigating the globe every hour or so, Sunday morning finally arrived.

We had a leisurely breakfast cooked over our campfire and plenty of hot cocoa.

After breakfast, we had a church service which was presided over by one of the fathers, who was a lay minister. We were all thankful that none of our Scouts had any boo boos, not even requiring a band aid.

We then packed all of our goods and tents back into our vehicles, putting all scrap wood that was left over as well as all of our trash into the back of a pickup truck. We then filled in the fire pit and raked sand and leaves over it, making sure that our entire area was well policed.

We left the area pristine, just like it never happened.

Chapter 39

Trip to Disney World

I was in the business of selling auto air conditioners and parts, both wholesale and retail. I finally hired Glenn, the parts man that I really needed. Not only was Glenn used to writing large orders, he was also very knowledgeable of the actual inner workings of the various components that went into making up an auto air conditioner. Glenn fit right in. He already knew all of the nomenclature of all of the associated auto air parts, and easily grasped our particular numbering systems. He had an excellent memory and within a month, could dial any of my busiest one hundred dealers without bothering to look up their number in the rolodex. He was always on time. I was relieved and thought that finally, I had a parts manager who would not need constant supervision.

Our parts business was booming, which led to the other parts of the auto air conditioning business to steadily increase also. Things were going well but after a few months I realized that there was a small potential problem. Glenn had a very close relationship with another man. No, he was not gay.

His close friend was a man named Jack Daniels. The man that he rented from told me that he often invited Glenn to share breakfast with him, but he always turned him down. Glenn's breakfast every morning was the same. Four fingers of Jack Daniels in a glass, topped off with a little coke. I soon began to realize that any time you wanted to contact Glenn after work, you did not call his home, rather, you would call Big Daddy's. Big Daddy's was a popular bar group, that served inexpensive drinks, and had various bars located all over the county. You did not call just any of the bars, but only one, as he hung out at just one particular Big Daddy's when he was not working.

As the months passed by, he was still a consistent worker and was always prompt in his attendance. By the time that the second Christmas rolled around, he was courting a cute little blonde girl named Claudia.

Claudia was a teetotaler, as far as alcohol was concerned, and she realized that Glenn had a serious drinking problem. Glenn was trying to coerce her into going with him to visit his parents in Georgia at Christmas time, and that they would stop at Disney World on the way up. Claudia finally agreed that she would accompany him to see his parents, but only on one condition. That was, that he would not drink one drop of alcohol while they were gone.

Glenn really liked the girl and would have done anything that she asked him to do, if she would just go with him. Three days before Christmas, they loaded up their traveling duds into her late model car, drove to Orlando and got a room for two nights at a motel near Disney World. The first evening, the next day, and that evening, apparently went by without a hitch. At five o'clock in the morning of Christmas Eve, the telephone at my home rang. When I answered it I was dumfounded to hear Glenn's voice on the phone.

He said, "Richard, a former co-worker, has followed me to Orlando and is harassing me." He sounded disoriented and I said to him, "Please put Claudia on the phone." Claudia got on the phone and said. "About four o'clock this morning, Glenn started hearing voices in his room, He must have been getting the d.t.'s(delirium tremens), and that he has ripped apart two pillows and is trying to get the mattress off of the bed." She sounded very distraught.

I tried to comfort her a little, and then I said, "Get your things together and move out of the motel as soon as possible, and go directly to a restaurant and get him something to eat. I know that he does not drink coffee, but try to get him to drink a lot of orange juice." Claudia did as I suggested, moved out of the motel directly, and had a big breakfast at a local restaurant.

That done, she was driving north on I-4 towards Daytona Beach at about sixty miles per hour, when a car started to pass her. Glenn, seeing the car, pointed a finger toward it and exclaims, "Look, there is Richard, and that S.O.B. is going to shoot me." With that, he opened the car door and jumped out of her car moving at sixty miles per hour.

Claudia brought the car to a screeching halt and pulled to the side of the road. She is miles from nowhere, has no phone and does not know how bad Glenn is hurt. She is devastated.

She runs back to where he is, lying in a heap, but obviously still alive. Just then a good Samaritan pulled over and stopped. When she explains her problem, he said, "I will go and call an ambulance for you immediately." He then sped away. Very shortly thereafter, a highway patrolman stopped to see what was the matter and immediately called for an ambulance. The ambulance arrived, loaded Glenn into it and headed towards the hospital in Daytona Beach. Claudia followed along, well behind.

When they got him to the hospital, they found that Glenn was not seriously injured, but realizing what his condition really was, would not admit him into the hospital. She took him to two other hospitals, but none would have anything to do with him. By this time, Claudia is beside herself. She doesn't know what to do. She then called me at my home, fortunately I was there, and she explained in a frantic voice as to what had transpired. I got from her the address of where they presently were and said to her, "Stay right where you are, don't go anywhere or do anything, I will send Paul up there to take care of everything."

Paul was one of my sales representatives, who was a little older and a little wiser then many of us, and I knew that he could handle this delicate situation. I called Paul on the phone and gave him a brief rundown on the situation. I then asked him to stop by my office. I went directly to my office to await his arrival. When Paul came by, I handed him a note with the address of where Glenn and Claudia were, the address of two local rehab hospitals and five hundred dollars, and said, "I want you to go to Daytona Beach to this address, pick up Glenn and bring him back to this area. Do not bring him here. Do not take him to your house, and do not bring him to my house. Check him into one of these rehabilitation centers and I will see you the day after tomorrow."

The day after Christmas, Paul came by, we settled the money situation and he gave me the address of where Glenn was staying. That evening, I stopped by to see Glenn on my way home. I said, "How are you feeling?" "Fine," He said. "Have you called your parents?" I asked. "No, I have not been able to get to a pay phone." He replied. "Do you need any money to make a phone call, or anything else?" I inquired. "No," was his response.

Glenn, I am going to come by here tomorrow evening and if you have not called your parents by then, I am going to call them myself.

When I went by to see him the next evening, I said, "How are they treating you?" "They are treating me fine." He responded. "Did you call your parents?" I asked. "No." He replied. "Well, then I am going to." I said. Staying there with him and talking with him for about a half an hour, I drove on home and fixed myself a double martini, got out my phone book to get his parents phone number, and braced myself for the call. I knew that it was not going to be easy.

When I finally got enough alcohol in me and enough courage to make the call, his father answered the phone. I said, "Have you heard from or about Glenn?" "No." His father responded. I went on to tell him where Glenn was and why he was there and his only remark was, "Does he need any money?" He replied. "No," I said, and that was the gist of our conversation.

I was confused and hurt that his father did not ask for the name of the facility where Glenn was staying, did not ask for the address or even the telephone number, only, whether he needed any money? That told me something about the father and son relationship.

Glenn spent three weeks in the rehab center and then came back to work for me. Glenn stayed away from all alcohol altogether and was back to his old self, doing excellent work. Then, after about three months, when we went out for dinner, I noticed he would have one glass of wine. Within another three months, he was back on speaking terms with his old friend, Jack Daniels. He continued working for me, but by this time it was affecting his performance at work. Finally, I had to give him a thirty day leave of absence, to try to get his act together.

Two weeks later, his father flew into town and took Glenn back home to Georgia in a straight jacket. He never came back to work for me.

Chapter 40

MOUNTAIN VACATION

My wife Joan and I were on holiday with my son Dan. Dan had recently been inducted into an organization that was popular at that time, known as "Dare to be Great." To prove just how great he really was, he bought a new Lincoln Mark IV. Also, Dan's mass had increased from a modest two hundred and ten pounds to two hundred and eighty pounds, to prove he really dared to be great.

The Lincoln Mark IV, with Dan behind the wheel, would pass anything on the road, except a restaurant. No matter whether we had traveled one hundred fifty miles or forty miles since our last stop, when Dan saw a restaurant sign, that Mark IV just automatically whipped into a parking spot. We had motored over quite a bit of the southeastern highways, but were ultimately headed for the mountains of North Carolina. I had a customer who lived there and had some rental cabins.

Since this was the off season for him, he had tendered the invitation for us to come and be his guest for a few days, just to see how quiet and peaceful the life was there, compared to the hustle and bustle of life in South Florida. After God only knows how many eating places we had been in and out of, we finally arrived at our destination. Jim, the owner was at home and he and his wife Nita gave us a gracious welcome.

Jim had a large cabin that he and Nita stayed in when they were there and then had three slightly smaller cabins that he rented out in the summer when the folks from warm South Florida were looking for a cooler climate to spend their vacation. We fished, we played cards, we drank, we ate, we drank and we ate some more. Jim was telling us that when he first went to this area, he had bought seven acres on a medium sized lake and built one small cabin on the property. The next summer when he went there, he built a second small cabin. After that, each year, he would build one more cabin. In the meantime each summer he was renting out the completed cabins, and by doing most of the work himself, was able to pay for the additional cabins from the income that he garnered from renting the completed ones.

He and Nita operated a retail service business in Coral Gables, Florida and once the word was out that he had rental cabins in the mountains of North Carolina, he had no trouble at all in keeping them rented during the spring, summer and fall.

He now had a place for himself and three cabins completed for rental and expected to build two more for a total of five rental units.

He felt that even if he did not desire to live there, he would be able to get a caretaker to live in his larger cabin and do minor maintenance and look out for his interests in exchange for free rent, and thus Jim would have a substantial income every year from his rental cabins as long as he lived. By the time we had spent three days relaxing there with no customer complaints it certainly seemed like something that we wanted to look into.

When we returned home, we decided that we would be interested in buying a larger piece of mountain property, create a private club with a clubhouse on it and twelve chalets, each with a name of a sign of the Zodiac for our members use and call it Zodiac Development.

We expected to sell forty eight lifetime memberships, at $25,000 each, even with the maximum number of memberships sold, each member would be entitled to a minimum of three months visitation rights, by reservation, with six weeks to be taken during the winter months, October through March, and six weeks to be taken during the summer season, April through September.

Those visitation rights might be changed or even extended, depending on the needs and requirements of other members. Only a minimum of annual dues to cover, taxes, insurance and maintenance would be required, and depending on how the stock market stayed, even that might not be required.

That time would be guaranteed, by reservation, by the member, or made for by the member, for their family and friends. Aside from the clubhouse and chalets, we visualized having a private swimming pool, a private fishing pond, a rifle range, a skeet shooting range, a dirt track bike trail and probably a short ski slope. We expected to have two outdoor barbecue pits, one near the clubhouse and the other at an area to be set aside as open space for recreation.

These were big dreams, but we were seriously interested in doing just that and try to make our dreams come true.

Chapter 41

REAL ESTATE EXCURSION

Our family often spoke of the good times and the relaxed atmosphere of our trip to the mountains when we visited with Jim and Nita and we relived our thoughts about building a resort in that area. I spoke about our plans to my friends Joe and Vera, and they thought it was a good idea and that they would be interested in becoming one of my first members. I told them that I was going to contact a real estate agent in that area and have him try to locate some appropriate property for me.

About a week later, Joe called me on the phone and told me that a man that he worked with had some mountain property that he was anxious to sell. I told Joe to give the man my phone number and have him give me a call. A few days later I received a phone call from the property owner and I told him that we were interested in purchasing some property and that if he would give us the details and exact location of the property, we would consider it.

He gave us as much information as he could over the telephone and assured me that he would get back to me in a few days, with exact location of his property as well as explicit directions of how to get there and a contact person once I was in that area. Another few days passed and then he called again and gave me the name and telephone number of a friend of his, A Mr. Buckhannon, who lived near the property that he owned. He told me that if I decided to take a physical look at the property, I should call this man and talk to him. Then when I actually got to the general area, I should call him again and make arrangements to meet him near the property and he would personally direct us onto the property.

I realized that the operation of my business was starting to get to me and this looked like an opportunity to make some changes for the future. Our family discussed it for another week or so and finally one afternoon I called Mr. Buckhannon and told him who I was and that I would be driving up there the next night and to expect a phone call from me the following day, so that he would be prepared to join us then.

My son Ross and I were now on an expedition to look at some property to purchase. After driving most of the night and half of the morning, we finally arrived in the area. We stopped at a small gas station/convenience store and they assured us that we were in the general area. Using a pay phone there, we called Mr. Buckhannon and he said to wait right there and that he would be there within the hour to show us the property.

He arrived at the station in just a few minutes, and then we followed him down a narrow paved county road until he pulled to the side of the road. There it was, in all of its glory. Our first view of what was to be our project property. It appeared to be virgin territory, with the exception that one could see where and old mining trail had been scraped into the side of the mountain, a trail that was to be used as a logging trail at a later date. Mr. Buckhannon then walked with us to show us where the boundary markers were near the paved road, and gave us a verbal description of the lay of the land. We thanked him for taking the time to show us the property and he went on his way.

The appearance of a new red Porsche on that narrow mountain road certainly caught the attention of the local population, in an area where most folks traveled in five year old pickup trucks or ten year old Jeeps. We found out later that most folks there figured that we were revenue men, searching for the still that was in operation at that very moment, on the property that we were considering, because of the wonderful fresh spring water spring that was available there. We were probably very fortunate that we did not traverse every foot of the ground there that day, because if we had stumbled onto a moonshine still in progress, we may not have left the property alive.

After Mr. Buckhannon left, we walked from the paved road down a small embankment to a new bridge, that the property owner had

Mr. Buckhannon build, so that we could cross the trout stream that bordered the bottom of the mountain.

Although the bridge looked new, to us it did not look very sturdy. We declined to drive our Porsche across it as we did not desire to have to take a bus or a plane to return home. We did start walking up the old road, which was by now pretty deteriorated, with small brush growing up through it and green briers growing across it. There were gully's washed across it in several places, as there were no culverts installed to divert the rain water.

We could see several nice sized trees on the premises now. The property had been bought by a timber company about fifteen years earlier, and after they cut everything profitable from the land, then sold the land to the present owner, who now was trying to dispose of it to try to regain his investment and perhaps even make a profit on the deal.

As we walked up the old road we came across of what was left of an old mica mine. All that was left was two small rail road tracks disappearing into a pile of mud that must have been the mine entrance, an old rotted down shed which contained a crowbar and a shovel with the point well rounded off and the handle rotted away.

A little further up the road we came to a fairly large level spot, with a beautiful view of the area below. After looking around the area, we determined that there was a nice fresh water spring just above it, nearby. We thought that this would be a wonderful spot for a clubhouse, with the water and the view. As we walked over the area, we began to realize that it would take quite a bit of money to make this project work, but we never dreamed what the biggest deterrent would turn out to be.

Our neighbors.

We then decided that since we did not have an actual survey map to look at, that we would go back home and discuss the place. That we would check the distance to the closest airport, to various cities and particularly to ski resorts, as we were right in the midst of several of them.

As Ross was driving south through Georgia, he saw a blue light flashing in our rear view mirror. After pulling to the side of the road, the officer asked to see his driver's license and registration, he then had us follow him back to a local police station.

At the station, the officer informed us that his radar had clocked the Porsche at seventy two miles per hour in an area that had a speed limit of 55 and that the fine would be $72.00. At that point Ross asked him, "How far is it to the Florida line?" "Sixteen miles," the officer replied. "If you will give me a one minute head start, I will pay double the fine if you catch me in Georgia or nothing if I cross the Florida line before you do." Ross said.

The officer came back with, "No, I will just take the $72.00 now and then another $72.00 if I catch you speeding before you cross the state line."

So it was.

Chapter 42

Convoy to the Mountains

School was now out and my son Ross had graduated from high school and said that if we wanted to buy that property in the mountains, that he would postpone his starting into college by one year and contribute this next year of his life to starting the development of that property. My wife, Joan, and I discussed it and decided that it might be the best way to feel out the cost and opportunity of our dream development. We contacted the owner of the mountain and obtained the documentation, signed and paid for the land. I had a customer who was a local developer and he volunteered to check out for us, the quality and workability of a used bulldozer, which I located from and ad in the local newspaper. He certified as being good and very usable for what we intended to use it for, and we went ahead and purchased it. We then bought a used Jeep, which we knew we would need to go up and down the mountain property.

We also bought a twenty four foot, dual wheel box truck, into which we purchased and placed inside, a complete shower for a chalet, a toilet and lavatory, a four burner electric kitchen range, a small refrigerator, and a large assortment of wall switches, outlets, rolls of electrical wire, table lamps, two bunk beds and assorted other household items. An eight by twelve foot aluminum shed, unassembled, was also purchased and placed in the box truck.

We then purchased an old dual axle lowboy trailer to transport the bull dozer to the mountain and had an appropriate hitch installed on the box truck. We purchased a motor cycle trailer and had a hitch installed on the back of the Jeep to pull that trailer. With everything loaded and two dirt motorcycles on the trailer, Ross, along with three of his high school buddies, with extra sleeping bags, headed out in the two vehicles. With a thirty five cent set of plans on how to build a chalet, and a lot of high expectations, the little group convoyed out of our driveway en route to the mountains.

They had traveled no more that twenty five miles up the turnpike, when on the second time Ross applied the brakes, one of the tires on the trailer blew out. He pulled to the side of the turnpike, unloaded the bulldozer, put on the one spare tire that he had for the trailer, pulled the dozer back on the trailer and were off again. Another fifty miles up the road, as he again applied the brakes, another tire on the trailer blew out. At this point, Ross realized that he had a problem, that the trailer we had purchased was old and had a six volt electric brake system, hooked to a truck with twelve volts, and that he was not going to successfully make the journey all of the way to the mountain property.

With that realization, he again unloaded the dozer, pulled it well down away form the pavement, locked it up, removed the wheel with the flat tire from the trailer and convoyed back to our compound with a trailer with only three wheels on the pavement.

This time, we rented a lowboy trailer that did, in fact, have a twelve volt braking system and early the next morning, Ross headed the convoy north again, stopping to retrieve the bull dozer that he had left parked along side of the turnpike. With that reloaded, nothing was going to stop them now. An overnight stay at a motel in South Carolina would be the last time that they would sleep in a regular bed for some time to come. As they were going through the mountains of North Carolina, they stopped at a roadside diner. While eating there, the diner's owner, realizing that there was a dozer on the trailer parked outside, convinced Ross to do some work with it, and after lunch Ross unloaded the dozer and picked a few peso's with his new equipment before he ever reached our property.

The rest of the trip was uneventful.

Chapter 43

FINAL DAYS

I was continuing going to work every day, trying to keep building the business and keep my forty or so employees gainfully employed. In the meantime, our son Ross had built the first chalet on our mountain property and was renting it out on a weekly basis, since we had not yet started selling memberships. Two of Ross's schoolmates had found that mountain life was a little too rugged for them and had returned to Florida. He and his buddy were still living in the 8 x 12 aluminum shed while they rented out the one finished chalet. They continued to clear some of the property and improve the roads with ditching and adding culverts.

Since Ross was not experienced with running a bulldozer, he found it necessary to purchase a used backhoe to make his construction work possible. Then feeling that the used bulldozer was not a safe item to use on the mountain terrain, since it had no roll bars on it, we traded the used dozer for a new International dozer that had roll bars and a front blade that you could change the angle of while in motion, which was extremely helpful.

Back at work, I was starting to get distressed at going to the hospitals to visit my fellow business men following their triple and quadruple heart bypasses and going to the funeral homes and signing the guest book as another prominent business man had departed this earth, and all because of stress. With the cost of insurance rising in leaps and bounds and new

SLY FOXX

taxes to be paid every quarter, it started to seem to me that I was no longer working for myself but rather I was working to make money available for other people, most of whom I did not even know.

One of the things that finalized my decision, was on one Tuesday evening a long time employee came to me and said, "Boss man, I need to get an advance of six hundred dollars. I responded with, "What in the world would you do with six hundred dollars? It would take you a month to drink that much beer." "No, I need it so my daughter can get an abortion" he replied. I complied and was not concerned about it because I knew that he would work it off.

At this time in our business we were installing a lot of air conditioners in local dump trucks and over the road tractors. We had a program worked out in the business, that if the owner-drivers would bring their vehicle in on Friday afternoon, then we would install the air conditioning unit for them over the weekend, and that way they would not even lose a single days work, which in most cases would save them more than the cost of the unit. We had one such vehicle in our shop on this Friday.

The truck owner brought the vehicle in at about two o'clock on Friday afternoon, and I had two of my installers working on the vehicle the latter part of the day. At quitting time I walked up to Leroy and said, "Leroy, how about coming in tomorrow morning and give these fellows a hand. With the three of you working on it, you can knock it out by noon?" His response was, "I would love to, boss, but I can't, you see I belong to the softball team down at my neighborhood bar and we have a big game tomorrow morning."

I thought to myself, "Am I going to have a heart attack and end up in the hospital or the morgue by worrying about whether I would have ten thousand dollars in cash to meet the payroll next Friday?" I don't think so. It was the tenth of January when I took my instant camera with me when I went to work on Monday and when my employees started coming in, I asked one of them, "Would you be so kind as to take my picture while I am at the front door, pretending to be unlocking the door?" He replied, "Sure, but why?" "Because you will never be seeing me here doing that again." I said.

And they never did.

I gave the keys to all of my stores to my nineteen year old son Ross, packed my immediate personal belongings, a television set and an antenna into a new Chevrolet van, drove north alone, and moved into the one chalet we had built in the mountains, never again to return to operate the business

196

Chapter 44

EARLY MOUNTAIN LIFE

It was wintertime when I arrived at the mountain chalet, so as soon as I unpacked all of my personal gear, I settled into doing what ever would be necessary to make life as easy and comfortable as possible. Since the weather was pleasant at that particular time, I set about to lay in a good supply of firewood for our wood burning stove and a large quantity of dry soft kindling. I then went into the nearest town and purchased a quantity of groceries to be sure that there would be adequate food in the event that I might be snowed in for a week or two. I did not find out until a little later that the weather was not going to be my biggest obstacle to having a happy mountain life. It would be my neighbors.

I climbed a seventy foot high tree, cut away enough of the branches to get a clear vision for a television antenna to be installed. After a multitude of trips up and down the tree, I finally had the antenna turned in the best direction for reception, so I was able to get three TV stations that were strong enough for comfortable viewing.

I had bought a St. Bernard puppy that we named Jackson, because I felt that if I was going to be living in snow covered mountains, I might as well have the appropriate pet.

Recently I had bought a new Chevrolet van and I took it in to the local dealer for service. While I was sitting in the waiting room, I heard a mechanic tell the parts manager, "There is the man who can fix that corvette air conditioner with which we have been having so much trouble." It turned out that the mechanic had worked at a Chevrolet dealership in South Florida and recognized me as the air conditioning man whom they had relied on down there. I agreed that if they could come up with the repair manual on the new Corvette, I would try to repair it for them.

They supplied me with the manual and since I had none of my own tools with me, I was able to borrow a few hand tools from a local mechanic and a couple of hours later the Corvette air conditioner was working as good as new. They gave me fifty dollars for my service and asked for my address and phone number, in case they got into a bind again, since there was not another repairman within ninety miles, who had any real knowledge of auto air repair. I was assured of getting calls from other dealers in the area, both new and used. It appeared that I now had an unexpected source of a cash income and at a time that I really could use it.

Hippy Gary, a young man who was single, contacted me and agreed to come to the mountain and help me for a while. He had been an employee of mine back in Florida, and he was sort of in limbo, waiting for another friend of his to complete his obligation to his boss on another job, and then together they were going to California. His arrival here made my life a little more pleasurable, as I now had someone to share a beer with and a card game or two, plus I now had another pair of hands to help me as I was starting to build the second chalet on the property

All did not remain serene in my new found paradise, because before my St. Bernard had matured, one of my neighbors had poisoned him. That was the first indication of the type of people of whom I was living in the midst.

I had a pretty good idea as to who might have poisoned my dog but was not really sure. I then bought a German Shepard puppy and took the puppy to our local convenience store and announced publicly, that if anything happened to my new dog before I buried this dog, I would be going to three local funerals.

I then went to the local sheriff's office and put a sign on the court house door that my property was posted and no trespassing would be allowed. I then purchased a quantity of posted signs and placed them around the perimeter of my property.

After that, if anyone wanted to speak with me, they would call first and ask permission to cross our bridge, or they would park down on the side of the county road and blow the horn of their vehicle to try to attract my attention. Our chalet sat on a small ridge up from the main road and the neighbors got to know that if my dog barked late at night, I would look to see which way he was barking. If he barked toward the road, I would merely take my twelve-gauge six shot pump shotgun and unload it in a sweeping motion toward the road. If the dog was barking up the mountain, I would take my thirty-thirty semi automatic rifle and unload it up the side of the mountain. One of my neighbors once asked me, "What if I found someone on my property the next morning?" I replied, "If I find someone on my property that is wounded, I would call for an ambulance, if I find someone who is dead I would call for a hearse and if I don't find anyone, then I would have to assume that my dog was just barking at some rabbits."

It did not completely keep all of my neighbors away from our property. Since I was in transition of our building program, the local telephone company had run a temporary telephone line into my chalet. During the time that I stayed there some of my neighbors cut my telephone line a total of fourteen times. Since the road to our property was a dead end road, all of the neighbors on that road knew every time that I left the property and had uninhibited access to our property.

As spring was now here but still very cold in the mountains, I could hardly wait to plant a garden as I had a large quantity of land available. I took a quantity of egg cartons I had been saving, filled them with rich top soil and planted a variety of seeds in them. I kept the cartons in the chalet with me where I watered and nurtured the seeds until by the end of April, when it was safe to set plants out into the garden, and I would be assured that I would have a quantity of radish, carrot, spinach, beans and lettuce to set on my table. The corn and potatoes I would plant directly into the ground.

Now I had my own pet little project to keep me occupied.

Chapter 45

GOLDEN SPIKE

I was back in South Florida for a few days of rest and rehabilitation from working on our resort in the mountains of North Carolina. I invited my son Ross, and neighbor Moe, to join me for dinner, to celebrate my arrival here. The three of us were in Moe's El Dorado Convertible, when Moe suggested that we dine at the Golden Spike Restaurant, where tonight they were offering an all you can eat Prime Rib dinner for only $7.95. We were all in agreement, that it sounded like a great opportunity, and we were headed there, full speed ahead.

We were greeted by the Maitre D' and I said, "A table for three for dinner, please." He replied, "It will be just a few minutes until we have your table ready. If you would care to wait in the bar, we shall call you as soon as we have your table ready." We nodded in agreement and were herded into the bar. We each ordered a drink and the bartender reminded us that the restaurant was serving raw clams and oysters on the half shell, that they were a part of the all you can eat buffet, and that we were welcome to partake of them while in the bar, waiting to be seated in the dining room.

We started taking advantage of that opportunity immediately. After sitting at the bar for almost two hours, we recognized some customers that we saw enter the restaurant after we were in the bar, paying their bill and leaving the premises, we then realized that we were being used as patsy's.

The drinks we were ordering were very expensive, and we had already spent much more for alcohol than we would for dinner. Ross was able to get the bartenders attention and asked him to have the Maitre D' step into the bar. When he came into the bar, Ross said to him, "We have been sitting here in the bar for almost two hours waiting to be seated for dinner, while other customers who came in after us, have been served, and ate their meal and left."

"Now, my father there, has consumed about ten dozen of your oysters on the half shell, Moe has eaten over seven dozen and I have eaten more than six dozen oysters. Are you willing to seat us now, or do we have to move on to some other restaurant to be served a meal?"

With that, he ushered us into the dining area immediately and we were seated. We had spent so much time there already that we were in no hurry to finish our meal now. We ate mainly prime rib, but also some delicious fresh baked rolls. We all deliberately tried to eat more than we needed, but then at the end I ordered, one at a time, four different French Pastries for desert, that on their regular menu, were $5.95 each, but were included in this all you can eat special.

We all had the feeling that we at least got a little revenge. Finished, we paid our bill, left a small tip and drove back to Moe's house. He invited us in and we went inside and started playing poker, his wife Dot joined in the poker game but after a few hands, she soon realized that she was in over her head, and she dropped out. We played poker until about one o'clock in the morning, at which time, Moe stood up and, rubbing his stomach, said, "I think I am ready for a little late night snack, Lets run over to the One Potato Two Potato and see what is on their menu."

The One Potato Two Potato was an around the clock restaurant, of an English pub design with several small private rooms, in which you would be served. They had a sister restaurant, located in a different area of town, called the Three Potato Four, of similar design and menus. I really, did not need anything further to eat, but since Moe and Ross wanted to go, I did not want to be a party pooper and stay back. Moe had won about twenty five dollars from the two of us playing poker, and declared that since he was the big winner that the treat would be on him.

We went there and had our little snacks and by the time that he took a little dessert home for his wife, his bill came to $46.00, plus the tip. But that was all right, Moe had more money than God and he could well afford it. When we returned to Moe's house, we started in playing poker again and played until the sun came up. This time he was not so fortunate, for between Ross and I, we won well over $100.00 from him.

Sometimes, it just doesn't pay to be the nice guy.

Chapter 46

GHOST STORY

It was the middle of June when a friend and ex-employee known as hippie Gary and I were holding forth in our little chalet in the mountains of North Carolina, when I was awakened by the crunch of tires on the gravel on the road in front of my chalet at six o'clock in the morning. As I looked out of the window, I saw my son Ross getting out of his white Firebird, only to be followed by two of his old high school buddies, Randy, who was a large dude and former football player and, Buzz, who was of smaller stature.

When I opened the door to invite them inside the chalet, a rush of cold air brushed by me, I did not realize it how cold it was outside until I looked at the window thermometer and saw the temperature was down into the mid thirties and this was the third week of June here in the mountains of North Carolina. I could see the sun trying to break through the trees as I looked towards the east and that assured me that we would have a pleasant day.

Hippy Gary, who was sleeping upstairs, came down and joined the group. After the introductions, he seemed to blend right in. Gary was helping me building roads and another chalet on the property. I put on a pot of coffee and started taking orders for what they wanted for breakfast. By the time we finished breakfast and everyone was well acquainted it was nearly nine o'clock. We were discussing what we could do, to best entertain our guests. I suggested that we climb to the top of our mountain, which topped out at over forty nine hundred feet high. I said "From the top of our place you can see Little Yellow Mountain, Grandfather's Mountain and Mount Mitchell, which is the highest peak east of the Mississippi River. You can even see well into Tennessee."

They thought it would be interesting and t we should give it a try. The five of us started up the mountain. The first phase of which was easy, as we were walking up the gravel road which I had refurbished with culverts and creek gravel on the base of the old mining and logging trail. Once we reached the first plateau, I walked over to a natural spring around which I had built a small dam, and was relieved to see several cans of beer were lying in the cool water awaiting their call. I asked, "Any one for a cold one?" They could not believe their ears. I continued, "I always try to keep a few cold ones here as one never knows when an emergency like this might arise." Each and every one had one and we were sitting around on a group of logs that we had been collecting to build a log club house on the level area there, particularly because of the ready supply of good spring water for the club.

After our brief respite, we continued our trek up the side of the mountain, but this was now tough going as we were climbing through virgin territory. The terrain was steep and sometimes very rocky. Buzz was starting to tire a bit and asked, "Isn't there any other way to get to the top besides this?" My reply was, "Only on those two legs of yours." Randy kicked into something that was on the ground under some dead leaves. When he reached down and picked it up, what he saw was a pint bottle with a rusty screw on cap, and a clear liquid inside. He exclaimed. "Oh look, I found a bottle of moonshine." He tried to unscrew the top but was unable to get it loose. I said, "Let me see the bottle a moment." He handed the bottle to me, I took it and banged the cap against the side of a tree a couple of times and I was able to get the cap loose. After smelling the contents of the bottle I determined that he had not found a bottle of moonshine, but rather a bottle of peppermint schnapps, that some hunter had probably dropped a year or two earlier. I then emptied the bottle and threw it away, not willing to risk drinking anything that may have been in the bottle.

We continued our trek up the side of the mountain and after about two hours from the time we started, we finally reached the summit. With our field glasses we could easily see Grandfather Mountain and Mount

Mitchell, but by now the new leaves were in full array and we were limited as to what else we could see and identify. Had we been there six weeks earlier, we would have had a clear shot at everything.

After viewing the scenery for a while, Buzz asked, "Isn't there an easier way to get back down to the chalet, other than the way we came up?" I replied, "Yes, the top of our mountain is known as Long Level Ridge, I pointed east, and if we walk down that way, it is a gentle decline and an easy walk down to the paved road, although it is a little further that way." They all agreed they would walk the extra distance, rather than to make the sharp descent down from where we were.

I had never been to this part of Long Level Ridge before, and thought we were walking through virgin territory, but after walking only about one quarter of a mile, we came upon quite a surprise. At the edge of a field was an old steel mowing machine. The area there, I suspected, had been a meadow, was approximately five acres in size and had a few small trees, but was mostly covered with scrub brush. The mowing machine was all steel and had a long cutter bar for severing the grass, large steel wheels with cleats on them, which, when properly engaged would power the movement of the cutter bar, and had a steel seat, mounted on a single leaf spring for the comfort of the driver. It would have been drawn by a team of horses and would have had a long wooden tongue, which by now was rotted away, but you could see the outline by the difference of the soil there. Everything on the mower was rusted solid as it probably had been sitting right where it was for fifty, sixty years or more.

Proceeding further on down the ridge another two hundreds yards we came to what had been an apple orchard. There were several old trees in all stages of disrepair but we found only four that still had leaves on them. These even had buds on them and little apples were starting to form from the blossoms, but we decided not to wait for them to mature to snack on, and continued on our way.

Moving on another hundred yards or so we came upon an old chimney, which was there, as though standing guard, maybe fifteen feet high, but you could see that it probably had been taller, but the top was eroding away through the years, from the rain and the wind. We could see the outline of what had been the shape of a house which probably was a log cabin, from the difference in the earth and it appeared to have been about thirty feet long and about twenty feet wide.

Near to what had been one side of the cabin, we found an old cast iron pot, twenty or twenty five gallon size, but almost completely buried in the ground. I was excited about finding an antique up here and could visualize it sitting on the front porch of my chalet. We took some old tree limbs we found nearby and dug and pried on the pot until we finally got it out of the ground. I was really disappointed to find that after all of that work, there was a big hole broken out of one side of the pot. We did not bury the pot again, but left it lying on top of the ground near where we had found it.

About thirty feet from the chimney we saw two large stones. The stones were sitting in the ground with about three feet high above the ground, two feet wide and about one foot thick. We all figured immediately that they were grave stones. There was a slight indentation on one side of both stones, indicating that there may have been an inscription chiseled into the stones at one time, but the wind and the rain had erased any message that may have been there. There were NO NAMES to be read. We lingered around the stones for quite a while, discussing the fact that in olden days many families buried valuable personal items with the bodies, when they were interred into the ground. Someone suggested that we should go back to our chalet and get a pick and shovel and come back here and dig into what we supposed were graves. Everyone else chipped in and thought that it was a great idea, including myself.

As we all agreed to the grave robbing, a cold breeze swept over us, and I do mean cold. All of a sudden I got that eerie feeling that someone else was watching us. As the others were talking, I interrupted them and asked if any one else had noticed anything unusual. A couple of them admitted that an uneasy feeling had crept over them, particularly right after the cold breeze had swept by us. Toying with the thought of digging up the graves, but not discussing it further, we walked the rest of the way back down to the paved road and then back up to our chalet. I still had that feeling that someone was watching me, like someone was following our group back to the chalet.

We unlocked the door and went into the chalet and by this time it had warmed up nicely outside, up into the mid-seventies and since it was warmer outside than it was in the chalet, we pulled back the drapes and raised the sashes of the two small windows that adorned either side of a large picture window.

Covering the window completely was a set of drapes so heavy that when they were closed at night you could turn on a light in the chalet and one would not even realize that a light had been turned on, if you were outside of the building. So that you will realize the reason that we had drapes this heavy, I will give you a little background on our neighborhood. We did not have a great group of neighbors.

When we first started building a chalet there, one of our neighbors poisoned our St. Bernard dog. We could not leave any tools or small items loose that were not locked up, as someone would steal them while we would go to town for food or supplies. The road leading to our property was a dead end road so most of our neighbors knew exactly when we came and went.

During the time that we were building the first chalet we lived in a small aluminum shed and we had a temporary telephone line running into our shed, and some one of our neighbors kept cutting that telephone line. Of course, reporting such actions to the local sheriff's office was a waste of your breath, as that department did very little to look out for the interests of newcomers into that area.

We were seated at a round dining table, which was located directly in front of the picture window and had a leisurely lunch, a couple of beers and then someone brought up the subject of our previous discussion of going back up to the top of the mountain and opening the ground by those stones. We were all one hundred percent in favor of doing just that, and as we arose from our chairs to get a pick and shovel from our shed, there was a sudden gush of wind and the heavy drapes hanging over part of the raised windows blew straight into the room and were so flat out that one could have played checkers on them. The room then turned ice cold, and the front door blew open.

Then the room started to warm up again. After about a minute or two, the front door blew shut, the room got ice cold again and the drapes blew out of the window and were left hanging limply outside of the window frames. At that point the room warmed back up to its normal temperature. We immediately disbanded any thought of digging up any graves that day, or any other day. If one had checked at that moment, you might have found that it was time for some underwear changes. There was very little talk, but some of the thoughts may have been about doing something more practical at that time, like doing some emergency laundry.

I ran into Buzz about twenty five years later back in Florida, and said to him, "Say Buzz, a bunch of us old boys are planning on going back to North Carolina on a grave digging expedition, would you be interested in joining the group?"

His reply was an emphatic, "No! You can count me out!"

Chapter 47

HUNTING TRIP

It was late in the fall when I decided to take a fifteen year old Ford car up to our mountain resort to use for casual transportation. Although the car was fifteen years old, it had hardly been used. My late father-in-law had bought the car new, drove it for ten years and put only nine thousand miles on the car. It was just parked down in Florida and we really could use it to run errands at the mountain instead of driving one of our gas guzzling trucks.

It was over a nine hundred mile trip to our resort, and although I had made the trip driving alone many times in newer vehicles, I did not feel comfortable driving a car of this vintage that far alone. I did not have a cell phone in those days but did have a Citizens Band Radio to help keep track of road and traffic problems as well as for warnings on the locations of the speed traps.

I could have asked one of my employees to take a week off to accompany me on my trip but that would not only mean that I would have to pay his salary for that time, but mainly that I would lose his production for that week. My best prospect for a traveling buddy would be my neighbor, Moe. Moe, like myself, owned his own business, only his was a pool cleaning and maintenance service, and would be able to be away from his business for several days almost any time he needed to be gone. He was a large man, standing at six foot seven inches tall but in excellent shape, weighing in at about two hundred and twenty pounds. His wife was loaded with money and he was used to driving a Mercedes Benz or an El Dorado convertible and two days of roughing it for him, would have been spending a weekend at the Fountaine Bleu Hotel on Miami Beach.

I talked the project over with him and he seemed generally agreeable to making the trip with me. A couple of days later he came over to my house and said, "I think I have changed my mind about going up to the mountains with you, I don't feel comfortable making a trip that far in a fifteen year old vehicle."

"If it will make you feel more comfortable, I will put all new tires and a new battery on the car. Even though the car is old, it is just broken in good, after all, it only has about fourteen thousand miles on it. We will take our guns with us and go hunting while there, I promise you that you will have a good time."

"Let me think about that and I will get back to you in a couple of days." He came over to our home on Tuesday evening and agreed that he would make the trip with me and he would be ready to go on Thursday morning. We shook hands on it and I was now mentally ready for the trip. I was up early on Thursday morning, had my small traveling bag packed and threw it into the back seat of the Ford. I then grabbed a cold six pack of seven up from the fridge and put it on the floor of the rear seat and I was off to pick up Moe.

Moe lived right down the block and when I arrived there he was ready to go. Like myself, had a small traveling bag packed, which he threw in the back seat and climbed into the front seat accompanied by a bottle of scotch and a snub nosed thirty eight caliber detective special revolver, and a hand full of small paper cups, which he placed on the front seat along side of my friend, a long barrel thirty eight caliber Smith and Wesson police special. I then drove to our local gas station and filled the tank for our trip. Moe suggested that he drive north until we reached the end of the turnpike and that I should take over the driving then, since I had made the trips several times before and would know just where we were going. That sounded good to me.

With Moe behind the wheel things were very uneventful on the turnpike, and after a couple of hours on the road, I opened his bottle of scotch and poured myself a little nip into one of the paper cups. Before we hit the north end of the turnpike I had hit his bottle two or three more times. I had Moe pull into a Racetrac gas station which was located near the end of the turnpike, we filled up with fuel and I drove out of there and over to a nearby restaurant, where we had a big meal, knowing that would be our last major stop until we reached the mountains in North Carolina.

I then pulled out onto interstate seventy five and headed north. I was driving for less than an hour when Moe noticed that my head bobbed a time or two. He said, very nervously, "Sly, are you all right, you are not sleepy are you?" He knew that I had a couple of nips from the bottle of scotch and was concerned that I might be trying to doze off. "No Moe, I am fine," and continued driving on for another hour, then nodding my head a time or two again. Moe nudged me in the ribs with his left elbow and said, "Damnit Sly, pull this thing over and let me drive." I meekly said, "OK Moe," and gradually pulled to the side of the interstate. Of course, he did not realize it, but that was what I had in mind all of the time.

After driving only an hour or less Moe said, "Sly, what does that red light on the dash mean?" I looked at the dash for a few moments and realizing what was indicated said, "Not to worry Moe, the red light merely indicates that the generator on the car has stopped charging, but you know that I just put a new battery in the car and we should be all right for the trip."

Wrong.

Moe drove along for another hour and then asked me, "Sly, do you have a match or a cigarette lighter?" I said, "No, I quit smoking fifteen years ago, why do you ask?" "Oh, it is getting dark out and I just wanted to check and see if the headlights were burning." Well, he certainly got my attention with that statement. I took a good look at my surroundings and realized that the lights did seem a little dim. I said to Moe, "Turn the headlights off but leave the parking lights on." As soon as he turned the headlights off, I noticed that the dash lights got nice and bright and when he turned the headlights back on, the dash lights got real dim again, which indicated that the battery was nearly dead.

Although I had just bought a new battery for the car, it had never been fully charged and we had started the car a multitude of times since the battery was installed and it really never got a chance to really get a good charge. I told Moe, "Go ahead and leave the headlights off, we can live without them but leave the parking lights on, that will give us tail lights so that some faster moving vehicle will not run over us. We will just stop at the first service station that we come to and get a full charge on the battery that should take us through the night, without any further problems."

He drove another ten or twelve miles and pulled off at the first exit we came to, and the second service station we came to was open, Moe pulled right up in front of the gas pumps and I said, "Keep the motor running and I will go inside and see if they have a good battery charger at this station." When I alighted from the car I realized that there were ten or twelve young black men hanging around the front of the station, with some more inside. I might have been concerned but I knew that we had two good friends lying on the front seat and had enough respect for Moe to know that he would not hesitate to use one of them if the situation demanded it.

I walked inside the station to speak with the manager, who was a short chunky black man who stood about five foot five inches tall and probably weight two hundred and fifty pounds. I said to him, "The battery in my Ford out there is about dead, do you have a heavy duty battery charger here that you can help me with?" He looked up at me and replied, "Yas suh, you jest pull around back to the second bay door and I will sho hook you up."

As I exited the station, I noticed that the rest of the young men who were inside then followed me outside. I walked around to the driver's side of the car and told Moe to please pull the car around to the rear and stop at the second door. As I entered our car, and closed the door, Moe put the car in gear, but apparently the number of blacks hanging out there made him nervous and did not give it any extra gas and the engine died. Of course when he tried to start it, it just went ugh and that was it.

I got back out of the car and walked over to where the group of young men were standing and said, "Would a couple of you fellows give me a hand to help push my car around to the back of the station?" To which one replied, "I have a bad back," another said, "I have a bad leg." They all seemed to have developed some physical ailment that prevented them from pushing our car, and at that point Moe got out of the car and said, "Aw, dammit, I can push the car around by myself." As he and I started to push the car, one of the young men did come over and help push the car to the rear, for which I thanked him profusely.

As promised, the bay door at the back was open and when we stopped the car and released the hood latch, the manager raised the hood and drug the long battery cables over and connected them to our battery. He said, "It will take about two hours to fully charge this battery." Which we said was all right with us. Realizing that we had some time to kill, we went over and opened both front doors of our car and poured ourselves a drink from the bottle of scotch. Moe said, "Let me see what type of guns that you have in the trunk." I opened the trunk and showed him that I had a twelve-gauge Remington six shot, pump shot gun, a Winchester semi-automatic thirty-thirty rifle, a semi-automatic Remington twenty two caliber long rifle and a four hundred and ten gauge shot gun.

When the station manager saw us standing at the rear of our car with the trunk open he started walking towards us. As he walked by the open doors of our car and when he saw the two revolvers lying on the seat, his eyes got as big as saucers. When he arrived at the rear of the car and saw all of the long guns lying in the trunk, he really got a surprised look on his face. He then walked over to Moe and started talking to him.

With the manager at five foot five inches tall and Moe at six foot seven inches, the manager looked up at Moe and inquired, "What do you gentlemen do for a living?" Now the manager was a man of color, but when he heard Moe's response he turned many colors and all of them different. Without one moment's hesitation, Moe looked down at him and replied, "We rob service stations." The manager instantly trotted over to the garage door, pulled it down until it was resting on the battery cables. Staying inside of the station, he then turned off all of the lights, except the one in the bay in which he was standing, but including the outside pole lights by the highway.

All of the young black loungers had instantly vanished. After about another hour had passed, the manager opened the bay door about three feet, bent over and came out and disconnected the battery cables, reached out his hand and said, "That will be two dollas, please. After I placed two one dollar bills in his hand, he ducked back inside of the building, slammed down the garage door, latched it and then turned off the final light. I mean that building was as dark as a tomb!

I got in the passengers seat as Moe slid under the wheel and we headed for the ramp leading to the interstate. As we pulled onto the entrance ramp we noticed that another car had pulled in behind us and while still on the ramp, the blue light on that car behind us came on. It turned out to be a Florida State Police car.

Moe pulled the car to the side of the road, stopped and put the lights on park. The one thought that instantly flashed through our minds was, that the station manager had called 911. I usually am pretty meek when it comes to times like this, but Moe had enough money that he was not concerned about fines or anything minor like that. When the patrol officer came to the driver side window, Moe, very boldly said, "What is the trouble, Mac?" The officer did not ask the usual, "May I see your drivers license and registration." He merely said, "I noticed that one of your headlights was not burning."

Moe's reply was, "I don't see how that is possible, we just pulled out of the service station there." "Yes, I know, I saw you pull out." The officer replied.

Moe turned the headlights back on, got out of the car and walked to the front of the car. Sure enough, the right headlight was not burning. At that point, Moe took the base of his right hand and hit the front of the headlamp a good jolt and the light came on nice and bright. Moe stepped back and admired his good work.

The highway patrol officer asked, "Where are you boys going?" Moe answered "Oh, we are just going up to the mountains of North Carolina to do a little hunting." The officer came back with, "Let me wish you luck and drive safely."

With that, he walked back to his patrol car and drove off. Moe then got back in the car and headed back north on the interstate towards my favorite Racetrac station in Brunswick, Georgia.

After gassing up our vehicle and using their facilities, we topped off our stop with a sandwich and some fresh coffee. I then volunteered to drive for a while and drove through the rest of Georgia and quite a ways into South Carolina before I noticed the headlights were dimming again. A quick flip of the headlight switch and the dash lights brightened up again. I was convinced that the battery was about gone, but I was afraid to drive in South Carolina with the headlights off, so I left them on and started looking for a service station.

At the next exit we found a large truck stop. I stopped, went inside and inquired if they had battery charging facilities. I was sure that they would have, and the attendant pointed to a large service building behind the gas station and was told, "That there was a night mechanic on duty back there and was sure that he would be able to take care of me there." I drove around to the service area and located the mechanic. I asked him, "Do you have a battery charger here where as you could charge the battery in my car for me?"

"Yes we do, I will be able to take care of you in just a little while." He said. I thanked him, and waited.

And waited.

And waited.

After an hour had passed and he had not even hooked the charger to our battery yet, Moe walked over to him and asked him, "Is there any way that we can help you to expedite getting our battery hooked up to your charger?" "I will take care of you, just as soon as I get this drive shaft back in this tractor, I have a customer waiting to take this rig out of here tonight." Realizing that the man was working alone, we may well be waiting another hour or so. Then Moe, in his seventy five dollar silk shirt and a pair of slacks that God only knows what he paid for, laid down on one of their greasy creepers and pushed himself under the tractor and said, "What can I do to help you expedite this job?"

The mechanic seemed relieved that he was getting some help and said, "You can stabilize this drive shaft until I can get all of these bolts started." With Moe's help within about twenty minutes he had his job completed and he very willingly hooked his charger to our battery. It was starting to break daylight as we walked back to the restaurant for breakfast while waiting for the battery to get completely charged.

With the battery charged and with day light on hand I felt comfortable in driving the rest of the way on our trip. We had only one more stop for gas in Columbia, South Carolina, and we arrived at the chalet just in time to take my son Dan, to the doctor to be treated for dog bites, resulting from an attack by our German Shepherd guard dog. At that time we owned two, one was a young female named Gypsy and the other was an older male named Prince. It seems that Gypsy was in heat and although Dan was the one who took our Prince through all of his training as a puppy, Prince was not about to mind Dan as long as there was a female dog in heat near him.

As Dan continued to try to keep the two dogs separated, Prince's desire for Gypsy turned to hate of Dan, and attacked him. Dan had to ultimately shoot Prince in self defense, as he was a large dog weighing one hundred and five pounds. When we returned from the doctor's office, we had the sad task of digging a grave and having funeral services for Prince, because after all, he was like a member of our family having been with us for about seven years.

This had not been a very auspicious reception for Moe at our chalet, but I assured him that things would get better. We then drove to Tennessee to replenish our supply of alcoholic beverages, since North Carolina was a dry state and we could not buy any liquor near where we lived. We did party some that night and things seemed a little brighter for Moe.

The next day we spent relaxing and having a fish fry with some nice Rainbow Trout that we caught from our own private fishing pond. One day though Moe, Dan and I did go hunting. We spent the most of one day in the woods. All in all we bagged three squirrels, a couple of snakes and one black crow.

All of the way back to Florida, riding in our Cadillac, Moe was still complaining, he did not think that the hunting expedition justified all of the problems that we had encounter. I finally told Moe, "Stop complaining, if you were to read about a trip like this in a paper somewhere, or hear about it on the radio, it would only be hearsay. You have just enjoyed some real life experiences."

Life goes on.

Chapter 48

Silver or Gold

It was late in the summer and my son Dan and I had gone to the big city to supplement our food and beverage supply. After spending a few seasons on the mountain we had learned to grow in my three gardens and a few fruit trees, most of our food needs. We gave up on making our own beverages as the quality was not there and was too risky, particularly when most of our neighbors would rather see us in jail or back in Florida. We were able to produce our own potatoes, beets, radishes, spinach, beans, peas, pumpkins, corn, peaches and with kind permission from a friendly neighbor, an unlimited supply of good apples.

We had a large quantity of blackberries and raspberries on our property and we were able to nurture a few strawberries. We raised and butchered our own pig for ham, pork chops, bacon and sausage. I traded construction work for fresh killed beef, from which I was able to secure steaks and beef to make my own mincemeat. Upon returning home this day, we took our little fruit basket and walked up the mountain road to one of my gardens to check and see what vegetables might be ripe for picking, something we did every two or three days.

When we came to a level area of the road, lo and behold, there sat a yellow Ford pickup. We called out and asked to whom did this pickup belong, with no response. We then walked around and could neither hear nor see anyone. Since our property was plainly posted with no trespassing signs, I went over to the pickup truck, raised the hood and removed the distributor rotor, placed it in my pocket, closed the hood and we walked back down to the chalet.

Upon arrival there, I immediately call the local sheriff's department and explained my dilemma and he assured me they would dispatch a deputy to our property immediately. We waited until the deputy arrived and then I strapped my thirty eight revolver onto my hip and Dan picked up an automatic twelve gauge shotgun. Feeling well armed and not knowing what lay ahead, we accompanied the deputy back up to the location where the pickup was situated.

Upon arrival at the scene, the deputy said almost immediately, "I know who this truck belongs to, it belongs to a Mr. Silvers who lives over at the other end of three mile road. He is probably up here digging for Ginseng roots. You two wait here as I do not want to have any serious confrontation with him."

We stayed by the truck and about a half hour later the deputy emerged from the bushes with Mr. Silvers in tow. Upon our request he handed over a small quantity of ginseng roots, and after an admonishment from the deputy about trespassing on posted property, the deputy walked back down the road.

I then proceeded to impress on Mr. Silvers that this property was well posted and what serious consequences would follow if I ever caught him on my property again. At that point I reached into my pocket and pulled out the distributor rotor from his truck and handed it to him. He immediately raised the hood and replaced the rotor in its proper place.

He got back in the truck and started the engine and just sat there for several minutes. At this point Dan's patience had grown thin and he walked over to the side of the truck and said, "If you are not off of this mountain in thirty seconds, I am going to start shooting out your tires and then your truck windows, I don't care if you are still in the truck or not." Almost immediately Mr. Silvers put the truck into gear, and spinning gravel, headed back down the mountain. Dan then fired a couple of shotgun shots into the air, to be sure that Mr. Silvers got the message.

After gathering a few vegetables we started our trek back down the mountain and about on third of the way down we came upon a series of small pebbles which were arranged to form the outline of a star accompanied by an arrow, which pointed to a small trail on the side of the mountain. We then realized that Mr. Silvers was waiting at the top for one or more accomplices to come back to the truck. We walked back the trail for some distance, but could catch sight of no one, so we fired a few shotgun blasts into the brush and continued back to the chalet.

A couple of weeks later I was visiting a neighbor, Mr. Speedy Reedy, and we were sitting in his living room talking when there came a knock upon his door. Speedy got up and went to the door, opened it and I heard a voice say, "Sir, I would like permission to go up on your property and look for some ginseng roots." Speedy replied, " I am sorry, but my property only extends about a quarter of a mile up the hill to the fence line there, however, the man who owns the property above that is visiting me right now and if you will just step into my living room, you can ask him yourself."

Coming in from the bright sunlight into a darkened living room, Mr. Silvers did not immediately recognize me and said, "Sir, I would like permission from you to go up on your property and look for some ginseng roots."

Recognizing who the speaker was I replied, "Mr. Silvers. I told you a couple of weeks ago that if I ever caught you setting foot on my property again that I was going to take my backhoe, dig a hole in the ground and bury you in it, right there."

To which Mr. Silvers replied, "Sir that sounds to me like a threat, Mr. Foxx."

"No sir Mr. Silvers that is NOT a threat, that is a PROMISE!"

To this day I have never seen Mr. Silvers again.

Chapter 49

Fun trip to Hickory

It was early in September and very warm for that time of the year in the mountains of North Carolina. My granddaughter, Nicole, had not yet started elementary school, but was enrolled in the head start program, an early learning program offered by the state. I felt charitable and volunteered to install a chain link fence around the playground of the head start learning center where my granddaughter was attending school. I shamed Nicole's father and my son, Ross into helping me. Ross and I had gone to the school grounds early that Saturday morning to find that the fencing, posts and other supplies had been delivered the day before. With our tape measure and chalk line in hand, we very carefully laid out the entire perimeter of the playground. We calculated that we had enough posts to place one of them every eight feet, so we took a can of white spray paint, that was especially designed not to kill the grass, and sprayed a small circle right on top of the chalk line every eight feet.

We then started digging the post holes down the entire length of one side of the play ground and then back to the side of the school building. We then mixed a wheel barrow full of concrete and with a level in hand and my transit level set up to make sure that the posts were perfectly aligned, we proceeded to install all of the fence posts in the holes that were already dug. It was just past noon by the time that we had put the last post in the ground and we were tired and thirsty. I decided that we would take a break and that I would go back downtown and pick up a bag of ice and some soft drinks, since drinking beer while working on the kids school grounds did not seem appropriate. Another determining factor was the fact that this was a dry county and alcoholic beverages were not readily available for purchase, unless one wanted to purchase such items from the local bootlegger, who just happened to live right next door to the local police station.

I am sure that no one from the police station ever realized as to what was transpiring right next door, with strange cars parking and knocking on his door at all hours of the day and night.

Right.

We also determined that we would need two additional bags of concrete, as we were digging the post holes deeper than we anticipated.

As I pulled out onto the main thoroughfare there was a young man standing there trying to hitch a ride. Having been in that same position in earlier years, I felt sympathy for him and I stopped and picked up the young man. After he was seated in my car and as I drove onward, I asked him where he was headed. He said "I am going down to Hickory." "Do you live down there?" I asked. "No, I just have a little business that I have to take care of there." He replied.

"I am very sorry, but I won't be of much help to you, you see I am only going to the convenience store and the hardware store next door, maybe you will be lucky and catch someone there who is going to Hickory." He replied, "I think that this would be a good day for you to go to Hickory, you never know what you may run into down there." "Oh no, not today, I have too much to get done today, and besides that, my son is waiting back at the school for me to return." I answered. Then, as the sharp point of his hunting knife punctured the skin next to the ribs on my right side he said, "I really think that this would be a good day for you to go to Hickory." "I really think that this would be a good day for me to go to Hickory," I said. So it was.

I drove on through the small town and started down the mountain towards Hickory. As soon as we headed down the mountain, he withdrew his knife from away from my side and then we continued to talk as normal as any two strangers might hold a discussion. He pointed out that a few of the leaves were already starting to change colors in the higher elevations and the fact that we have had very little rain during the past few weeks. We continued this idle chit chat until we passed the Greyhound bus station in

Hickory. As soon as we passed the bus station he said to me, "This will be a good place for me to get out."

I stopped my car and as he exited my car I called out to him, "Have a nice day!" He just stuck up his hand, waved and walked away. As I drove away, my first thought was, 'I have to find a police officer," but in those small towns one rarely saw a city patrol car on the streets. When I saw a man walking on the street I stopped and asked, "Sir, can you direct me to the local police station?" but he was as uninformed as I was and could offer no assistance to me. The second person that I saw was very accommodating and directed me to the Hickory city hall, which also housed the police station.

I parked and went inside and related my story to the officer on duty. He immediately summoned a subordinate, whom he directed to drive me back to the area to see if we could locate and identify the person who had threatened me. As we drove back towards the bus station, the streets were deserted because as I had mentioned before, it was mid day and very warm. We passed only one lady pushing her child in a stroller. When we arrived at the bus station we both went inside and the officer inquired as to whether a young man had recently purchased a ticket or inquired about one. The attendant assured us that not one person had been inside the station within the past hour.

With that done, he started slowly circling the area in ever larger circles to see if we might see such a person as my assailant walking the streets. We had no success as hardly anyone was out and about.

In looking back at the time, we might have had greater success in locating the young man if we had been traveling in an unmarked car, as a police car cruising the streets would certainly attract anyone's attention in that town. We finally gave up our search and returned to the police station, where the officer in charge proceeded to type up a report which he had me sign. I thanked both of them for their effort. As I left the station and started driving back to my original destination, I really figured that I would see the young man walking along the road somewhere, but no such luck.

I purchased my cold drinks, a bag of ice and two bags of concrete and returned to the school grounds. Upon arrival back at the school grounds, some two hours after I had departed, my son Dan inquired, "Don't tell me, the convenience store was out of ice and you had to go all of the way to Charlotte to get it." "No, I just ran into a little problem, but everything worked out all right." I did not even tell him at that time as to what had transpired. Some things are just hard to talk about.

The two hour delay in our work schedule meant that even by working until dark, which was nearly nine o'clock there; we were not able to finish the fence and had to return again on Sunday to get it completed, so that the kiddies would have a secure playground when they returned to school on Monday.

Chapter 50

CONSTRUCTION

I found another unexpected source of income while living on the mountain. I had bought some heavy equipment to do the development on my own property, and as soon as some of my neighbors realized that I had such equipment, they inquired if I might be able to do some work on their property. I was soon in the business of installing septic tanks, building driveways and roads for other builders and private parties in the area. I even learned the techniques of using dynamite. I must have been successful in my training as I never did blow myself up. I used the dynamite mostly for breaking up large boulders and for opening drainage ditches along side of the roads I would build.

I built a water reservoir, and ran water lines for my chalets, for which I had the approval of the local health department. I built two more chalets on my own property, and was getting some rental customers. I was still renting the property on a weekly basis as I had not yet satisfactorily started selling memberships.

I again was very fortunate because the local county plumbing and electrical inspector had previously lived in south and had been the service manager for a local Buick dealer for which I previously had done some favors and he remembered me. Any time that I was doing any of that type of work, he would always point me in the right direction to be sure that my work was done properly.

I once built a twenty two by forty four foot, two story log cabin for a neighbor. I mean from digging and pouring the footer to putting the shingles on the roof, including the plumbing and electrical work. The only thing that I did not build was the indoor fireplace with its large rock chimney, which was built by a specialty contractor.

During the summer months, I could always get more work than I had time to handle. I preferred to accept the opportunity to do auto air conditioner work over the construction type, as it was easier work and more profitable.

I finally hooked up with a developer who also was a South Florida resident and he was in the process of building a four hundred and fifty thousand dollar mansion near the top of a nearby mountain. I dug the footer for him, run all of his water lines, installed the one thousand gallon diesel oil tank and ran the lines for that. I improved the access road by adding culverts, gravel and opening the drainage ditches.

The three story home that he was building, was sixty four feet wide across the front and fifty feet high and the whole front, except for two stone pillars, was covered with Anderson Glass Windows. The third floor was basically a ballroom, with a small kitchenette and tables and chairs along one side. There were two nice bedrooms that took up one end of the floor. They each had a large walk in clothes closet and a private bathroom.

In one corner of the third floor, there was a floor that was suspended from the ceiling above, was about twelve feet wide and about fifteen feet long, and was well above the regular ballroom floor below. It had a small winding staircase leading to it and there was a table and chairs for four and a personal dance floor.

Since this mansion was located near the mile high level, the winters were very cold and severe and keeping a large building of this stature warm was a major project. They resolved that by having a large hot water heater that was heated by using diesel fuel from the one thousand gallon underground tank that I had installed for them. They ran water pipes through all of the floors and all of the ceilings, and the water pipes also ran through the three fireplaces, one that was located on each floor, so that if a fire was burning in any or the fireplaces, it would also help heat the water as it flowed through the pipes, thus reducing the demand from the diesel fueled heater. The water was circulated by a pump that was driven by an electric motor and they had a standby diesel generator, using the same source of fuel as was used for the water heater that would start automatically, should there be an electric power failure

This mansion was allegedly to be used for the photo shoot area for the girls of Penthouse Magazine, when it was completed. I do not know if any of them ever made the scene or not as I had left the area before the inside of the building was completed.

My father had been the owner of a large road contracting company, being responsible for building most of the public roads in West Virginia from nineteen hundred and five until nineteen hundred and twenty nine. As I was building my little gravel roads for individuals and contractors, I often wondered if my father could see me, and if he would have approved the roads that I completed. I once rerouted a creek for one farmer taking out all of the curves of the creek, thus almost doubling the usable size of the property. He repaid me by giving me one half of a steer that he butchered. The work I was doing was hard, but was rewarding. To see the happy smiles on my customer's faces when the jobs were completed made it all worth while.

Chapter 51

Blood on the Wall

I was living and working in the mountains while my wife Joan had gone back to Florida to baby sit our new grandson. During the time that she was there looking after our little grandson, a friend Lois, whom she had met here in the mountains called her and asked her, "Would you like to meet me at Disney World, I am going down there with Dee, you know her, and we would love to meet you there. Joan replied "I don't know, just what are your plans?" Lois said, "We are going to drive down on Monday. We have motel reservations for Monday night, Tuesday and Wednesday, and will drive back home on Thursday."

"Well, let me get back to you tomorrow, I have to check with my daughter-in-law, to be sure that she can handle it." After checking, Joan found that arrangements could be made to free up her time for about three days. She then returned the call to Lois, telling her, "I will drive up late on Monday, after my daughter-in-law gets home, go to Disney World on Tuesday and Wednesday with you, and then drive back down here on Wednesday evening."

Lois said, "That will be fine, we will meet you at our motel on Monday night." She then went on to give her the name and address of the motel near Disney World. On Monday evening, Joan drove to the Orlando area and met her friends. After spending two wonderful days with her friends, she then drove back to South Florida.

After spending two days walking around Disney World, and then having a four hour drive back down, Joan was getting exhausted, and instead of driving back to our son's house, she stopped off to visit with my Aunt Helen, who lived about twenty miles closer. Aunt Helen lived alone, and was surprised to see Joan, and was glad to have her spend the night with her.

After visiting with her and telling her about her trip and meeting her friends from the mountains, Joan said that she was exhausted, then excused herself and went back to her bedroom. Soon thereafter, Aunt Helen turned out the lights in the living room and retired to her bedroom.

Before either one of them had fallen asleep, they both heard a crash of glass breaking in the kitchen. They both got up and immediately ran into the kitchen. When they arrived there, they saw that someone was trying to break into the house and had broken out the kitchen window, knocking over some glass flower vases that were sitting on the kitchen window sill, which was the glass that they had heard breaking. They immediately reached for the telephone, which was sitting on the kitchen counter, to call the local police.

Wrong!!

They found that the telephone line had been cut on the outside. That, in itself was a good indicator that who ever was trying to break into their home either lived in a similar home or had helped build them, as the incoming telephone line was in an odd location. Once the two of them had turned the lights on in the kitchen, there were no further signs of any burglar, but just to be sure, both Joan and Aunt Helen armed themselves with a large butcher knife.

What they did not realize was, that the intruder had slit the screen and had secreted himself in the screened in back porch. After standing in the kitchen for a few minutes and not hearing any further noises, they finally decided they had scared the intruder away.

Wrong!

For some unknown reason, Aunt Helen then unlocked and opened the back kitchen door that opened onto the screened in porch.

The intruder, who was a tall black man hiding on the back porch, pounced on Aunt Helen, took the knife away from her, and threatened to cut her throat, if he did not get money. She did not have any money to give and Joan, having just returned from Walt Disney World, had only five dollars remaining in her wallet, which she offered to him and he accepted.

Joan then thought, "If I could just get him to let me go to my car parked out front, I could get my gun, which I always carried under the drivers seat in my car, when traveling alone." She said to the intruder, "I have a small purse under the seat of my car, which contains some traveling money, if you will take me out there, I will give you whatever is left in it" He thought about that for a minute and then replied, "No, I don't think so, that just sounds like some trick to get me out of the house."

It turned out that it was a lucky thing for Joan that he did not take her to the car, because later, the first time that she tried to shoot her gun, the bullet in the chamber misfired and he probably would have killed her.

Having refused her offer to go to her car, the man said to her, "I am going to rape you and then I will cut your throat." After that last remark, Joan decided she might as well make a fight out of it. She and the intruder went at it, dueling with knives for a minute or two, during which time, the intruder got cut in a couple of places, with blood on the sofa and on the wall.

When they took a break, Joan said, "Let me take my aunt to her bedroom and keep her out of the fracas, she is very old and cannot be of any help." He agreed, and Joan walked down the hall to where the two bedrooms were, with her left hand holding my aunts hand and the intruder firmly holding onto Joan's right hand. When they arrived at the two bedroom doors, she pushed Aunt Helen into her bedroom and told her to lock the door.

Joan then quick twisted her hand out of the grasp of the black man, and he was so surprised that by the time he realized what had happened Joan had slipped into the other bedroom and quickly locked the door. She then ran to the window, and with her bare hands, broke every jalousie out of the window, without getting a cut or scratch on her hand or arm, jumped out of the window, only to be confronted by another black man, who lived next door and had gone outside to see what the ruckus going on was about.

He took her inside his home and called the police. When the police arrived and walked into the living room, saw the upheaval of the furnishings and the blood on the wall and sofa, asked, "How many people were fighting this intruder?" They were stunned when Joan replied, "Just me." Then they asked her, "What is your name?" "Joan Foxx, " she replied." "Are you associated with Foxx TV?" they asked. "Yes, that is my husband," she replied. "Where is your husband now?" they inquired. "He is living up in the mountains, in North Carolina." She said. "Perhaps that is where you should be" they responded.

Joan gave to the officers a very detailed description of the intruder. After they finished writing up their report, they gave her a case number, and if she wanted to inquire about the progress of the case, or had any additional information, she should call and give that number so all information would be kept in one file. Two days later, as Joan was driving down the street behind the aunt's home, she saw a tall black man sitting on a lawn chair with his left hand and arm bandaged. She immediately went in and reported this to the police, with that case number, and even though they had the kitchen knife with his fingerprints on it, he was never picked up and questioned and no arrests were ever made. Great police work.

Apparently, the black man knew that Aunt Helen lived alone, and intended to rape and rob her. He was surprised to find on the one night he picked, she would not be alone, but had company staying over with her.

A few months after this terrible night, this same man was arrested for breaking and entering and rape. He had broken into the home of another elderly woman who lived alone, raped her and fell asleep in her bed. After his arrest, he admitted to several other rapes in that area.

Chapter 52

CHAIN SAW DILEMMA

When we first prepared to go to the mountain, I went to Sears and bought the most powerful gas powered chain saw that they offered for sale. Once arriving at the mountain site, the chain saw worked all right as long as there were two or more men on the premises, because it took so long and so many pulls on the starting rope to get it started, that by the time the saw was actually running, you would be too tired to use it and merely handed it to another person to use. Not long after arriving there this time, I found myself alone or with only my wife Joan, so I found it impractical to try to use that particular chain saw. Instead, I purchased a less powerful saw and it worked fine.

Three years have passed and the newer, less powerful chain saw was starting to give me trouble. It was in the fall and the harsh winter had not yet set in, but I knew it was coming and that I had to lay in a good supply of firewood as both chalets were heated only by wood burning stoves. The house we had built on the premises was heated with an electric furnace.

On the first day of October I gathered the large Sears saw and took it into the small nearby town where Sears had only an outlet store, which was a small store front with an office and a small warehouse which could accommodate the delivery and holding of any products ordered by the local towns people until such a time as they would come by to pick up their order. I took it into the store and was greeted by a lady who was very courteous. She got out a repair order and I explained to her that the saw worked fine once I had it running but was so hard for me to get it started that it was not practical for me to use She looked at the saw and could see that it looked like new and she inquired, "Is this saw still under warranty?" "I don't know, I have had it for three years, but has been so hard to start that I have used it very little." I said. "In that case, it would not be covered by a warranty, would you like an estimate on the cost of repairs?" She replied. "Do you think that I need one?" I answered. "Well, you never know what they will run into on a three year old piece of equipment." "OK, get me an estimate, but would you please put a rush on this as I really need to get it repaired before the snow starts falling, so that I can lay in my winter supply of firewood." She agreed, put a large red RUSH tag on it and took it to the rear to await the next delivery truck to arrive from their main warehouse in Charlotte.

I went back to my property and since the weather was so beautiful there with the changing of the leaves and very little rain at that time of the year, I took my old saw and tried to cut some firewood. It was a slow process since I had been using that particular saw for about three years it was well worn and the chain would keep coming off, but I tried to do what I could while the weather was nice.

About every ten days or so, I would call the local Sears outlet to check on my saw but they never had any word on it. Finally on the fourth of January the lady called me and said that she had an estimate on my saw and that the repairs would come to one hundred and eighteen dollars and seventy eight cents. I agreed to have the repairs done and asked her to try to expedite the repairs for me. About another week goes by and the lady called me and said that the truck had just delivered my repaired saw. It was then late in the afternoon and I told her that I would not be able to get into town that day but asked to be sure that she would be open on Saturday morning.

My wife Joan accompanied me into town, and with great anticipation I went to retrieve my newly rejuvenated chain saw. I wanted to pay for the repairs in cash but my wife insisted I that I keep my cash money as I might need it over the weekend and that she would give them a check to cover the cost of the repairs.

There was a little snow on the ground but not deep enough to bother me and I knew that I would now be able to cut some serious firewood.

Wrong.

On the way back to the mountain I stopped and bought a fresh can of gasoline, so as to be sure that I would not run out over the weekend. Arriving back at the chalet, I set the saw and gas can down on the front porch and went inside with Joan and put a couple of additional sticks of firewood in the stove.

It was very cold there in the middle of January and Joan was making a fresh pot of coffee for me as I went back outside and filled the tank of the chain saw with gasoline. Taking the saw back inside the chalet, I set it down in the middle of the room and went to the table and sat there waiting and when the coffee was done, drank one cup of coffee. When I arose and went to start the chain saw I was surprised to see a large brown circle on the carpet surrounding the saw. All of the gasoline that I had put in the tank of the saw had leaked out and was now in the carpet right in front of the fireplace, making for a very dangerous situation, in a wooden chalet with a wood fire burning.

I grabbed the saw and took it back outside and left it on the porch. I immediately tried to call the Sears outlet, but by this time they were closed. I was really devastated because I had just spent one hundred and eighteen dollars and still had no chain saw. Monday morning saw me walking into the Sears outlet with a defunct chain saw in one hand and a brown paper sack in the other one. The lady was surprised to see me back so soon, but immediately grabbed a repair order work sheet and started asking me questions again. I said, "Whoa, wait a minute, I am not going to let you send this back again for repairs. You see this red RUSH tag on the saw, well you put that on this saw on the first day of October and it is now the middle of January. I want you to get the repair section at Charlotte on the phone and let them know about my dilemma."

I then showed her the brown paper sack that I had in my hand, "In here are a bunch of sandwiches, and I am not going to leave this building until I have a good working chain saw in my hand, so you had better get cracking to get me a saw." (There really were no sandwiches in the sack, just a carefully folded towel to make it look like it.) The lady then realized that I was serious so she kept trying to get through to the warehouse in Charlotte, but always got a busy signal. She tried to explain about the busy signal to me, but I pointed out that I had previously had some problems in getting some satisfactory repairs done on a transit level and that I had the number of their direct inside line.

I opened my wallet and gave the lady the number which she dialed and was almost instantly talking to the manager of the whole repair section.

It took her quite some time to make him realize the seriousness of the situation that existed in her store but she finally got the message through to him and he then asked her to put me on the phone. I then gave the repair manager the complete history of the saw ordeal and he was finally able to calm me down enough to convince me that if I would go home quietly that a brand new chain saw would arrive at this store Wednesday morning and that I could pick it up at no charge.

Reluctantly I left the store and returned to the mountain chalet. In the meantime Joan had gone to her bank and stopped payment on the check that she had made out to Sears in the amount on one hundred and eighteen dollars and seventy eight cents for the repairs on the chain saw. Wednesday morning found me at the Sears outlet store awaiting the arrival of their delivery truck. When it finally did arrive, there it was; a brand new saw for me. I returned home in a very happy mood.

Friday came and about noon the Sears outlet store called and told my wife that they had a check from her that they could not do anything with. Joan assured them that she would be in right away and take care of that. Joan drove into town and went immediately to the Sears outlet store. When she entered the store the lady told Joan that she had a check from her that she did not know what to do with. Joan said, "Let me see the check and I will show you what to do with it." The lady went to her desk, retrieved the check and handed it to Joan. Joan took the check, looked at it and said, "Yes that is my check all right." She took the check, ripped it into tiny bits of paper, walked over to the waste basket and threw the pieces into it and said as the walked out of the store, "That should take care of it."

No further word from Sears was ever heard about that check.

Chapter 53

CLEAN UP TIME

Life was very good for my wife Joan and I. We now had our own game room, along with an ice cream parlor near the ski resorts. We took in craft items on consignment for sale to the tourists that were hand made by local crafts people. That consisted of everything from one dollar kitchen magnets to three hundred dollar quilts, blankets and throw rugs.

Then, our son Dan returned from Hawaii.

This time he had a live-in girl friend named Hattie.

The first few days he just relaxed at our resort, but then he started to come to our game room where he could play pool with our customers, and just generally mix with the public.

After a couple of weeks there with us, he decided that he liked the laid back quality of life here, compared to the hustle and bustle, and high prices of everything in Hawaii.

Then he started talking about buying our resort from us. Saying that we really were too old to handle all of the problems, and that he would be able to attract a lot of the younger crowd. After several days of beating up on us mentally, he finally convinced us to let him buy the property. He made a small cash down payment on the place and traded us a quantity of gold and silver jewelry for our four wheel drive Ford pickup truck.

We then rented, and moved into a small home near where our place of business was located.

We took with us only most of our clothes and our immediate personal items, leaving behind a lifetime collection of books, pictures, etc. A couple of weeks later, we went back to the resort to pick up a few of our items that we had left behind.

We were dumfounded when we entered the first chalet, only to find that it was completely barren, except for the furniture and the space heater (wood stove)!

When we entered the second chalet, we found the exact same condition. We waited for Dan to return, to give us an explanation. When Dan returned I asked him "what happened in those chalets?" He said "I don t know, I haven't been in them, what is wrong?

"WRONG! There is nothing left in them; someone has stolen everything out of both chalets!!"

"Let's go take a look," Dan replied.

We went to the first chalet and when he opened the door, he looked surprised. When we went to the second chalet, he found the exact same situation, except that there was a lot of our clothes still hanging in the clothes closet. Dan then went on to try to explain what had probably happened.

Dan said that he had hired Hattie's brother and his friend to come down from Virginia, to straighten up and clean up those two chalets. These two chalets had not been rented out for about a year and a half, and contained largely a collection of odds and ends, and was a depositary for everything that one did not know what to do with. Well, they cleaned it up all right! They just threw out everything from both chalets into the back of the pickup truck, and with several trips, hauled it all down to the creek and threw it into the creek, since we did not have an open pit for them to throw things into.

When Dan told me what had happened, I immediately drove down to the creek and walked along the creek bank. I picked up three little trinkets that had landed on the creek bank and did not slide into the water. Any papers, pictures or books would have washed downstream long ago. We went back to the chalets, to see if they may have moved some of our collection onto the shelves in the clothes closet or kitchen cabinets. No such luck, everything was gone! Pictures and scrapbooks dating back to my childhood were gone forever. Pictures of my time in the Air Corps, with my crew and the B-17 bomber were gone.

Gone forever.

The pictures of the resort, as we converted it from virgin woodland to what it is, never to be seen again. The decoration medals that I received in the service were gone. Drawings that Joan's brother, who was killed in the war, had made. Hundreds of little items that I had collected over a period of fifty years went down in Henson Creek.

I had some matching bird houses and bird feeders that I had made and expected to sell in the craft section of our store.

Gone.

I told Dan that what has happened to me here is the worst thing that has ever happened to me in my lifetime, or ever will happen, except for possibly a death in my immediate family.

Life does go on, but it will never be the same.

Chapter 54

RETURN TO THE SOUTH

My most profitable business while in the mountains was still my auto air work. This was true for two reasons, first I had essentially no competition within one hundred miles, and second, I was good at what I was doing.

I had a Porsche come down from Washington, DC for me to install an air conditioner in it, also an MGB came all of the way from Canada for an installation.

Aside from used cars, I installed air conditioners in bulldozers, backhoes and dump trucks.

I once installed an air conditioner on a sand barge parked out in the middle of the Catawba River, where I had to haul the parts as well as my welding equipment out to the barge in a small boat.

My wife Joan was not at all happy living in the mountains and I finally tired of the brutal winters and especially my neighbors. Almost every time we would leave our premises, someone in my immediate vicinity would steal anything that was movable, even if it was nailed down.

We talked it over and decided to pack most of our personal items into our travel trailer and head back to Florida.

So it was.

Chapter 55

The Fortune Teller

It was Thursday and we were set up in our usual location at the Sanford Flea Market, selling our wares which consisted of sterling silver and Indian jewelry, 14k gold chains and charms, and a few antique bottles. We were doing exceptionally well with our bottles on this day because a bevy of antique dealers had come in and set up at this market for only this one day. Not only were there dealers there that were selling antiques, but there were specialists who could repair minor chips on dishes and cups to enhance the value of some genuine antiques.

Early in the afternoon a young man who appeared to be of Middle Eastern descent, seemed to show considerable interest in my gold and silver jewelry, checking the price of several pieces, and I was beginning to think I had a live one.

Wrong.

He then burst my bubble when he asked me "From whom do you purchase your gold and silver jewelry?" I replied "I buy most of my gold from New York, and most of my silver from Denver and my Indian jewelry form Phoenix. At that point he introduced himself and said, "My name is Najah and I am a jewelry wholesaler, and after seeing your pricing, I believe that I have jewelry at values that you might be interested in. Do you think you will have a little time to take a look at what I have to offer?"

"No, I said, but I could give you some time this evening." We discussed my proposal and agreed that we would meet in the parking lot of the Day's Inn Motel over on SR46 at 6p.m. that evening.

I arrived at the parking lot of the Day's Inn a couple of minutes early and found that Najah was already inside seated at the lunch counter. I entered and joined him in a cup of coffee, after which we went outside to the rear of his car. He opened the large trunk of his car and slid out a couple of showcases full of nice looking jewelry pieces. He then unrolled a large roll of 14k gold chains and laid that on top of the jewelry cases.

At that point, I said, "Whoa wait a minute! If you keep displaying any quantity of this type of jewelry here in the parking lot, we would be likely if either of us get back to our homes alive."

After discussing it for a few moments, he agreed that I probably was right and shoved everything back into the trunk of his car. We finally agreed that I should come to his home in Deltona the following afternoon. He then took a piece of paper and put his address and telephone number on it and drew a crude map as to how to get to his place. I assured him that I would be at his home between 1 p.m. and 2 p.m. the following afternoon. We then both departed for our respective homes.

Arriving at Najah's place the next day he greeted us graciously and invited us into his home, where he introduced us to his Mother, a small slender lady who spoke to us in very broken English. We sat and discussed the jewelry business while his mother brewed a fresh pot of tea.

When we finished our tea, his mother asked if either one of us would like for her to tell our fortune. I declined, because I always felt that any thoughts that a fortune teller might put into my mind, might influence some decision that I might be required to make at some distant future and I did not relish the thought of that.

My wife Joan, agreed though, and I started looking through some of his wares. I then asked him if he could come up with two cartons, one was to put merchandise into that I would purchase and pay for that day and the other carton was to be for merchandise that I liked but did not desire to buy on that day, as living the way we did, we always had to have a considerable amount of cash money available at all times. I will call him first, but come back on Monday or Tuesday to purchase the rest of my selections. On most weekends, when it did not rain, we usually would gross about three thousand dollars. With that in mind, I would feel comfortable in coming back and pick up the rest of my selections.

As we were about halfway through with our jewelry selection, Joan came out of the other room with a perplexed look on her face. When we asked her what the problem was, she said that she did not know. She said that his mother had been reading the tea leaves in her cup and checking the lines in her hand, and told her things that she could not possibly have known, such as the fact her father had been a school teacher and she was an adopted child. She said that all of a sudden she stopped talking and walked away into another room.

Nijah said, "Let me go speak with my mother and see what I can do." He then went into the other room and after a few minutes he emerged and his mother appeared at the open door and motioned for Joan to return to the room with her.

Joan was smiling as she emerged again from the back room, just as we were finishing up with my purchase, and Najah had a calculator in his hand, running a total on my days purchase.

Nijah walked us out to our car and wished us good luck on our sales for the upcoming weekend.

Joan was bubbly and talkative as we drove toward home and was telling me that toward the end of her fortune telling adventure, that Najah's mother moved her arms in a rolling motion, and telling her that much money would be rolling in. Of course, we both assumed that would be from selling some of the jewelry that we purchased from her son

Wrong again.

As we were proceeding west on SR46, within a half mile from our home, a young man, apparently high on drugs, pulled directly into our path from a side road, and we struck him broadside.

Neither of our car doors could be opened after the crash, so I put both of the windows down and crawled out of the driver's side window. By the that time a few people had came to the scene and an off duty police officer helped me pull Joan out of the car through the passengers side window, as we were fearing that a fire might envelope the whole car.

The accident occurred near a convenience store and after hearing the crash, the manager of the store immediately called 911 and ordered an ambulance.

The police arrived first and called for a wrecker and then proceeded to process the accident scene. Shortly thereafter, the ambulance arrived and whisked Joan off to the local hospital.

When the wrecker arrived, it turned out that it was the property of a local body shop and the driver was the owner of the shop. Not knowing any of the repair shops in the area, I readily agreed.

I walked over to the convenience store and bought a six pack of beer, sat down on the seat of the wrecker and rode with my car in tow to the body shop. Once there, using his telephone, I phoned an old school mate of Joan's, who lived in the area, telling her of the accident and the fact that I was really stranded.

She understood and assured me that she would have her son come and pick me up. I gave her the name of the body shop and address. I then unloaded all of my jewelry out of my car and stacked it out on the sidewalk in front of the shop. There I was, with approximately $25,000 dollars worth of jewelry in my possession, sitting on the sidewalk on a jewelry case, with stacks of display cases on either side of me, a thirty eight caliber revolver lying on top of one of the showcases and a six pack of beer on the sidewalk, between my feet, waiting for a ride at 11p.m!

When my friend's son arrived, driving a van, I loaded all of my goods in his van and he drove me to the hospital. We found that Joan had several cuts and pieces of glass from a broken windshield in her head, a broken right wrist and a severely cut left wrist. Joan had to sign a release, but they let her leave the hospital in our company.

We did not go back to where we were staying, but instead spent the next few days with her friend, who was in a position to give Joan some much needed. I continued going to the flea markets, Joan was at home with her host, and feeling very badly that she was not able to assist me in making a living. At that point her friend said to Joan, "Well, I can use my son's van and you and we can start a lawn service.

Right.

Joan, who has one broken wrist and the other one severely cut, who cannot even use them to make change, is going to work as a lawn maintenance worker.

I don't think so.

Time passes, and after multiple visits to the doctors, dentist, and lawyer's offices, Joan gradually healed, both mentally and physically.

Five weeks later, the repair on our car was completed and I happily went and recovered my pride and joy. However, on my way back home I realized that the braking system was not working properly and I had to drive very slowly to avoid another accident.

The next morning I returned my car to the body shop, not knowing whether the brake problem was a result of the accident or just deterioration form sitting idle during the time of repairs.

That afternoon, as my car was reposing in the fenced in compound of the body shop, a severe storm struck the area, with hail stones one to two inches in diameter. The hail stones destroyed my new windshield, my rear tail lights, my hood, my trunk deck and did severe damage to the entire right side of my car. The damage was so severe to my car that my insurance company elected to just pay me a cash settlement and let me keep the car, rather than trying to run it through the auto body repair shop again.

Months passed and we finally received a cash settlement from the insurance company. We realized then, that what the fortune teller lady had seen was the terrible car accident and walked away form Joan, without telling her about what she saw. When she returned to Joan and continued with her reading she told her of the money coming in, but did not tell her why she would be receiving all of that money.

We assumed that she meant much money would come our way as a result of reselling the jewelry we had bought from her son, but in reality she foresaw the car accident and the monetary settlement that we would derive from it.

Chapter 56

Two Bad Weeks

It was Sunday in mid July and very hot under the tin roof of the Frontenac Flea Market Shed. My wife Joan and I always rented two tables in row "C" and they were fully loaded with everything from antique bottles and two dollar sterling silver bracelets to $500 dollar gold chains and Silver Thunderbird Indian necklaces.

We had some hundred year old hand blown glass bottles to current Coca Cola bottles with Bear Bryant's picture and records printed on the sides of the bottles. All of these items were neatly placed inside of glass covered display cases. I kept all of my sterling silver rings in cases, each holding 72 rings. I kept on display one of $3.00 rings, one case of $5.00 rings, one case of $10.00 rings and one case of $20.00 rings. If I were to sell a ring, then I would immediately replace a penny in that ring slot until I had a chance to replace it from my reserve stock. That way I could tell instantly if someone had or was trying to steal any of my rings. I also kept the trays of rings well separated to reduce the chance of a group of customers from grabbing rings and switching trays on me. The more expensive gold rings and silver bear claw rings I kept inside the glass show cases.

Two young ladies came by and were trying to decide on buying a ring. They were obviously ring buyers as each already had rings on two or three fingers of both hands. Joan was working with the girls and after about a half hour and trying on dozens of rings, she threw up her hands and said, "You wait on them, I can't take any more of this!" and walked away from the stand. I said, "Go ahead I will take care of the young ladies."

After another half hour passed and they were still trying on different rings, finally one of the girls had on a $5.00 ring and said, "I really like this ring but it is just a little too big, do you have it in a half size smaller?" I smiled at her, happy to finally see a ring that pleased her and said, "I will have a look see." I then pulled out my case of rings and looked through my back stock of $5.00 rings, but to no avail. I told her that I had some in the right size but they were slightly different, but no, she wanted only that ring, she was not interested in any of the others. I told her not to worry, that I would fix it so that ring would fit perfectly. With that I reached under the table and pulled out a small hammer. "What are you going to do with that?" she asked. With that I reached our and grabbed her hand and said "I am going to slightly smash your finger and then when it swells up, the ring will fit your hand perfectly."

She pulled her hand away from mine and replied, "That won't be necessary" as she reached into her purse and handed me a five dollar bill with a very perplexed look on her face. I thanked her and she walked away.

A short time later another young girl, maybe in her mid teens, stopped by and started looking through my case of $10.00 rings. After about ten minutes she walked away without buying anything. However, I noticed immediately that one of the $10.00 rings was missing. I walked fast and caught up with the young girl and when I confronted her she was wearing my $10.00 ring that she had not paid for. I told her, "Young lady, I am going to give you three choices."

'First, you can pay me $10.00 for the ring or,

Second, you can stand in front of my booth, holding a sign declaring that you are a thief, or

Third, I will call the Deputy Sheriff, who is half owner of this market and have you thrown in jail."

She meekly responded, "I do not have ten dollars and I do not want to go to jail." She came with me back to my booth and I made up a cardboard sign which read "I am a thief, do not do what I did" and stood out in the middle of the aisle. Each time that a customer would walk by she would flash the sign.

After about five minutes I called her back to the table and let her select at no charge a ring from the $5.00 tray and asked her to think twice before she ever did anything like that again. She thanked me for the ring and walked away with a sheepish look on her face. I hope she learned something from that episode.

This was the time of the month that I would make my two week trek to the Mid-Atlantic States where I would sell my wares in North Carolina, Virginia and Tennessee.

Joan had not yet returned to your tables and as I was going through my wares trying to sort our what I wanted to take with me, while at the same time leave enough behind for Joan to have a representative display, as she would still be coming back to this market with the assistance of a girl friend while I was gone.

As I was sorting things out, I was keeping my eye on a couple of scruffy looking young men who had been eyeing some of my better jewelry. When they realized that I was watching them closely on of them spoke, "If I had this much valuable jewelry here, I would have an armed guard sitting behind the table." I merely walked to the table and whipped back the corner of the blanket, exposing my 45 automatic lying there on the table. I said, "I do have, and it is loaded with hollow points, if I have to stand before a judge, I do not expect some thief to be standing opposite of my and lying to the judge as to what had happened. With that statement, they moved on, never to be seen by me again.

By three o'clock in the afternoon the traffic at the flea market was winding down and I was loading my selections as well as card tables and some show cases into my Monte Carlo. That done I topped it off with a cooler, a pillow, and a light blanket and I was ready to roll. I never tied anything down on the top or back of my car, everything had to be inside as far as I was concerned. With my car loaded, I carefully placed the remaining products back into a shed which we rented that was sitting directly behind our tables, so that it would be easy for Joan to get at while I was gone. I spent a few minutes visiting with my fellow venders who all hoped that I would have a successful selling trip.

I kissed my wife goodbye and I was off like a herd of turtles.

Once I hit the interstate, I pushed in a Charlie Rich tape, knowing that I had a double length of Eddie Arnold to play when Charley ended and that would take me to my favorite Racetrac station in Columbia, SC for my next stop. The rest of the trip to Tazewell, Va was uneventful and arriving there I went directly to the flea market, arriving there at 4:00 a.m.

Knowing that I would be arriving there early on Monday morning and also knowing all of the selling spaces would be sold out, I phoned Ted, a friend of mine who lived near Trazewell and would be going to that flea market, I asked him to purchase a selling spot for me there also.

When I entered the market, I was happy to see Ted's van parked there and also that there was a vacant spot right next to where he was parked. I pulled into the vacant spot and let the seat back and catch forty winks before I had to start setting up my tables for the day's sales. It seemed as though only a few seconds had passed when I heard someone pecking on the side window of my car. When I opened my eyes I realized that it was daylight and Ted was standing by the side of my car. I got out and shook hands with him, reimbursed him for my spot, thanked him and seeing his wife Wilma at her area, walked over and chatted with her for a few minutes. The weather was cooperative and we had a beautiful day. My sales that day were very good, particularly on my sterling silver products. I had been selling my jewelry there for about four years and had a good following because I stood behind everything I sold.

One young girl brought back a small light chain that she had bought from me when I was there the month before. The chain was broken. I immediately reached over and handed her another chain just like it. The girl said, "I didn't tell you HOW the chain got broken. I was playing with my dog and his paw came up and caught it and broke it." I said, "Listen, when I sold you this chain, I said it was guaranteed, I did not say it was guaranteed against everything except playing with your dog. However, it is obvious that you really need a heavier chain, so I cannot guarantee it again. She agreed and started looking at some heavier chains and she ended up buying a nice rope chain for $10.00, less the $3.00 credit that I gave her for her old chain. That was the type of operation that kept bringing me repeat customers.

The fact that sales were always good there was the reason I was willing to drive all night on Sunday night to get there

After packing away the remaining goods, I went over to talk to Ted and Wilma, to thank them again for reserving my spot for me and reassuring them that I would see them in Kingsport, Tennessee on Saturday morning, since we would be going to different markets on the rest of the week.

Saturday morning I arrived at the market early, paid my fee and had just barely pulled into my location when Ted and Wilma arrived. This time they had their Granddaughter Jessica with them, they were babysitting her as their daughter and husband had gone to Florida on a selling trip.

We walked for a few minutes then went ahead with the work of setting up our stand for the day's sales. The weather held good for one more day, but we did not have a very good sales day as the crowd was very thin. It seemed to be over by one o'clock and we both started putting some of the less desirables away. By two o'clock we were both packed up and ready to move on.

Since we both were going directly to the flea market at Jonesboro, Tennessee, we agreed that we would convoy over there. Before we left town, we stopped and bought some more beer and food for sandwiches because once we arrived at Jonesboro, we were there for the duration.

Arriving in Jonesboro, I selected a spot that I wanted, backed my car in and went to the office to pay my fee. The reason that we went directly to the market was because all of the selling spaces would be sold out by Saturday afternoon.

I then walked over to where Ted was parked to get a cold beer. He was driving a large van and had plenty of room for a mattress, blankets and sleeping bags plus room for the large cooler which contained our food and beer.

Wilma made a sandwich for everyone and Ted and I took our sandwiches and a cold beer and walked back to my car because I had seats with six way adjustments to make yourself extremely comfortable, where we could eat, drink and relax in comfort.

The rest of the afternoon was spent that way with Wilma drifting back and forth between our car and watching three year old Jessica, who was playing in the van.

About five o'clock when she went back to the van to get some more beer for us, she noticed that Ted's bottle of blood thinner tablets was on the floor, empty and with the cap missing. When Wilma confronted Jessica, she admitted that she had opened the bottle and swallowed all of the pills.

We recognized the seriousness of the circumstance and I volunteered to drive the whole family to the emergency room at the hospital in Johnson City, Tennessee, to get Jessica's stomach pumped.

With the family in my car I drove as fast as I reasonably could until I arrived at the hospital. Arriving at the emergency room, Ted, Wilma and little Jessica all got out but I said that since I was not really a hospital person, I would just wait in the car and listen to my radio.

About eleven thirty all three emerged from the hospital, all smiles. They had pumped her stomach and gave her some kind of liquid to drink and assured them that she would be just fine.

Chapter 57

First Food Tour

My wife Joan and I had gotten our feet wet in the food catering business, entering only such events as art festivals and kids shows, we were really not making any money, but after the disastrous Bath Tub races and ensuing tent fire, we began to realize what it was that we were going to have to do if we were to make a living in the catering business. We had observed that if the festival attracted a goodly crowd, and good food was served promptly and fairly priced, a profit could be made in the business. First we realized that the deep fryer had to be at the back of the tent, so as not to endanger your clientele. Then, the grills needed to be right up front, so that the potential customers could see and smell the food as you were preparing it, and that you could not produce enough product with just one grill and one deep fryer to make any money, or to handle your customers in a reasonable manner.

As the season progressed, we decided that we would try our hand at taking our food business up north in the coming spring. Having originally lived in West Virginia and still having a few friends living there, we decided that would be our first try. We contacted the West Virginia chamber of commerce and they mailed to us a book that contained the various festivals that would be going on during the coming year. It contained the name of the festival, the town where it was to be held with the dates and the name of the contact person handling the vendors. We tried to work out a schedule, which would accept us as a food vendor serving Italian sausage, spiral fried potatoes and lemonade. We ended up the first year with only four festivals on our schedule. They were all on consecutive weekends, and thus minimizing our hotel or motel costs and we were excited to try our hand at it.

In the meantime we traded our Cadillac automobile for an extended body Ford van. When we neared time to head north we loaded into our van our new ten by twenty foot food tent, two grills, two deep fryers, a small deep freezer loaded with two hundred pounds of Italian sausage, fifty dozen hoagie rolls, two boxes of lemons, five fifty pound boxes of potatoes and all of the equipment and supplies that we thought we might need to operate.

Since this was to be our first trip away from our home base, we had no idea as to what facilities we might find to supply us with product out there on the road, or what would be our ability to obtain any local help, if necessary.

Our first festival was to be a coal festival. We arrived at the town the day before that the festival started, checked into a motel and went to a small restaurant to get something to eat. As the young waitress was taking our order I spoke to her "Do you know anyone who might be willing and able to work for us at the coal festival on Saturday and Sunday?"

"What would you expect them to do?" she asked

I told her mostly just take the sandwich that I had prepared, or pour out a glass of lemonade, collect the money from the customer and put it in our cash box."

"What would you pay them?"

"Five dollars an hour in cash with no deductions, plus free food."

How many do you want?" she replied.

I realized then that getting help at our festivals probably would not be a problem. I told her that we would start with just two girls and that we would supply them with one' shirt and apron.

The first day of the festival went very well and the highlight of the Saturday night's festivities was to be a Michael Jackson look-alike contest.

Ordinarily one might not think too much about a contest like that, except for the fact that there probably not a black family that lived within fifty miles of the festival.

When the contest started, what we had on the stage was a bunch of Al Jolson's, wearing long sleeved shirts and one glove, mimicking a Michael Jackson current record, while dancing around wildly and continually gyrating and grabbing their crotch. I will admit that most were very good and I am glad that I was not one of the judges that had to select the winner.

After the festival closed on Sunday evening, we packed everything back into our van and spent the night at the same motel.

Our next festival was to be a railroad festival, but when we arrived in the area, instead of checking into a local motel, we had been invited to stay with an old family friend who lived in the general area.

They turned me on to a produce wholesaler, and to a local independent grocery store who agreed to discount to me any products that they sold such as ketchup, mustard, relishes, steak sauce, etc. They also introduced me to two young ladies who agreed to work for us during the festival.

It turned out that one of the women was a very good worker, and attractive enough that she was able to keep a steady flow of male customers lined up waiting for her to serve them food, and I paid her well. Although she had a full time job as a seamstress working for Wrangler Jeans, she would end up making more money working for me on the two day weekend than she did working the other five days in the factory.

Anytime thereafter that I had a festival that was within about one hundred miles of where she lived, I would pay for a room for her and she would come and work for me.

The amount of planning and all of the activities that the promoters had put forth at the railroad festival really surprised me. Although the antique railroad cars and the museum were open for festival goers viewing all week long, and there were round trip train excursions to scenic spots and places of historical interest, the actual festival for food vendors, the music, the celebrities and special events were held only on Saturday and Sunday.

I learned more about the American railroad system that one week while there, than I had in all of the rest of my life. I found that the railroad buffs were loyal too. They came from as far away as Chicago and New York, and attended these railroad festivals where ever they were held, always looking to buy that unusual railroad lantern or some other paraphernalia that a local vendor might have to offer.

We did not know what type of returns we should make on these weekends, but we were satisfied with the results. We did better here at the railroad festival than we did at the coal festival.

Monday was a day of cleaning all of our equipment and tools, straightening out our truck and visiting with our hosts. On Tuesday we thanked our hosts and departed for our next adventure, which was to be an Italian festival, sponsored by a local church.

Upon arrival at the festival city, we checked into a Days Inn hotel and immediately went to check out the festival site. We were fortunate enough that Mario, who was in charge of the food vendors, was at the site and we introduced ourselves to him. He showed us around and showed us where the stage would be and about everything that we would need to know to properly prepare for the weekend festival.

At the end of our little tour he casually asked me, "How much do you charge for your Italian hoagies?" "Three dollars and fifty cents," I said.

"Oh my god," he said "You will never sell any of those sandwiches here at that price, this is a family oriented festival, these people are used to paying one dollar and fifty cents for an Italian sandwich. Let me go and see if I can find the priest, and maybe I can get him to refund your setup fee which you have paid in advance."

"Wait a minute, Mario, how many people did you say you have come through here during the weekend?"

"We had forty thousand through here last year, not counting the little kids." "Mario, you show me where my stand will be and I will show you how to sell Italian hoagies."

He showed me where my booth would be and as we drove away from the festival site I told my wife Joan "We are in a heap of trouble" "Why are we in trouble?" She asked.

"Forty thousand customers in two days, I have never seen a crowd like that, let alone try to make Italian sandwiches and fries for that many!" At least I had three days to try to get my act together.

Early the next morning I was able to locate a sausage manufacturer and ordered an additional seven hundred and fifty pounds of mild Italian sausage, to be delivered to me at the fairgrounds early Saturday morning. I was fortunate enough to find a bakery that promised to deliver another two hundred dozen, six inch hoagie rolls, sliced three quarters of the way through the bun, to be delivered at the same early morning hour. I went to a restaurant supply house and bought an additional thirty six inch grill and another gas tank, which I took with me.

Going to a produce house, I picked up eight fifty pound sacks of onions, fifteen fifty pound boxes of potatoes and two cases of green peppers. This was in addition to what I already had.

I next went to a wholesale distributor and picked up some additional supplies, such as catsup, mustard, hot sauce, paper towels, napkins and aluminum sandwich foil wrap.

Thursday was a day of relaxation and anticipation. Just sorting things out.

Friday I went to our site and unloaded most of my goods and then went and had all of my propane tanks filled. Coming back, I got everything set up the way that I wanted, with all of my signs and banners in place. I felt that I was finally ready for the big day.

We were on site early on Saturday morning and we were met by Mario who told us that it was all right to go ahead with all of my food prep, but we were not to make any sales until after the priest held mass.

We were seriously looking for additional help. So far we had hired only one lady, who later turned out to be a street person. I had already fired up both deep flyers and two of my grills. I loaded up both grills with Italian sausages, while noticing that the other food vendors were getting no food ready at this early hour, and although there were only a few people milling around at that time, anytime any young people came by our area I always asked if they were interested working for us for the weekend.

When the first of my sausages were done, I lit the third grill, but left it on very low heat, just to use it as a serving grill.

As mass was being conducted, I noticed that although it was nowhere near lunch time, that two couples were standing in front of my booth waiting for sandwiches.

When mass was over I made the four hoagies and handed them to our new employee. When I looked up, there were six more people waiting in line for food.

Two older teenage girls stopped by and when I spoke to them about working for us, they asked, "What will you pay us?" I told them, "Five dollars an hour in cash to each plus your food free."

They thought about it for a while and seeing a line in front of our booth asked, "When do we get to take a break?"

"Anytime that we don't have customers" I replied.

They stood there for a few more minutes, watching the ever increasing line in front of our booth then said, "No, we don't think so," and started walking away.

I yelled to them, "Wait a minute! You never gave me a chance to tell you about our medical and hospitalization program and our retirement benefits!" as they continued walking farther away.

We finally hired two brothers who were high school students, one was our cashier and the other was the runner, who brought the sandwiches and fries to the front where his brother gave them to the customer and collected for them.

Joan noticed that he brought a lot of twenty dollar bills to her to change for a ten and two fives. Finally she went and checked his cash box to see if he had an adequate number of fives and tens and found that he had plenty. It turned out that although he was a senior in high school, he could make change from a five or a ten all right, but was unsure of how to make change from a twenty.

A local high school football coach saw that we were in dire need of additional help and recruited one of his players and brought him to us to work. He was an Italian kid and I had him making all of the sandwiches.

At the end of the weekend I asked him, "What if your mother serves you Italian sausage for dinner?"

He emphatically said "I never want to see another Italian sausage as long as I live." We were never without a line waiting for food the entire day and about six thirty Mario came by our booth and said "Sly, you have to do something to move your line, your customers are lined up and have many of the other booths blocked."

I said "Well, you can make change" and I handed him and apron and he stayed right on the counter until the line died at eleven thirty that night.

Mario took off his apron and as he started to walk away from my booth, he stopped and shook my hand and said "Sly, you have made a believer out of me."

We closed up our booth and as we started back towards our hotel, Joan said that she would like something different to eat. We were driving through a very bad neighborhood and I declined to stop anywhere. When we got back into our room I told her that I would walk to the hotel concession stand that was open all night and bring something back for her. They had pre-made sandwiches there as well as an assortment of snacks, candies and soft drinks.

As I was walking along the side of the hotel I met a young black man coming towards me with not a stitch of clothing on, only a piece of cardboard that he was holding in front of his privates with both hands. He said, "Good morning," gave me a big smile and kept on walking. As he went by me I turned and looked and saw that his bare butt was shining in the moonlight.

When I got to the concession stand I asked the clerk what that was all about. He told me that the kid had been in a room with two other boys and one girl and the boys tricked him and told him to get undressed and he would get to have sex with the girl. Once he was undressed, the boys asked him to step outside of the door, as the girl did not feel comfortable in getting undressed in front of him. That once she was undressed, she would turn out the lights and open the door, he could come in and she would have sex with him.

Once he got undressed and stepped outside of the door the boys locked the door leaving him trapped outside in the nude.

The clerk then said that the boy had asked him to call the police, who agreed that they would come by and pick him up and take him to his home.

When I returned to our room with a sandwich and drink for Joan, I found her sitting on the edge of the bed with money strewed over the whole bed. We had never seen money of this quantity since we had been in the catering business.

I had some rubber bands and as she was counting the money, she would put a rubber band around the stacks of one hundred dollars with the ones, the fives and the tens. The twenties she put in stacks of one thousand dollars.

The festival on Sunday was a repeat of the day before. Once we were able to start serving food in the morning, we were never without a line until the festival closed at six o'clock.

When we returned to our room the light on the telephone was flashing and when Joan called the desk, they asked her to come to the office. Once arriving there, the lady handed her two one hundred dollar stacks of ten dollar bills, which the cleaning lady had found under her pillow. They felt sure that it was a mistake and not a tip.

We were beat and after a good night's sleep, I arose early and went back to the festival area to make sure that I had loaded all of my equipment and banners and that my area was left reasonably clean.

When I returned to the hotel, Joan was still in bed. I told her, "I am ready to roll down the road." "I am too sick to go, you just go ahead without me," She replied.

With that, I reached in my pocket and pulled out six one hundred dollar bills and threw them down on the bed.

"What is this for?" She inquired.

"That will keep you going for a little while, I am leaving now and I will pick you up when I come back through here next year to work this festival again," I said.

"Wait, I am going with you," as she jumped up and started grabbing her clothes.

Chapter 58

Second Food Tour

Back at home for the fall and winter, and after seeing the potentiality of some big shows up north, we started planning for our next summer tour. We contacted the chamber of commerce of other neighboring states, to see if we could arrange a larger schedule. After reviewing the brochures, we still started our schedule in West Virginia. The first event that we scheduled was a three day event in a small town in southern West Virginia, on our way up. The set up fee was only seventy five dollars. We arrived there one day early to get our location and case out the place. The promoters gave us a location which we thought was great, near the stage and center of attraction. We expected to do great.

Wrong!

After the close of the event, we found that we did not make enough profit to even pay our hotel costs, not to mention, travel expenses, set up fee, propane and wasted food. After talking to some of the other vendors, we determined that only the established locals made any money. For all of the others, like us, it was a financial disaster. We then moved on to the Strawberry Festival. This time we had made arrangements in advance, with our regular sausage supplier, to ship to us five hundred pounds of sausage to our motel there. We hired the same two girls that had worked for us last year. We found that we had a following and did even better than we had last year.

When the festival was over, one of the promoters, seeing how busy we were came up to me and said, "You should do the Italian Festival that is held Labor Day weekend. You would do well there." He went on to give me the name of the lady in charge of vendors and how to get in touch with her. After packing up everything, we spent another night in the area.

The next day we drove to the area of the Italian festival. As we were driving into town we notices that several business buildings were boarded up. When we arrived at the courthouse building, where the lady worked that handled the vendors, we saw that there were several wino's hanging around. I was a little nervous as I got out of the van, because I had several thousand dollars on my person, but figured that nothing too bad should happen to me on the court house steps. I was right, too, as I entered her office no worse the wear. I explained to her that I was just a good old West Virginia boy trying to make a living and she agreed to sell me a vending space. I paid the lady in cash, and left the building very happy.

As I was driving out of town, we realized that there were other business buildings boarded up, also. While driving, I told my wife, Joan, "Well, we are good to go in the big Italian festival here on labor day weekend. "How much will it cost to set up?" She asked. "Fifteen hundred dollars." I said. "You didn't pay her yet, did you?" She replied. "Yes, I paid her in cash, why?" I said. "You just turn this van around and go get your money back, you saw all of those bums at the courthouse, and all of those businesses boarded up. Why we would be lucky to gross fifteen hundred dollars in this town. We have never paid more that three hundred dollars, for just the set up fee." She said.

I did not stop, but kept on driving to our next festival. We kept on doing our festivals, until one day we went to the post office to pick up our mail that a neighbor back in Florida had bundled up our mail and sent it to us in care of general delivery. When we opened one letter, we found that the show that was scheduled the week after the Italian festival had been cancelled and they returned my check. So now we had to search for another festival for that weekend. We located another Italian festival in Ohio, but the fee to set up was seven hundred and fifty dollars, and we did not feel like spending that much until we saw how this Italian festival worked out.

Again I had previously made arrangements with my Florida supplier to send twelve hundred and fifty pounds of good Italian sausage to us our hotel, which we were very happy to receive.

The festival was great and the weather was wonderful. Again, the two local girls came to work for us. When we went back to hotel room that night we started counting the money. We would wrap a rubber band around groups of one hundred dollars of ones, fives and tens. The twenty's we packed in one thousand dollar groups.

We had done well enough on Friday, that when the post office, which was right behind our stand opened on Saturday, I went in and mailed a money order to the Italian festival in Ohio for seven hundred and fifty dollars. Saturday was another great day. When we got back to hotel room Saturday night, the telephone in our room was flashing. When we called the desk, they told us to come to the office. Arriving there, they handed us a bundle of five dollar bills, which the maid found under our pillow. She felt sure that it was not intended to be a tip. That night we were very careful as to where we put our bundles of money as we counted it.

Sunday was another great day and shortly after noon we ran out of Italian sausage. Not too long after that a couple ran up the incline to our stand and the man stuck up two fingers and said give me two of those bad boys. I said to him, "I am very sorry sir, but we just ran out of Italian sausage subs, however I can offer you a German bratwurst with peppers and onions or sauerkraut." He replied, "Listen fella, I didn't drive over fifty miles to come to an Italian festival to eat a little German weenie." And he went on looking for another Italian sausage vendor.

On Sunday night, we just closed up and left everything where it was and came back on Labor Day to pack up everything. When everything was secured, we still noticed one problem that was since one of the grills was at the back of the tent, the gutter that ran down the slope from where our booth had been was filled with grease. I just shook my head and said, "Well I guess the committee can use part of that fifteen hundred dollars to clean this gutter." And walked away.

We drove on to the next festival in Ohio. On Tuesday we just relaxed, as we needed some rest. On Wednesday I went to the fairgrounds, where the next Italian festival was to be held to scope it out. This festival was to be held indoors, and all of our equipment had to be adjusted to operate on city gas, instead of the usual propane. Mario, who was in charge of vendors was there, and told me that there were only twelve vendors and the only reason that I was able to get a location, was that one of the regulars was in the hospital.

He asked me, "What do you charge for your Italian sausages?" "Three dollars and fifty cents." I said. "Oh my God, You'll never sell any here, this is a family oriented festival. The vendors here sell them for one dollar and fifty cents. Let me see the priest, and see if I can get your money back." He replied. "How may people did you say came to this festival?" I responded. "Last year, we had over forty thousand adults, not counting the children." He said.

Knowing that I had just sold twelve hundred and fifty pounds of sausage and ran out, at my last festival, I said, "You just show me where I set up and I will show you how to sell Italian sausages." I said. He did, he showed me where my location would be, and that I could set up either Thursday or Friday. I thanked and went back to our hotel and told Joan, "We are in a heap of trouble." "Why is that." She said. "Because we are going to see forty thousand customers in two days with no help!" I replied. I located a local wholesaler who agreed to provide me with all of the Italian Sausage that I would need.

We went back to the Festival area on Thursday, set up our equipment and hung our banners. We talked to every young person that we saw to see if any were interested in working here this weekend. We were able to hire only one lady.

We went to work early Saturday morning. Mario told us that we may light our equipment and start cooking, but that we could not start selling until the priest held mass. I lit everything and loaded up two of my three grills. When mass was over I noticed that we had four people at our stand. I went ahead and started making four sandwiches. By the time I had served them six more people were in line. Then two young girls walked up and asked if we needed any help. I said, "Yes." "What do you pay?" They asked. "Five dollars an hour in cash and free food." I said. "When can we take a break?" They asked. "Anytime that there is no one in line." I replied

As the girls stood there for a few minutes and saw the line growing longer, the girls said, "No, we don't think so." And walked away. I yelled to them, "Wait a minute. You never gave me chance to tell you about our medical and hospitalization program and our retirement benefits," as they continued walking away.

A local high school football coach seeing that we were in dire need of help recruited for us one of his players. He was a large Italian kid, and I had him make all of the sandwiches. We also were able to hire two brothers who were in high school. We used one as the cashier and the other as a runner. Joan noticed that the cashier was bringing a lot of twenty dollar bills to her to get change for them. She then went to check his cash box to make sure that he had adequate fives and tens. He did, he was just unsure as to how to make change from a twenty.

After the festival closed on Saturday night, we drove without stopping directly to our hotel room, as we had to drive through a bad neighborhood. Once we were settled in our room, Joan said that she would like a little snack. I told her that I would walk to the hotel concession stand and get her something. As I was walking along side the hotel, I met a young black man coming towards me with not a stitch of clothing, only a piece of cardboard that he was holding in front of his privates with both hands. He said, "Good morning." When I got to the concession stand I asked the man there, what the nude boy was about. He said, "He was in a room with two other boys and one girl. The other boys told him that if he would get undressed, the girl would have sex with him." Once undressed, they said that the girl did not feel comfortable in getting undressed in front of him and that if he would step outside, she would get undressed and have sex with him. Once he stepped outside the door, they locked him out. He came down here and had me call the police, and they agreed to take him home.

There was never a time either day that we did not have a line of people waiting for food. Early Saturday evening, Mario came by our stand and said, "Sly, you have got to do something to keep this line moving. They are blocking the other vendors." "You can make change." I said and handed him an apron. He worked until the festival closed at eleven o'clock, when the line finally ended. He then handed me back my apron and said, "Sly, you have made a believer out of me." As my Italian boy was leaving, I said to him, "What are you going to do if your mother serves you Italian sausage for dinner?" He replied, "I never want to see another Italian sausage sub as long as I live."

I arose early on Monday morning and went to the festival to make sure that the area was reasonably clean so that I might be invited back next year. When I returned to the hotel, Joan was still in bed. I told her, "I am ready roll on down the road." "I am too sick to go, you just go without me." She said. I reached into my pocket and pulled out six one hundred dollar bills and threw them on the bed. "What is this for?" She inquired. "That will keep you going for a little while, I am leaving now, I will pick you up when I come back here next year, to do the festival again." I said. "Wait, I am going with you." She said as she jumped up and started grabbing her clothes. With that, we were on our way to our next festival.

Our next festival was the Black Gold festival in Hazard, Kentucky. On our way there we passed through the area where Colonel Sanders had opened his first Kentucky Fried Chicken restaurant. I was not impressed with the place, but am glad that we at least stopped by to see it. The first thing we noticed when we entered Hazard was how narrow the streets were. This was the first year that we pulled a trailer for our products, and I was very cautious meeting other vehicles. Then we found out the good and bad news. The good news was that the festival was so widely known that the two major hotels in town had been sold out for weeks in advance, guaranteeing a good crowd. The bad news was that we could find no place to stay in the area.

We finally located another run down hotel, but even then they were reluctant to rent us a room. It was only when we offered to pay for a week in advance, were we able to get a room on the first floor. The first night we got little sleep, as apparently the room directly above us was occupied by a prostitute. From about eight o'clock on, the telephone there would ring and shortly thereafter there would be a knock or their door. We would hear heavy footsteps, the sounds of excited voices, and the squeaking of the mattress for a few minutes. Then the sounds of voices again, heavy footsteps and then the slamming of the door.

This continued until after three o'clock in the morning, when things quieted down. We went to the festival area early Thursday morning, to set up and find out how much of a hassle the health department would give us. We ended up with a decent location and thanks to the certificates from the health departments from both Florida and West Virginia, which were highly regarded, we had no hassle with them.

We were selling our Italian hoagies, but mainly potatoes. We offered them as spiral fries, shoestring fries, butterfly fries and as English chips. We offered them as traditional American style and as Cajun style. It became almost instantly obvious that the various potatoes were going to be our main attraction. By the end of the festival we had sold over forty two, fifty pound boxes of good old Idaho's.

For an area that was supposed to be one of the most depressed areas in the country, we ended up with twenty one, one hundred dollar bills and thirty nine fifty dollar bills. And that was besides the other ones, fives, tens and twenty's. This was certainly one of the festivals that we would look forward to coming back to.

We loaded everything back into our trailer and headed south. Soon after entering Tennessee, I noticed two new looking big rigs passing us at a good clip. Shortly thereafter a Pontiac passed us at a real high rate of speed. Traffic started slowing down, and we were able to come to a stop in the middle of I-65. After sitting there for a few minutes, I got out and walked forward to see what the problem was. I soon realized that the Pontiac driver had lost control of his vehicle and crashed into the second big rig, right at where the trailer was connected. The Pontiac went off the road and the rig ended up with the right side of the tractor up against one side of an overpass and the back of the trailer against the other side of the overpass.

I realized that since the rig was going to be stuck there for sometime, I went back to the trailer, opened up, lit my grill and fryer, and was open for business. I had my wife, Joan, out taking orders. When the local press arrived and saw me open, he took my picture and said, "This is what I call American ingenuity in action." About two hours later, the state police directed traffic into one lane of the northbound lane, and eventually everyone was back in the southbound lane at a normal speed.

We continued south into Georgia, and when about half way through it, a truck came close to me and when I swerved to avoid an accident, the wheels on the right side of the trailer, caught the curb and ripped both axels with wheels out from under my trailer. The trailer was sitting flat on the interstate. My wife got out with a red flag to try to direct traffic away from us until the police arrived. The police arrived and called a wrecking company, and about two hours after they arrived, they had my food trailer loaded onto a flat bed trailer and hauled it back to their service area.

They then determined that they would have to get a new wheel and tire plus a new axle for the trailer and it would be at least until late the next day before it would be ready. We then got a room at a local hotel for the night. The next morning after breakfast, we went to the service area and waited around all day until late at night they finally had it welded back together. It cost us only a little more than we had brought in at the previous road escapade.

We continued on home, without any further interruptions, looking forward to a little leisure time before starting our next tour.

.

www.ingramcontent.com/pod-product-compliance
Lightning Source LLC
Chambersburg PA
CBHW030917090426
42737CB00007B/225